BANGOR & AROUND

THROUGH TIME

Steven Dickens

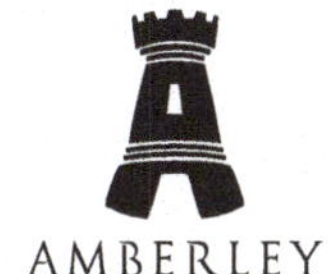

Mae'r llyfr hwn yn ymroddedig gyda chariad at fy nan Olwen Williams, gynt o Heol Well, Gerlan, Bethesda.

First published 2016

Amberley Publishing
The Hill, Stroud, Gloucestershire, GL5 4EP
www.amberley-books.com

ISBN 978 1 4456 3278 0 (print)
ISBN 978 1 4456 3289 6 (ebook)

British Library Cataloguing in Publication Data.
A catalogue record for this book is available from the British Library.

Origination by Amberley Publishing.
Printed in Great Britain.

Introduction

The city of Bangor in Gwynedd is noted as one of the smallest cities in Britain. It is the oldest city in Wales and was historically in Caernarfonshire before the 1974 boundary changes. Bangor is also a university city, with a population of 18,808 in 2011, including 10,000 students. It was founded by the Celtic St Deiniol in the early sixth century. The word 'Bangor' is an old Welsh word for a wattle enclosure, the type which originally surrounded the site of the cathedral. The Bishopric of Bangor is one of the oldest in Britain.

Bangor apparently has the longest High Street in Wales and the United Kingdom. It also has a rich ancient heritage, which is exemplified in Friars School, founded as a free grammar school in 1557. The foundation of Bangor University occurred in 1884.

Bangor lies on the north Wales coast, close to the Menai Strait. Bangor Mountain lies to the east of the main districts of the city. The large housing estate of Maesgeirchen, which was originally council housing, is also to the east of the mountain and near to Port Penrhyn. Another ridge lies to the north of Bangor High Street and south of the Menai Strait. It creates the district known as Upper Bangor. There are also two rivers in the area: the River Adda is culverted until it reaches the Faenol estate in the west, and the River Cegin enters Port Penrhyn at the eastern edge of the city.

Culturally, Bangor has been the host for the National Eisteddfod in 1890, 1902, 1915, 1931, 1940 (via radio), 1943, 1971 and 2005. There was also an unofficial Eisteddfod, which took place in 1874. To cater for the ever-increasing needs of day-trippers and holidaymakers, Garth Pier was opened in 1893 and has served consecutive generations, despite the ravages of wartime and ailing finances. It is the second longest pier in Wales, the ninth longest in the British Isles and is Grade II listed. Bangor Cathedral Church of St Deiniol is a Grade I-listed building and is located in an oval, sloping churchyard. The present building dates from the twelfth century.

One of the most notable and influential families to aid the economic and social development of Bangor was that of Morris Wartski, a migrant who fled the terror of the Tsarist pogroms. He established a jewellery business on Bangor High Street and later a drapery store, which his son Isidore inherited and further developed. Isidore also redeveloped the Castle Inn on the High Street, which later became the Castle Hotel. He eventually became the Mayor of Bangor and a patron of local sports and charities, with Wartski Fields given to the city and the people of Bangor by his widow, Winifred Marie, in Isidore's memory. Other notable people from Bangor include: Duffy – singer, songwriter and actor; Sasha – DJ and record producer; Tom Ellis – actor; and Aimee Richardson – actor.

The town of Bethesda, inland from Bangor, is also covered extensively in this volume. Its importance lies mainly in the development of the Penrhyn Slate Quarry and the emergence of transport links, both road and rail, in order to move slate in bulk to Port Penrhyn for export around the world. At its peak the quarry employed in excess of 3,000 quarrymen, although today a much-reduced operation employs around 200. Most of the former workings of the quarry are flooded. The development of leisure activities has now taken over – there is a zip-wire at the quarry and walking and sightseeing are popular. The town is now a gateway to the Snowdonia National Park, via the A5 Holyhead Road and the Ogwen Valley.

This book also covers some spectacular views along the Ogwen Valley of the Carneddau mountain range. Through the Ogwen Valley the Nant Ffrancon Pass can be reached. This is a fine example of a glacial valley, along which the River Ogwen flows. The valley leads us to the Ogwen Falls, Llyn Ogwen and then through some of the more desolate mountainscapes of the Snowdonia National Park to Capel Curig. Here we can see the Snowdon massif in all its glory, the road then leading us through the Llanberis Pass into the village of Llanberis, where we can find the Snowdon Mountain Railway and the Lakeside Railway. From here we return to Bangor, via Tregarth and Bethesda, or can head towards Caernarfon and its spectacular castle. Also included are some of the coastal towns around Bangor, such as Llanfairfechan and Penmaenmawr and those coastal regions of Anglesey that border the Menai Strait. It has to be admitted that there are many panoramic and beautiful landscapes that cannot be shown in this selection but I believe that those included more than adequately represent Snowdonia's beauty, tranquillity and diversity.

Finally, in relation to language, I have tried to keep Welsh/English translation in the text to a reasonable level, so that it does not become an issue, or the sole purpose of the book. The headers to photographs have been written with Welsh name titles, where appropriate and English translations in brackets, where necessary. The text has been written with Welsh or English translations in brackets, where necessary or where deemed appropriate. At all times the length of word counts has to be considered, so where there are a number of translations it may not be possible to include them all and discretion has, therefore, been used when selecting those to be translated.

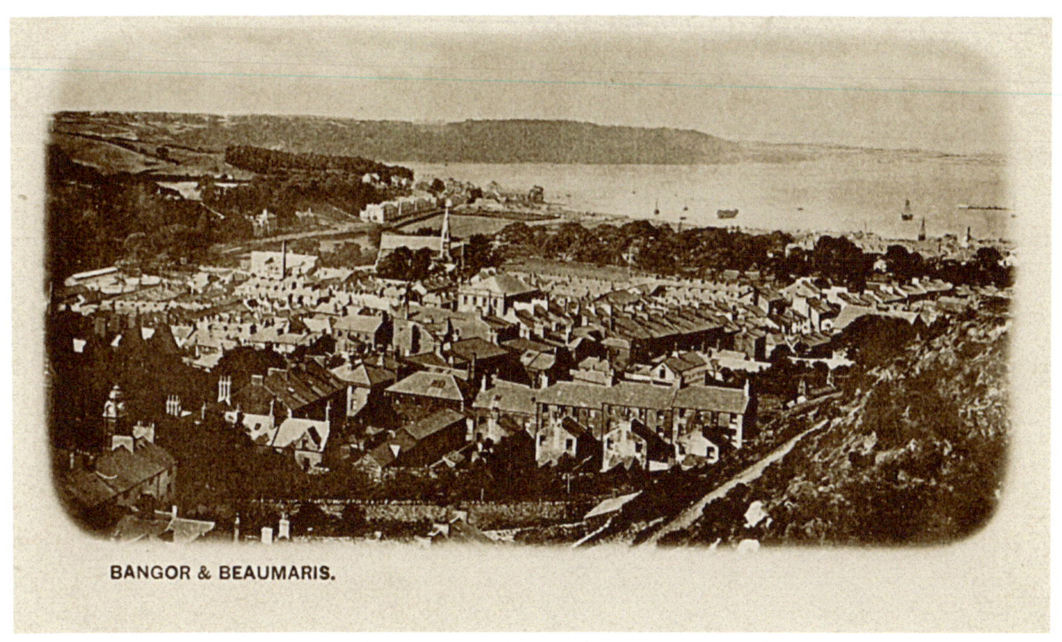

BANGOR & BEAUMARIS.

Bangor and Biwmares (Beaumaris), 1900

Bangor developed from the establishment of its cathedral, around AD 530, and the growth of slate quarrying in the nineteenth century. Beaumaris is a former royal borough and county town of Anglesey (Ynys Mon). Once a Viking settlement, Beaumaris began to develop in 1295, when Edward I defeated the Welsh and built Beaumaris Castle as part of a chain of fortifications along the north Wales coast, which included Conwy, Caernarfon and Harlech. The name Beaumaris originates from the French castle builders title of '*beaux marais*' (beautiful marshes).

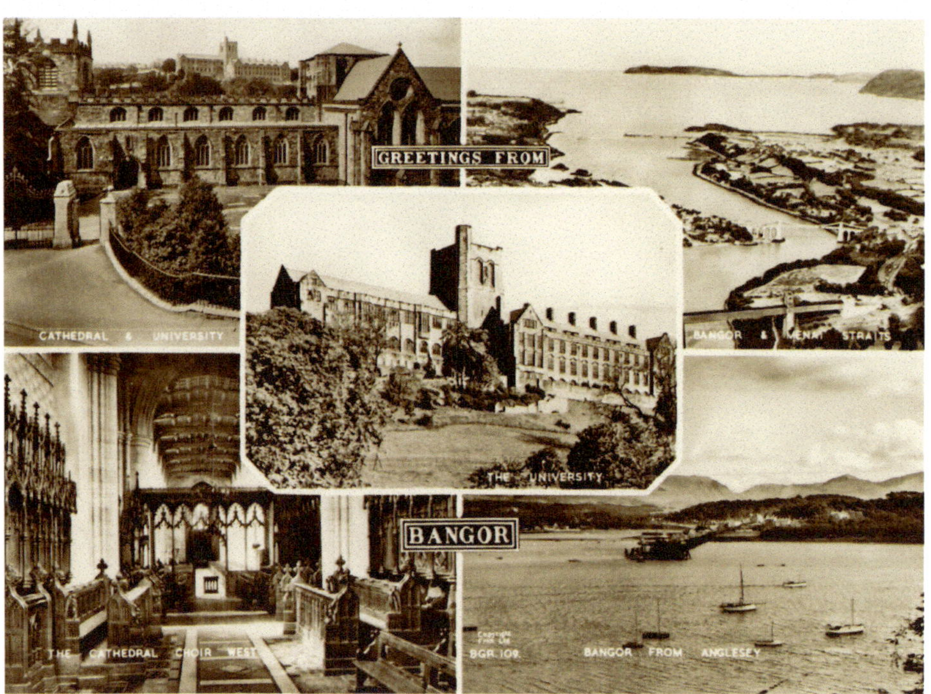

Bangor and Afon Menai (Menai Strait) from Anglesey (bottom right), *c.* 1950
The Menai Strait is a narrow stretch of tidal water around 25 kilometres (16 miles) long, separating Anglesey from mainland Wales. Between Thomas Telford's Suspension Bridge of 1826 and Robert Stephenson's Britannia Tubular Bridge of 1850, there is a small island in the middle of the Strait, Ynys Gorad Goch, surrounded by disused fish traps, once a staple industry. At Garth Pier the Strait is around 900 metres (1,300 feet) wide. The distance from Puffin Island (Ynys Seiriol) to Penmaenmawr is around 7.5 kilometres (4.7 miles).

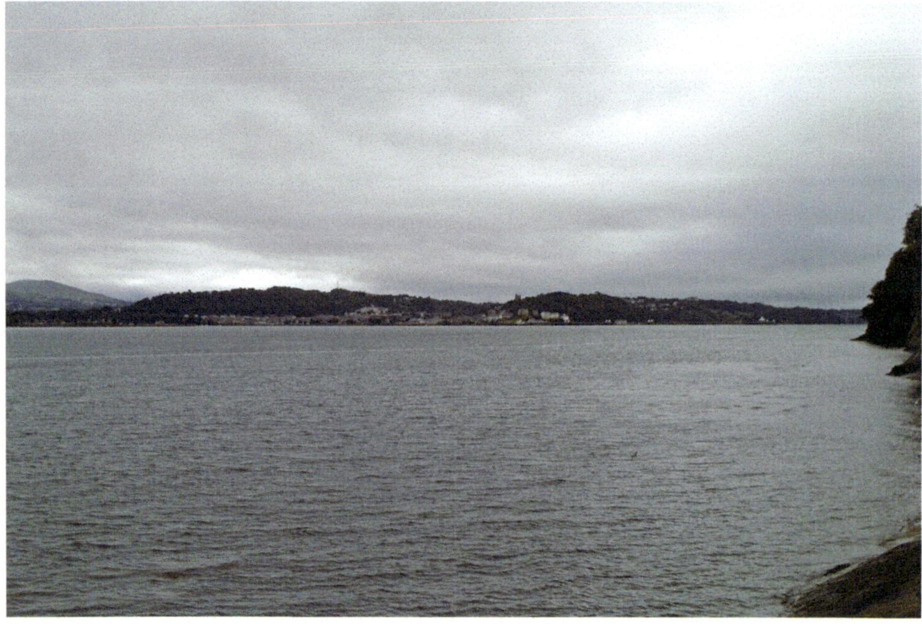

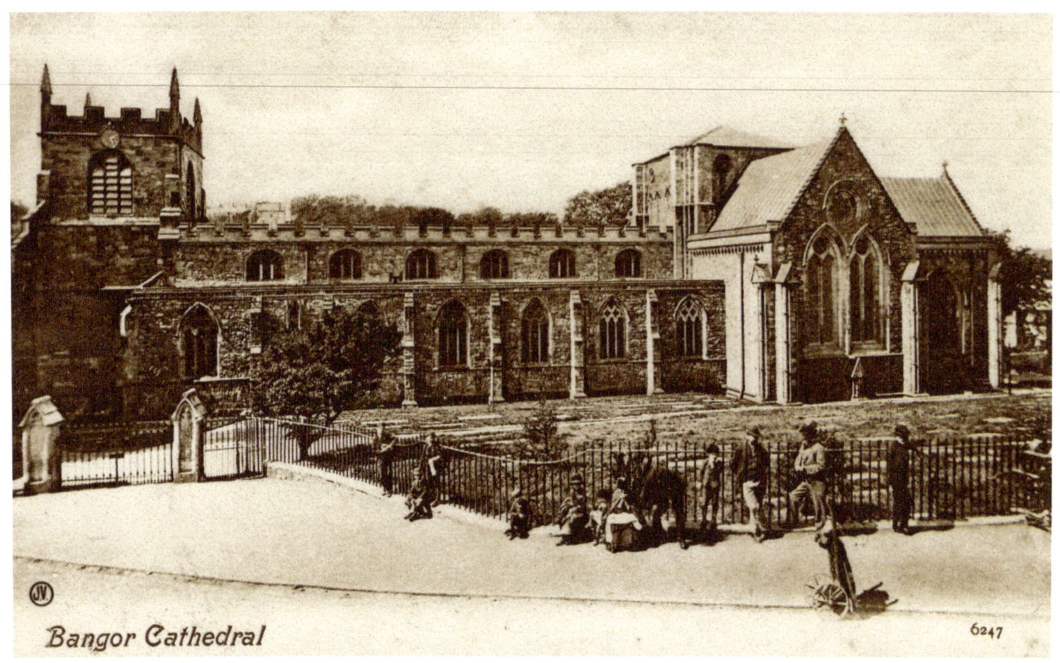

Bangor Cathedral, Cathedral Close, 1907

In around AD 530 Deiniol, a noble Welshman, was given land by Maelgwn, King of Gwynedd, which he enclosed with a fence known as 'bangor'. Deiniol then built a church inside the enclosure, surrounded by huts in which his followers lived. Acting as missionaries, they increased the number of inhabitants, encouraging them to worship in the church. A Celtic monastery (Clas) was established because of this. In around 546 Deiniol was consecrated as Bishop, reputedly by St David, and the church became a cathedral. Deiniol died in around 572.

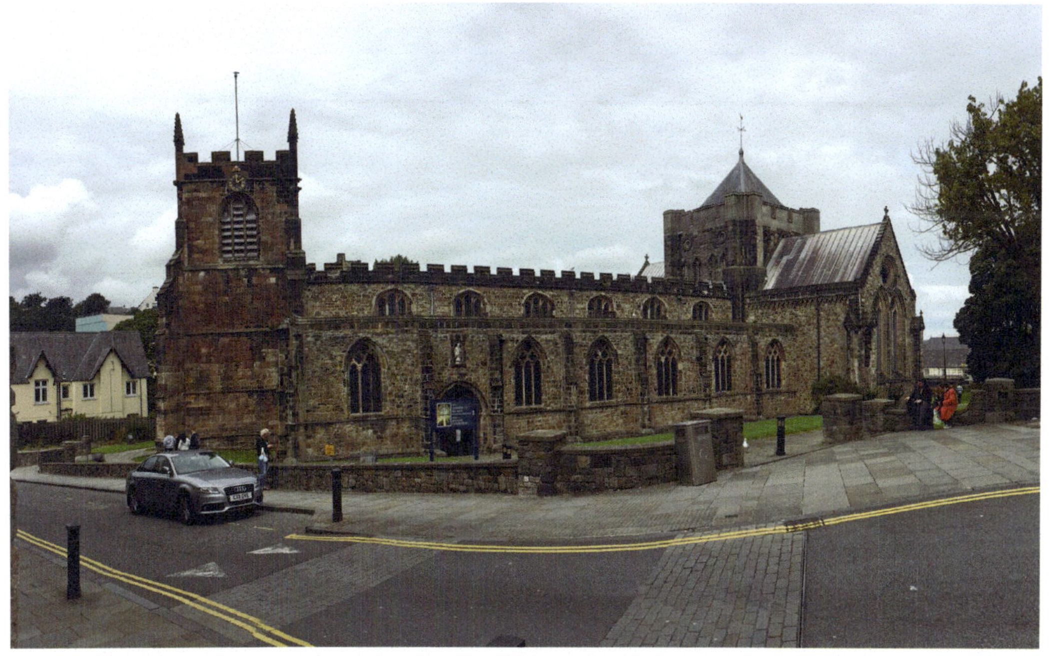

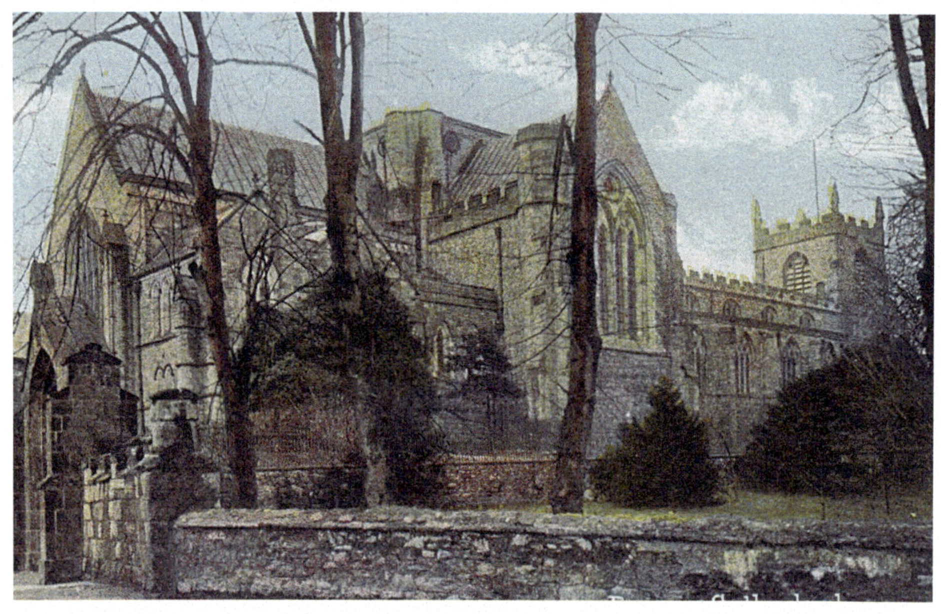

Bangor Cathedral, Cathedral Close, *c.* 1910

Bangor Cathedral has a rich library and also contains the 'Mostyn Christ', a carved figure believed to date from the late fifteenth century, unusual because Christ is shown prior to the crucifixion, seated on a rock and wearing a crown of thorns. The organ, which dated to 1779, was replaced in 1873. Outside, the Bishop's Garden is planted with flowers and shrubs traditionally associated with the medieval church and the Bible, and that are able to survive the Welsh climate.

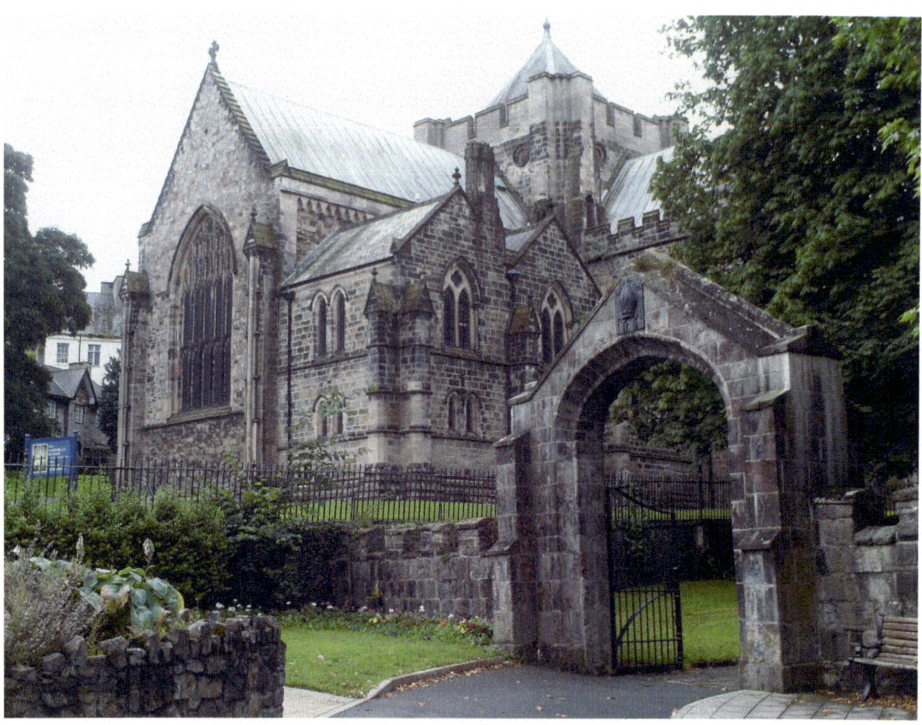

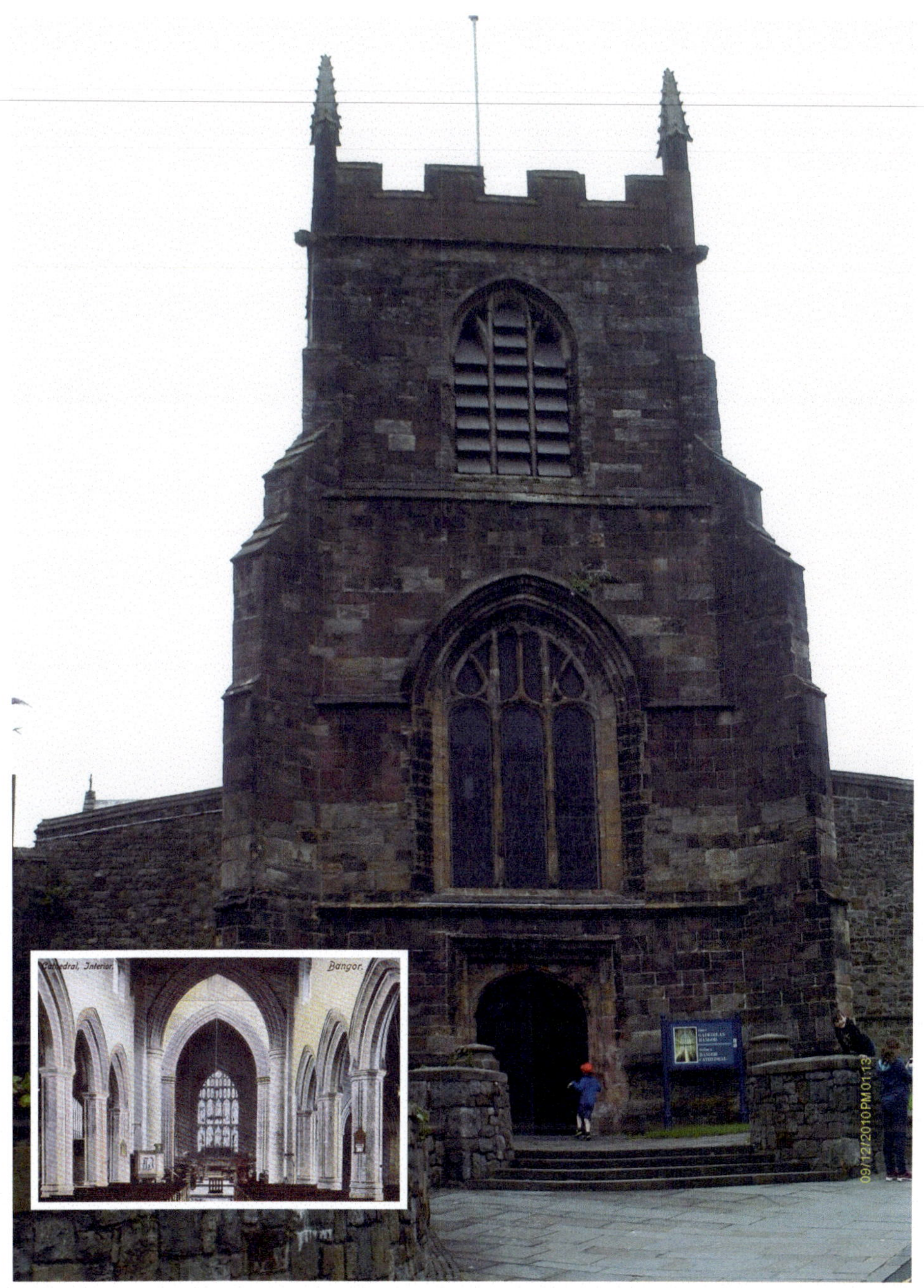

Bangor Cathedral Interior, Cathedral Close, *c.* 1910

The site of the church is low-lying, possibly to avoid detection by Viking raiders. The earliest part of the present building was constructed during the episcopate of Bishop David (1120–39), with the financial help of the King of Gwynedd, Gruffudd ap Cynan, who was buried by the high altar on his death in 1137. His son, Owain Gwynedd, and brother, Cadwaladr, were also buried here. Much of the present building is the work of George Gilbert Scott, beginning in 1868.

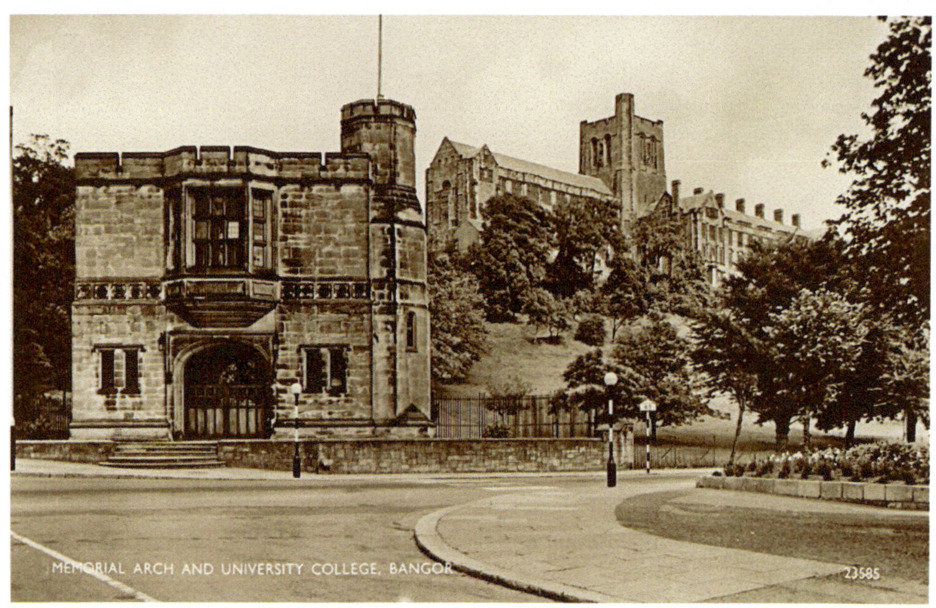

Memorial Arch and University College, Junction of Ffordd Deiniol and Allt Glanrafon (Glanrafon Hill), *c*. 1960. *Inset*: Memorial Plaques

The winning design for a war memorial was built in 1923, the architect being D. Wynne Thomas. It was opened by Edward, Prince of Wales, on 1 November 1923. It takes the form of a Tudor, two-storey gateway. The rectangular upper room is reached by a stone staircase and has all-round wood-carved panels listing 8,500 names by parish, and bronze double doors. It was constructed by John Laing & Son Ltd (Carlisle) under contract for £8,078, with the total cost £15,000.

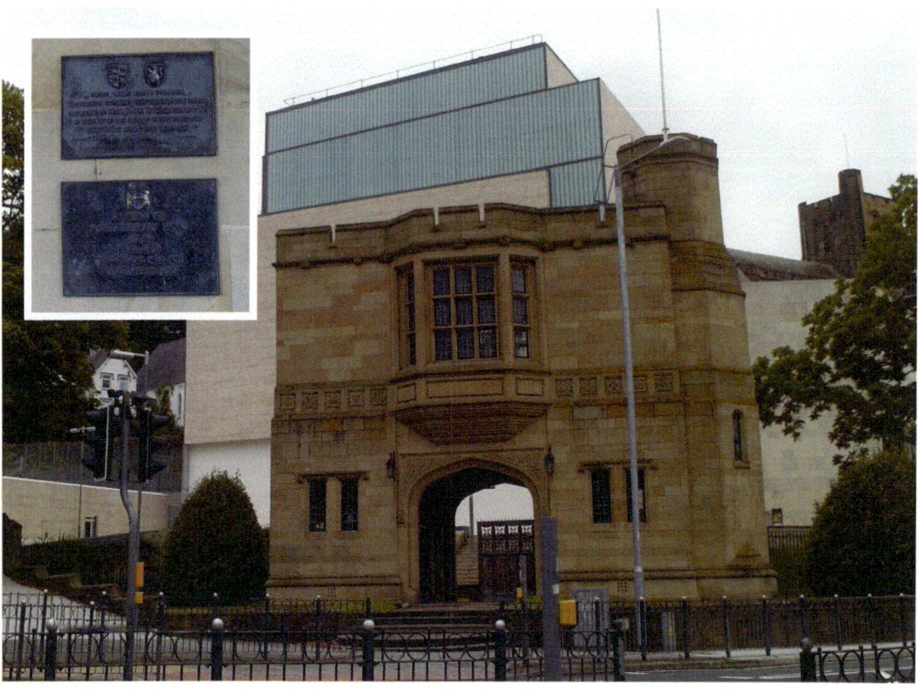

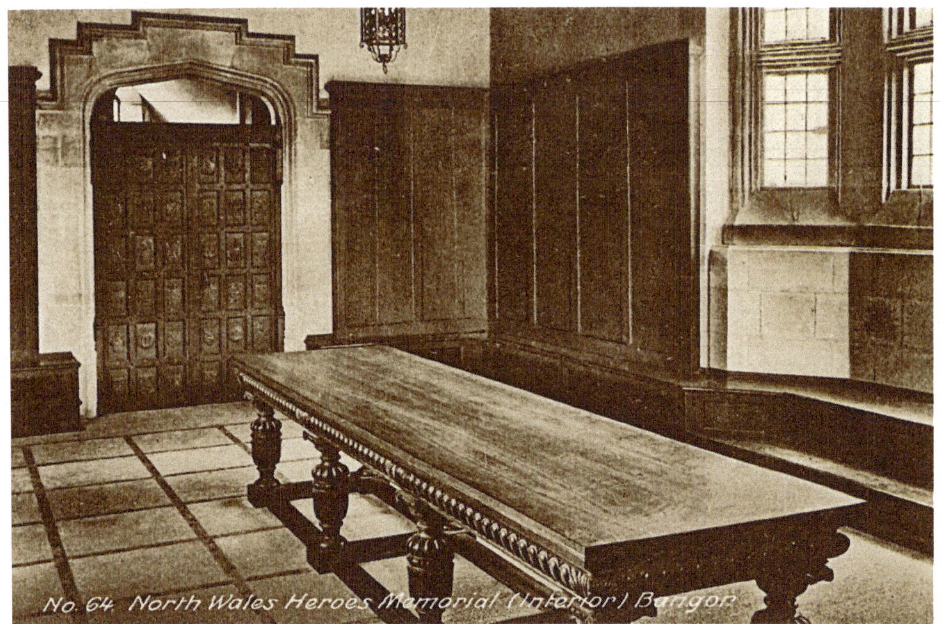

North Wales Heroes' Memorial Interior, Junction of Ffordd Deiniol and Allt Glanrafon (Glanrafon Hill), *c.* 1950

The interior's oak panels list those who fell in the First World War, arranged by the parish and county. Funded by public donations, the project began in 1917 when Bangor University was given £20,000 by Sir Robert Thomas. An arch and new university buildings for science, opened at the same time, were planned. Prime Minister David Lloyd George became one of the patrons. In 2007 the memorial was restored, as the floor of the upstairs room was unsafe and there was water in the basement.

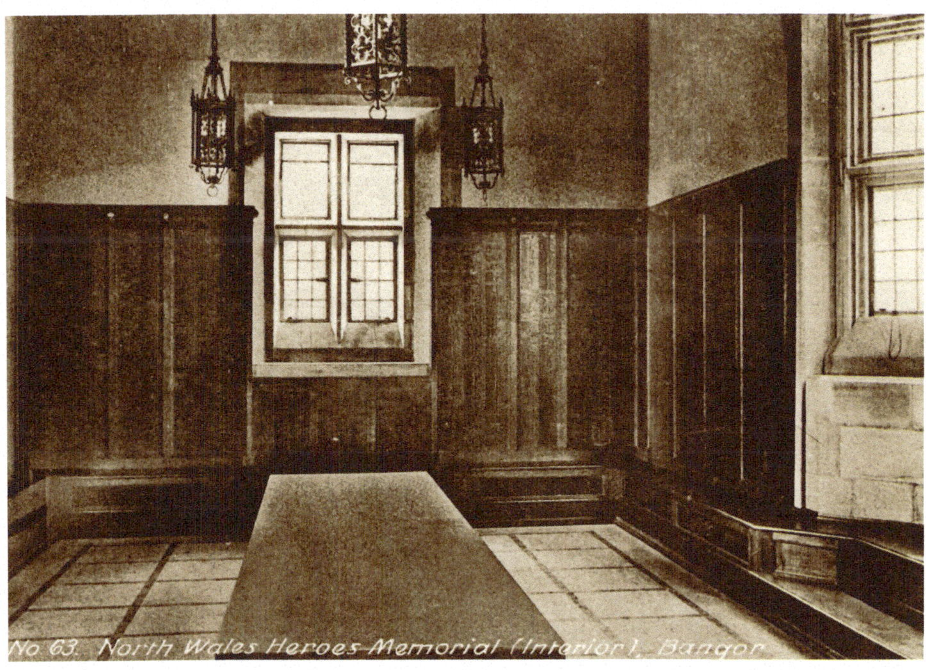

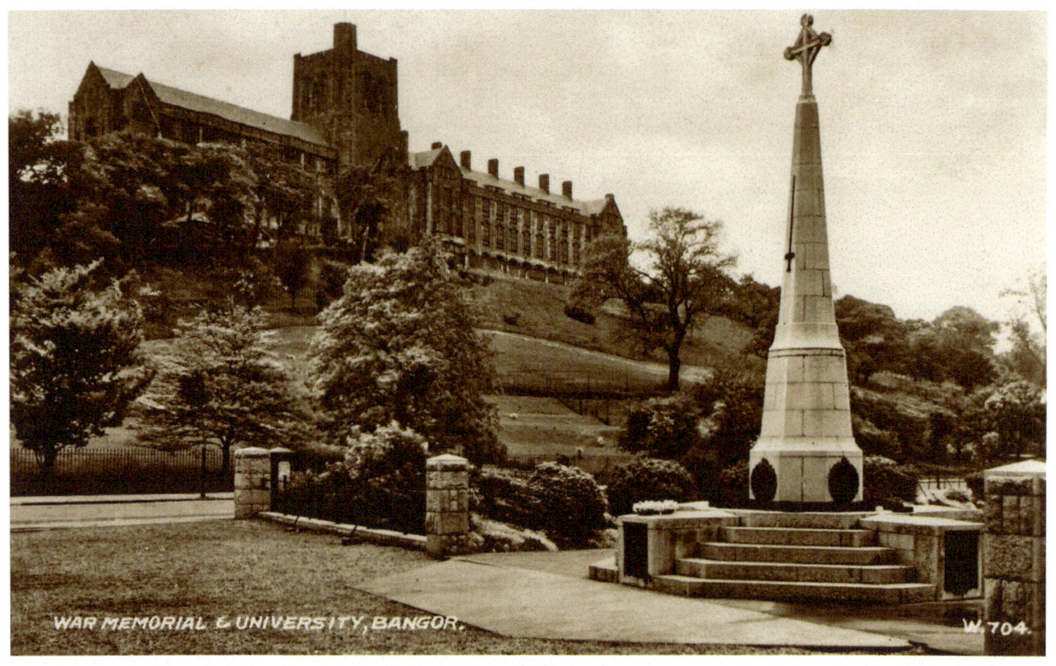

War Memorial and University College, Ffordd Deiniol, Bangor, *c.* 1930
The war memorial (*inset*) stands opposite the North Wales Heroes' Memorial and commemorates the war dead of Bangor. The main memorial lists the local people who died in active service in the First and Second World Wars. There is also a slate memorial listing members of the Royal Garrison Artillery, who died in both wars. The loss of the SS *Pamela*, once owned by Lord Penrhyn, is recorded, as is the death of the only son of the 1st Baronet of Faenol (Vaynol) Park.

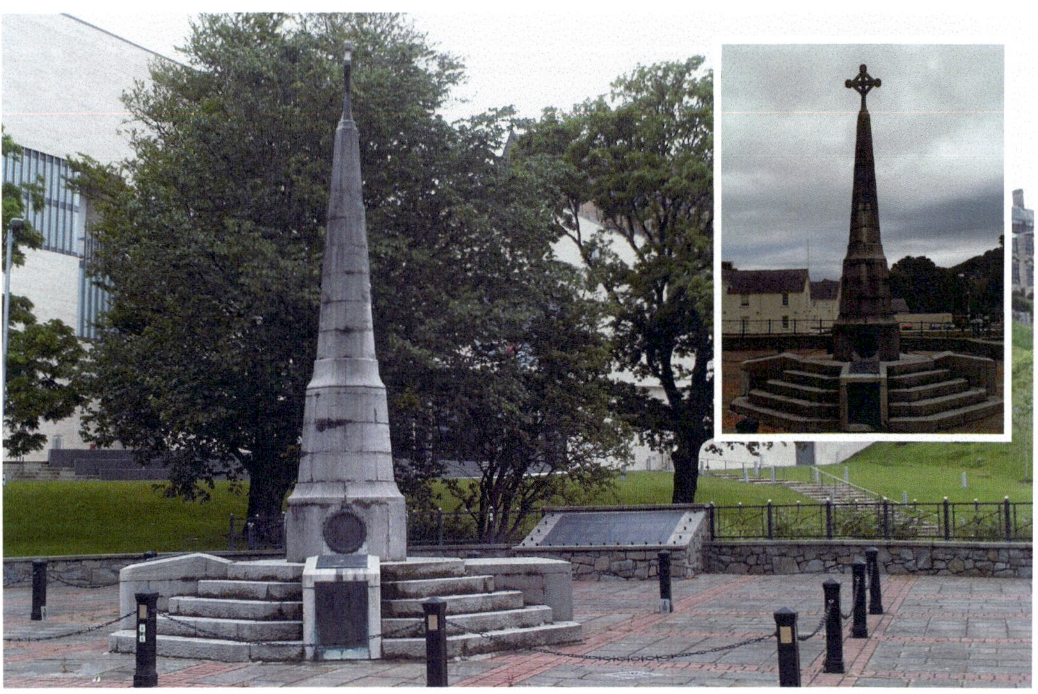

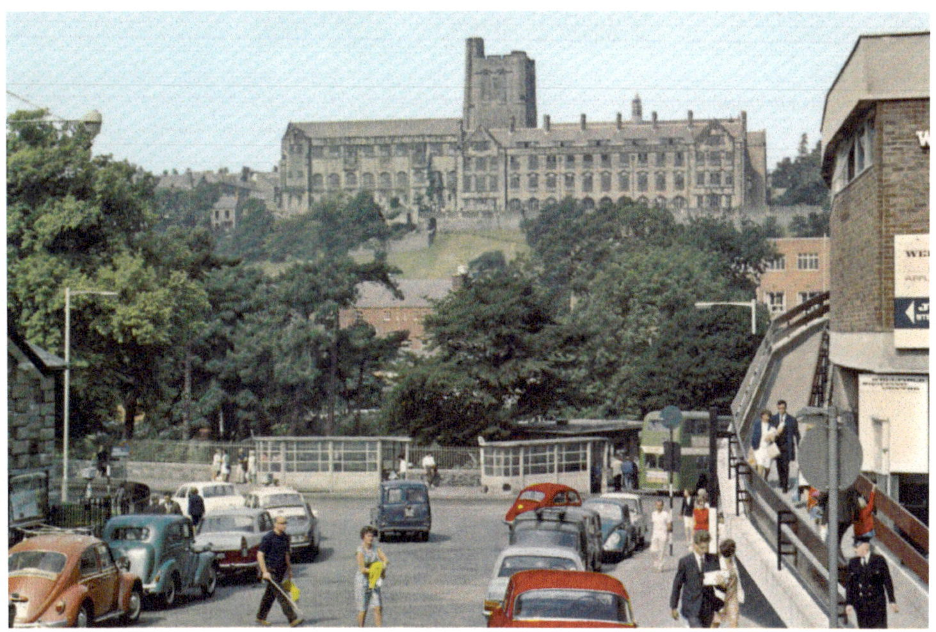

Bangor University and Wellfield Shopping Centre, Ffordd Garth, *c.* 1970

The university was founded as the result of a campaign to improve higher education provision in north Wales. Funds were raised by public subscription and voluntary contributions, including those from quarrymen's wages. It was founded as the University College of North Wales, opening on 18 October 1884, in an old coaching inn, the Penrhyn Arms. There were fifty-eight students and ten members of staff. In 1893 the University of Wales was founded, with Bangor one of the three original founding colleges.

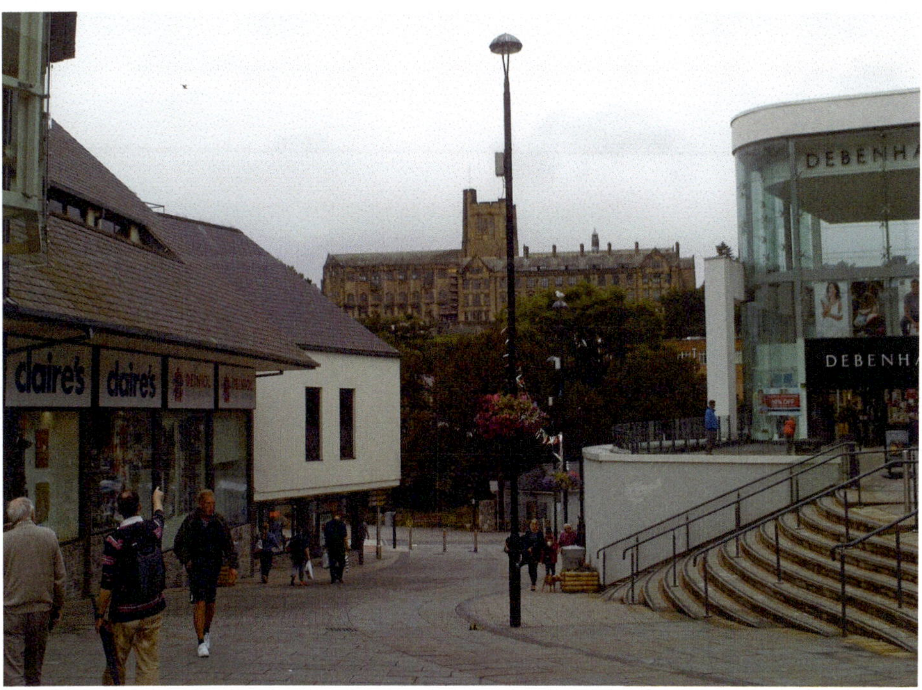

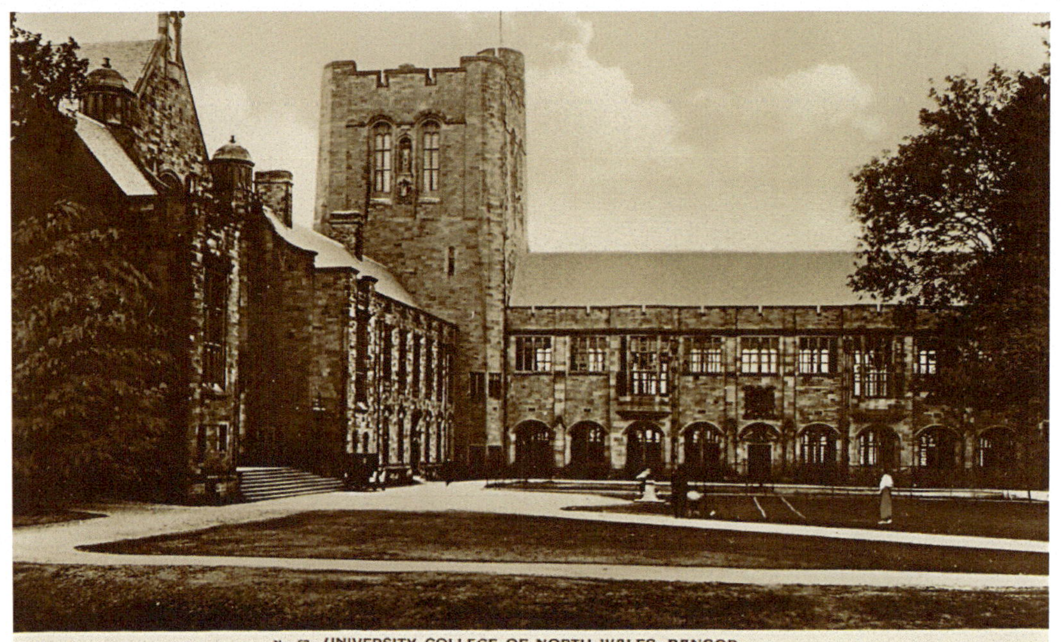

No. 67. UNIVERSITY COLLEGE OF NORTH WALES, BANGOR.

University College of North Wales, Ffordd Deiniol, Bangor, *c.* 1900

In 1903 the City of Bangor donated a 10-acre site overlooking Penrallt for a new building with money raised by public subscription. The foundation stone for the new building was laid in 1907, with the main building opening in 1911, together with some arts and social sciences buildings and part of the library. The science departments remained in the Penrhyn Arms Hotel until 1926, when they moved to a new purpose-built headquarters, constructed with the North Wales Heroes' Memorial.

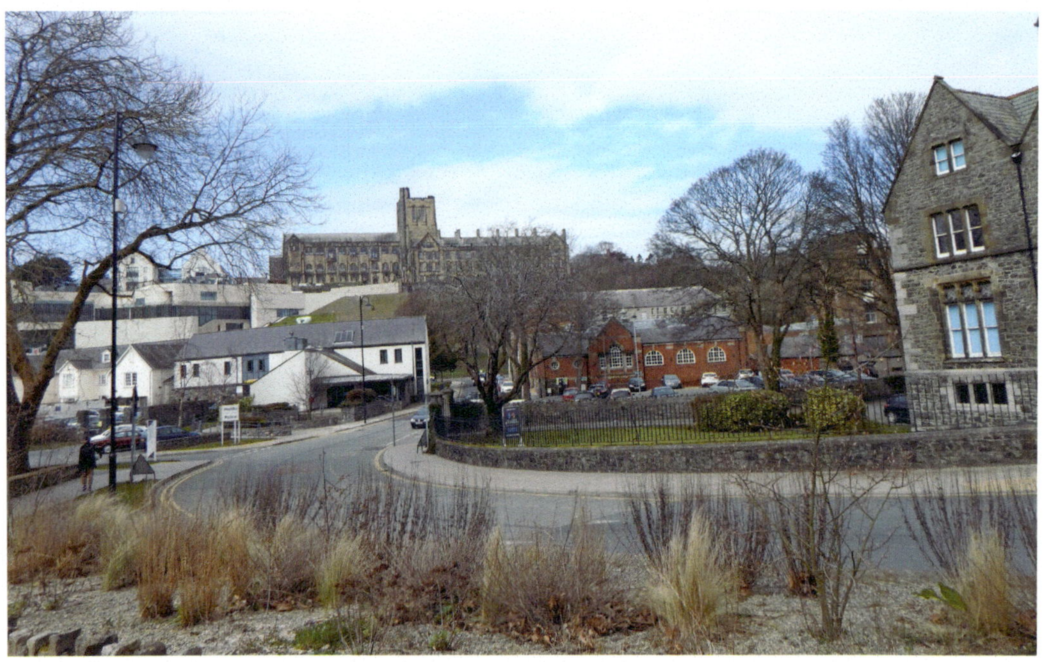

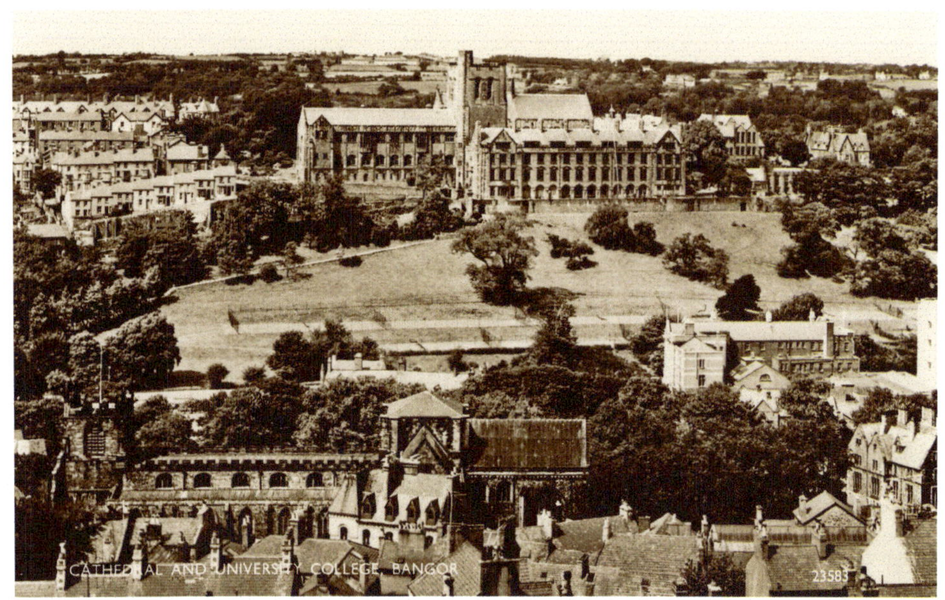

Aerial View of Cathedral and University College, Bangor, *c.* 1950. *Inset*: Bangor from the Recreation Ground, *c.* 1940

When the University College opened on 18 October 1884, an inaugural address was given by the Earl of Powis in Penrhyn Hall. This was followed by a procession to the university of 3,000 quarry-workers, from Penrhyn and other quarries, who had contributed over £1,200 to fund the institution's opening. The new building, designed by Henry Hare and opened by King Edward VII in 1911, is now the old part of the main Arts Building. Today there are over 12,000 students and 2,000 staff.

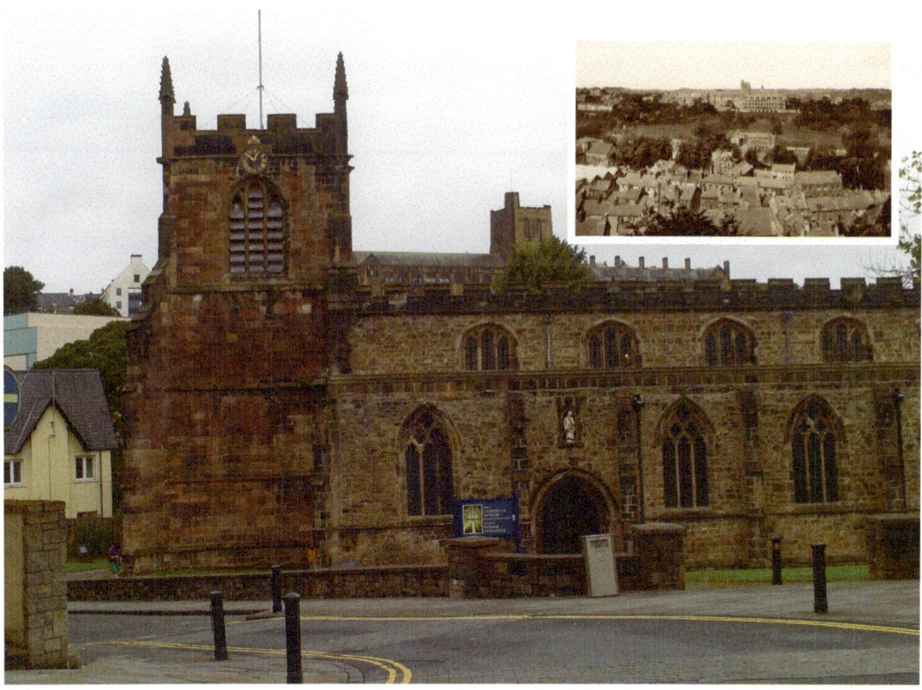

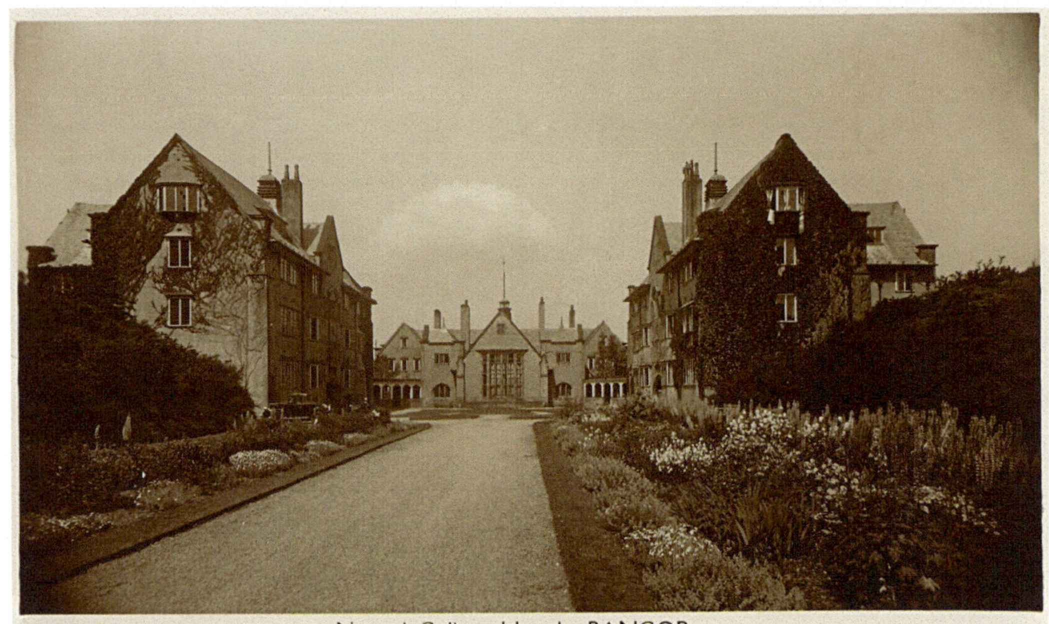
Normal College Hostels. BANGOR

Normal College Hostels, Ffordd Caergybi (Holyhead Road), Bangor, 1941

Normal College is now a part of the university's Department of Education, but in the 1950s it was at the centre of a political storm. One student objected to the strict rules, specifically designed for female students. Her case was taken by the National Union of Students and the NUT teaching union. MPs eventually raised the issue in the House of Commons. However, it was fifteen years after her expulsion, in 1969, before the rules changed. She managed to finish her course at another college.

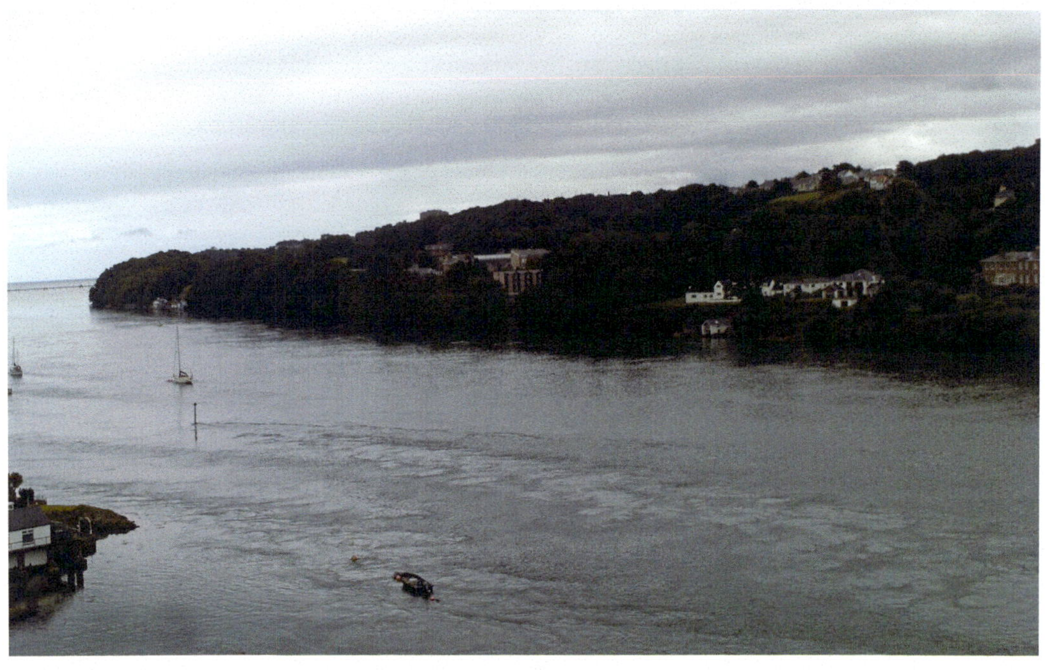

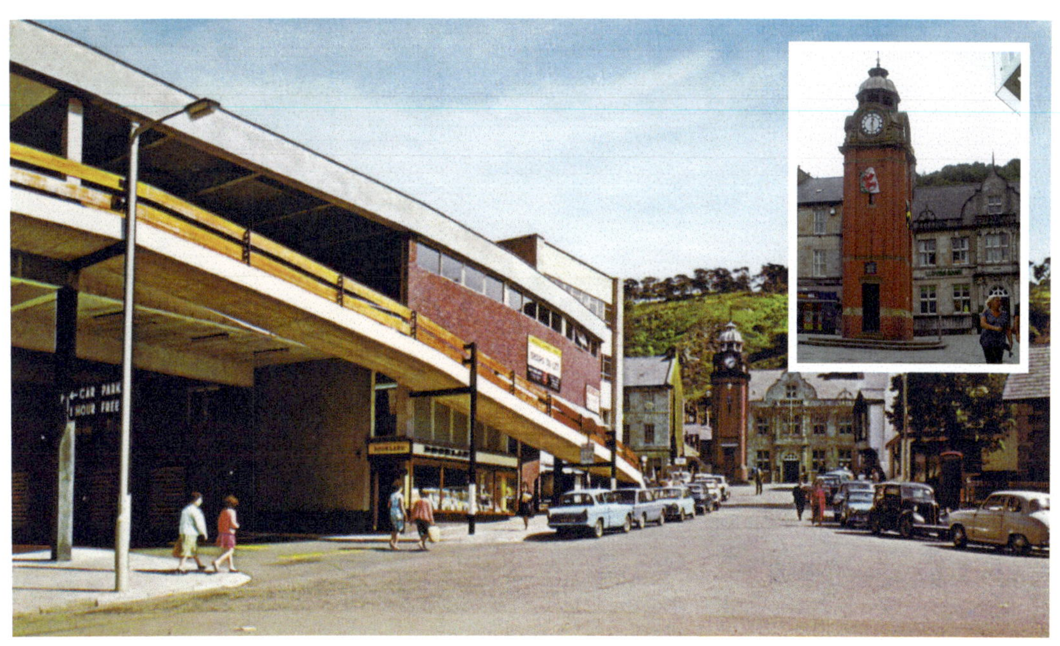

Bangor Shopping Centre and Clock Tower, *c.* 1960

At the junction of the High Street and Garth Road stands Bangor's Victorian red-brick Twr y Cloc, or Clock Tower (*inset*). It was the gift of former mayor Thomas Lewis and was presented to the city, according to an inscription on it, by 'Alderman Thomas Lewis J.P. during his Mayoralty as a token of his interest in the welfare of the city, 1886/7'. The Clock Tower was restored in 1986 and is a well-known landmark, making it a popular meeting place.

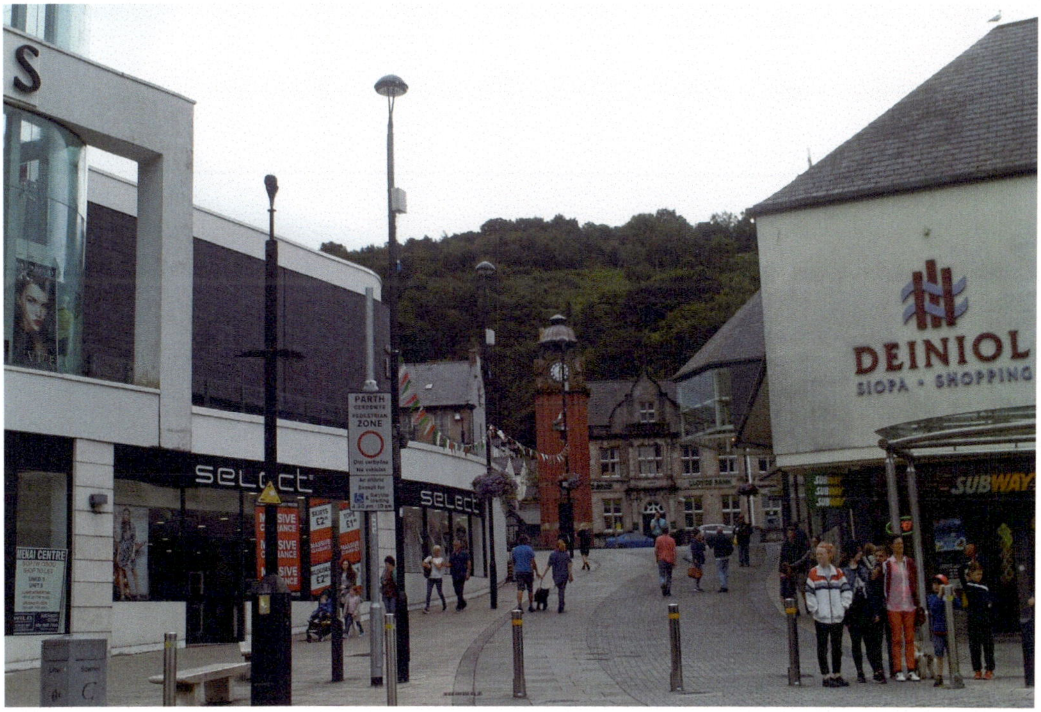

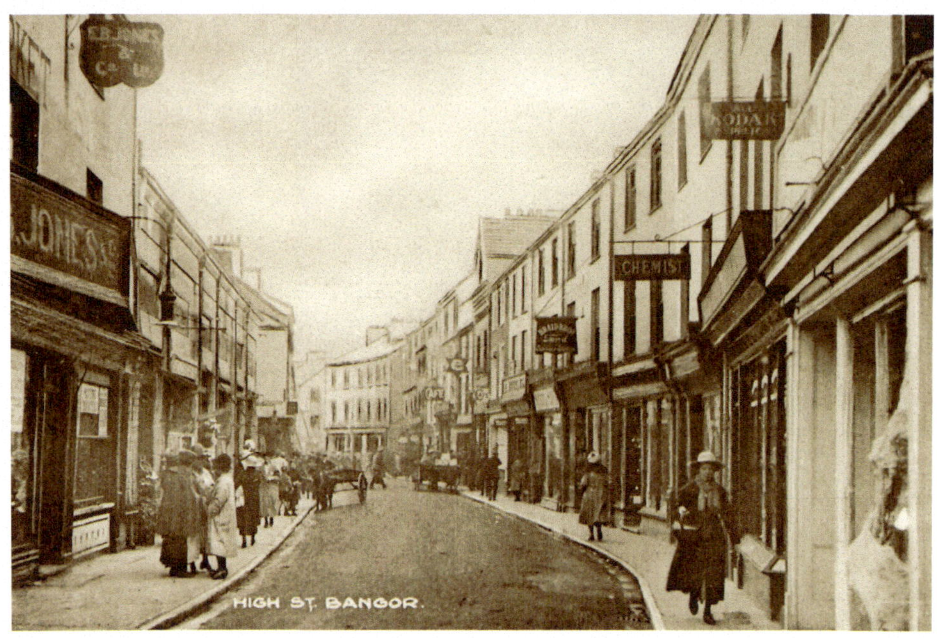

Stryd Fawr (High Street), Bangor, *c.* 1910

Today traffic has restricted access to the shopping centre. The city centre has two modern shopping centres (Menai and Deiniol) and was redeveloped in the 2000s. There is a range of larger stores and smaller, independently owned shops, a cinema and a theatre. Bangor is one of the smallest cities in the United Kingdom, but it is also a city with a strong cultural identity, where Welsh is the chosen language of the vast majority (despite the official figures).

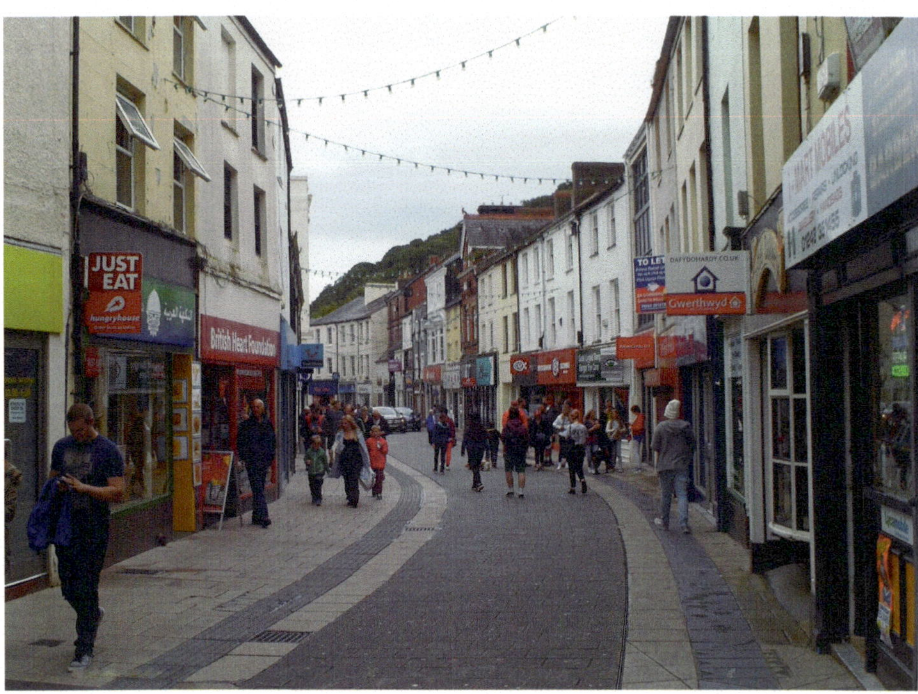

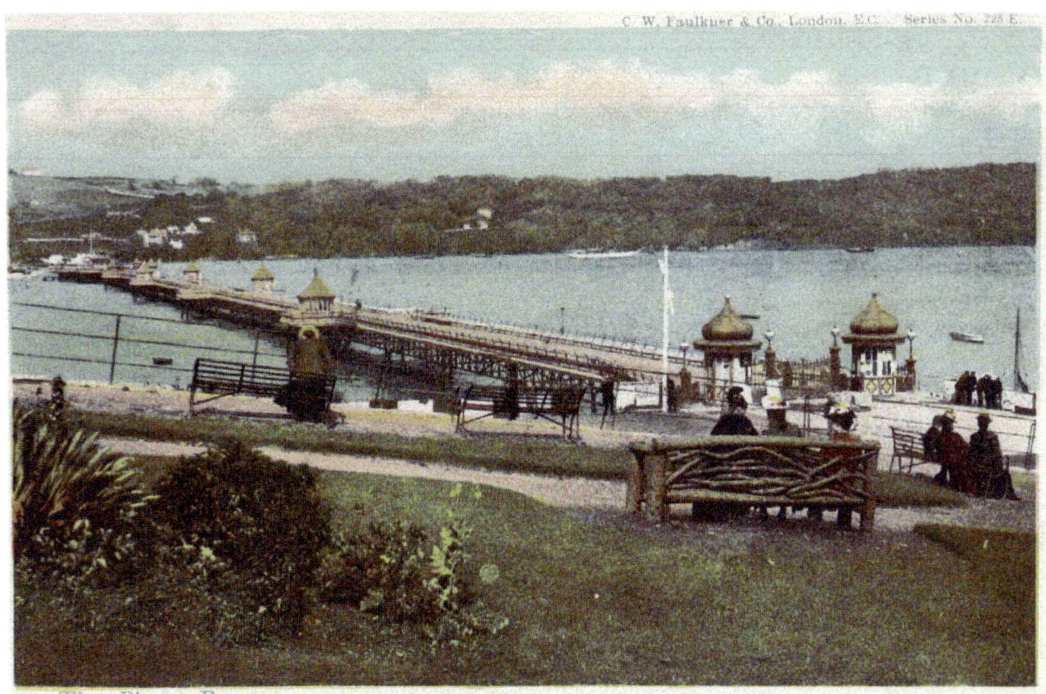

Garth Pier, Ffordd Garth, Bangor, 1905

The pier is a Grade II-listed structure and is currently 460 metres (1,500 feet) long, making it the second longest pier in Wales and the ninth longest in the British Isles. It was designed by J. J. Webster of Westminster, London. Originally 470 metres (1,550 feet) long, the pier has cast-iron columns, with a metal structure of steel throughout, including the handrails. It opened on 14 May 1896, the opening ceremony being performed by George Douglas-Pennant, 2nd Baron Penrhyn.

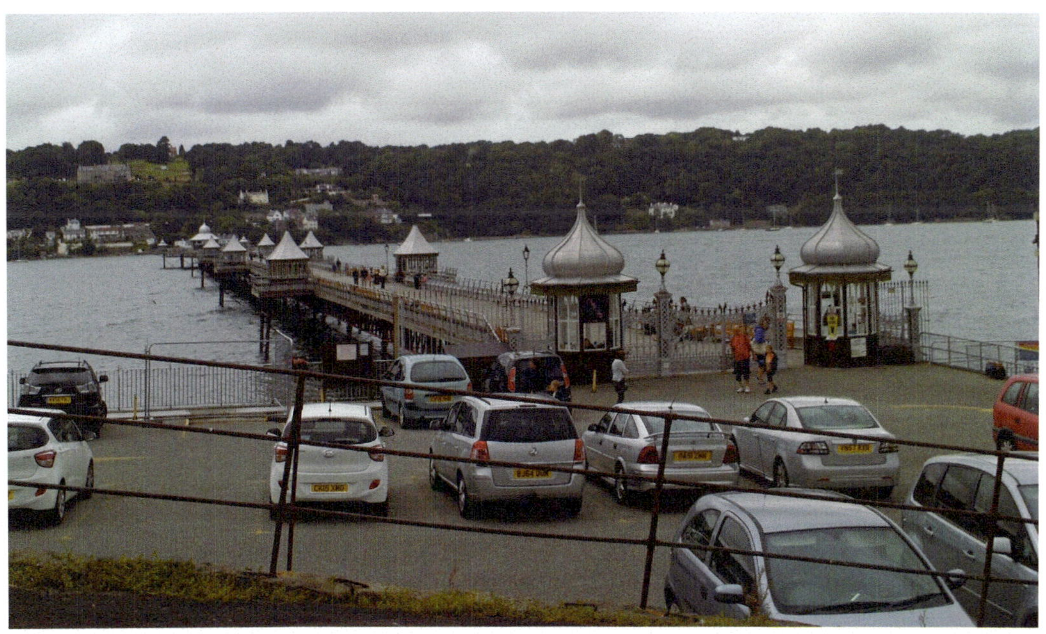

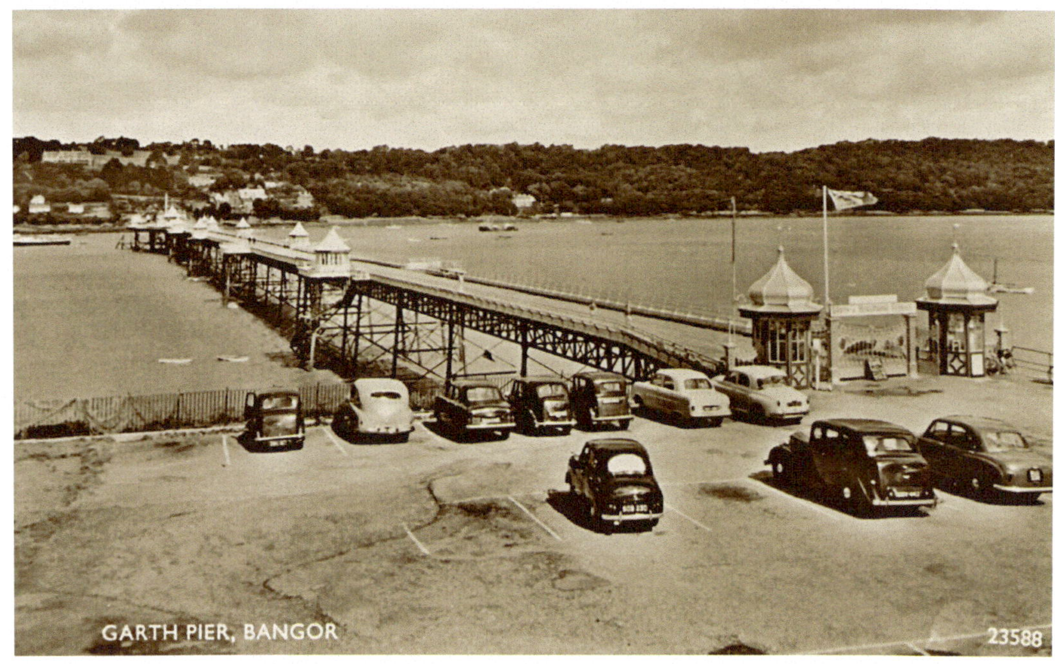

Garth Pier, Ffordd Garth, Bangor, *c.* 1950

The pier cost £14,475 to build and opened on 14 May 1896. Over the next eighteen years an annual average of 34,000 passengers disembarked at the pier, while over the same period 442,000 walked on the structure. Included in the design of the pier was a pontoon landing stage and a 90-centimetre (3-feet) gauge railway for baggage handling. Steamers from Douglas, Liverpool and Blackpool regularly used the pier head until 1914. Today, although the steam excursions have gone, the pier remains popular with holidaymakers.

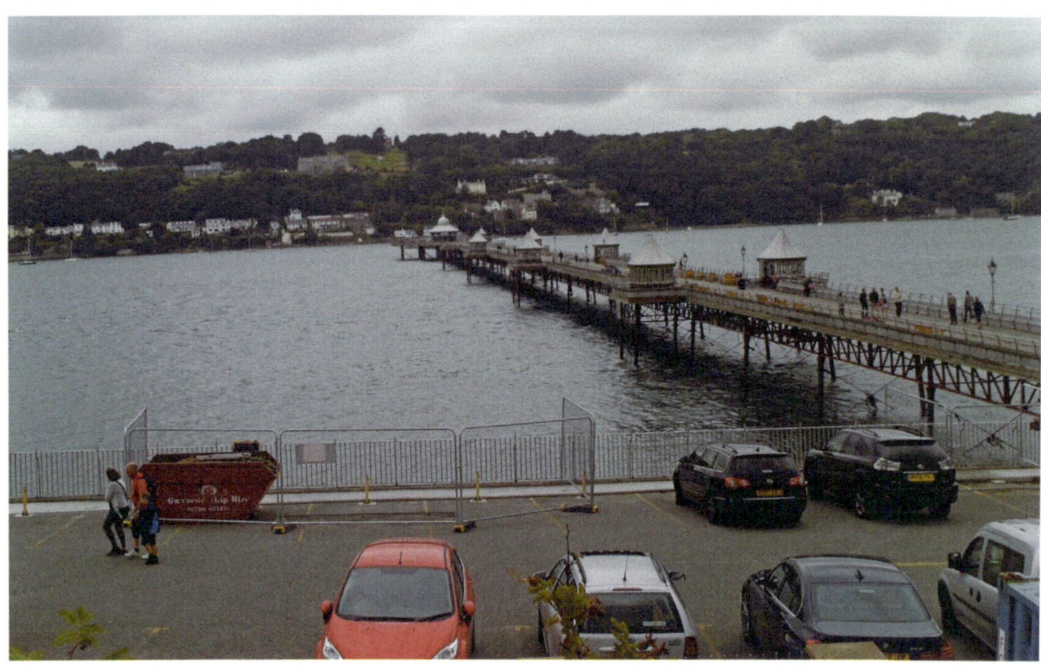

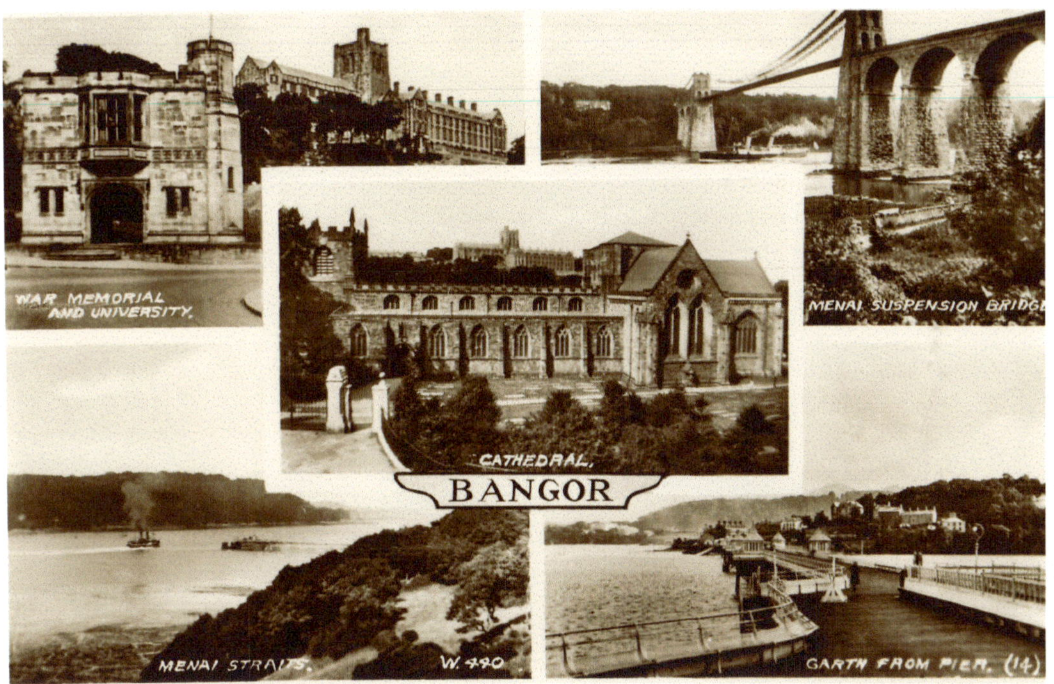

Garth as seen from Garth Pier, *c.* 1930

In 1971 Garth Pier was closed to the public and it was acquired by Arfon Borough Council in 1974, who deemed it should be demolished. However, Bangor City Council successfully obtained Grade II-listed status for the structure, becoming its owners for £1 in 1975. Following a six-year programme of refurbishment, Garth Pier was reopened by the Marquis of Anglesey, in May 1988. Today, it is the second longest pier in Wales and the ninth longest in the British Isles.

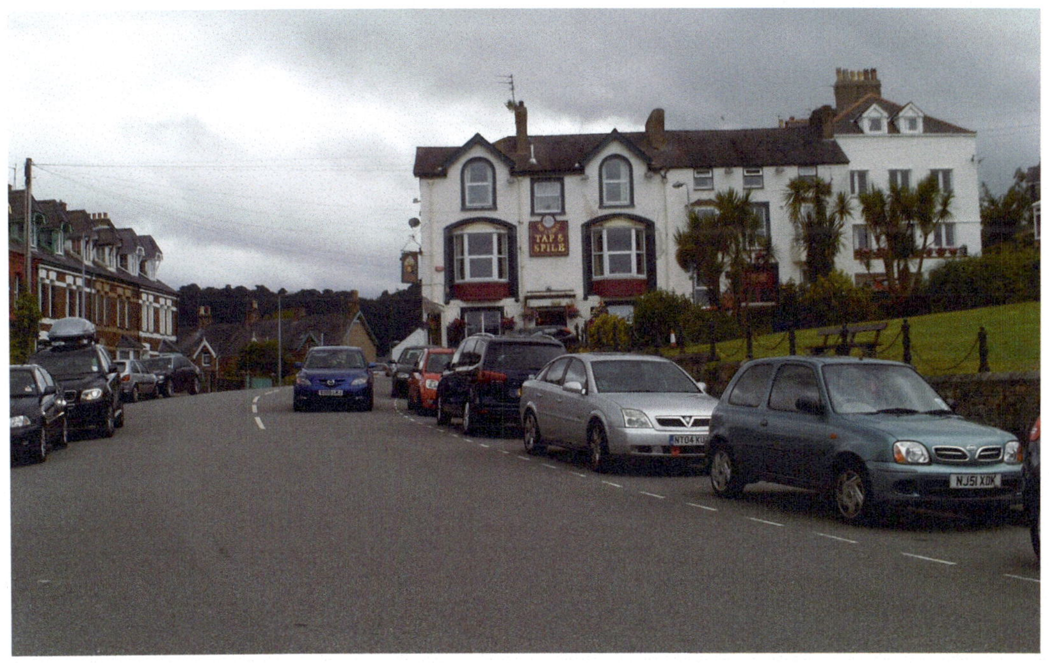

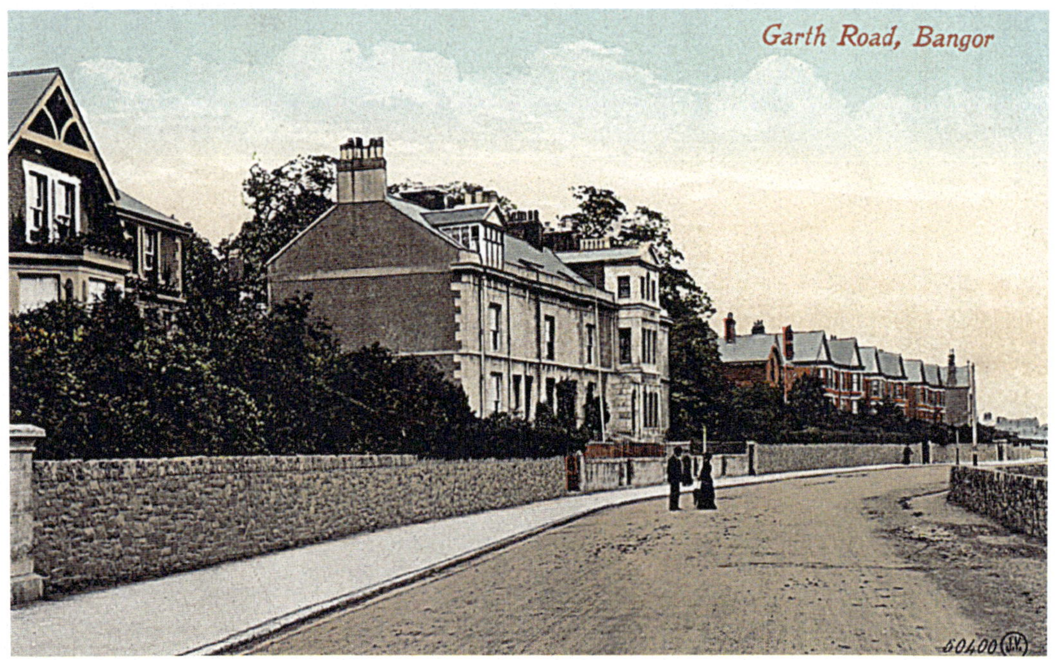

Ffordd Garth, Bangor, *c.* 1900

The substantial houses shown in this picture of Garth Road are still here today, although many of them are now obscured from the road by trees and some have been converted into hotels and boarding houses. Bangor Public Municipal Swimming Baths are also located on Garth Road, opposite the terraces shown in this picture. They opened in 1965 and are now the headquarters for the City of Bangor Swimming Club. Facilities at the baths include water slides and diving boards.

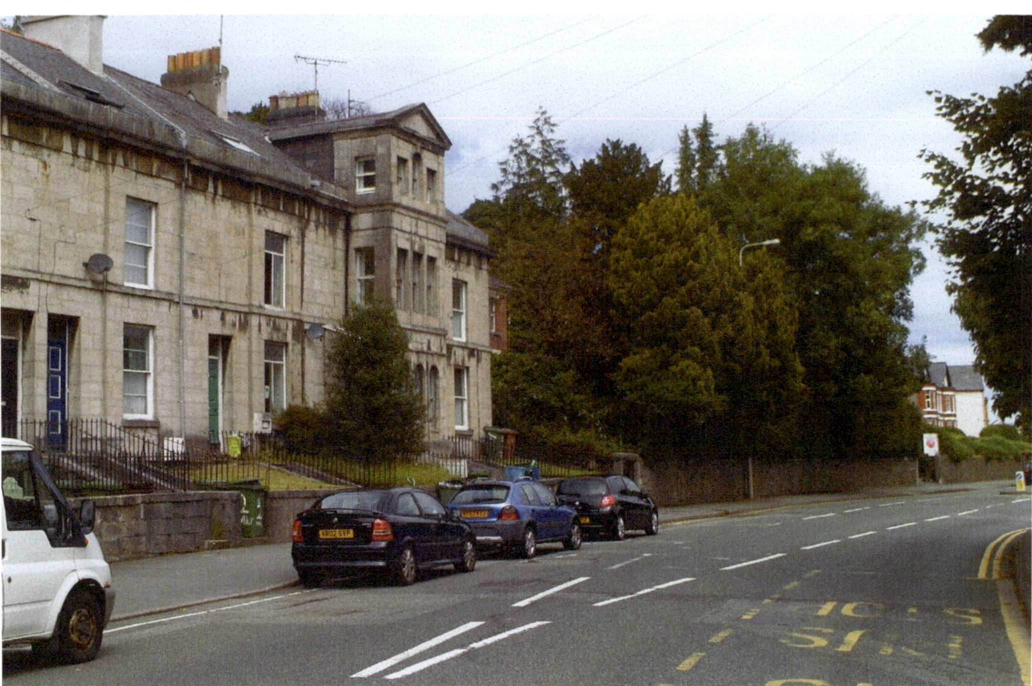

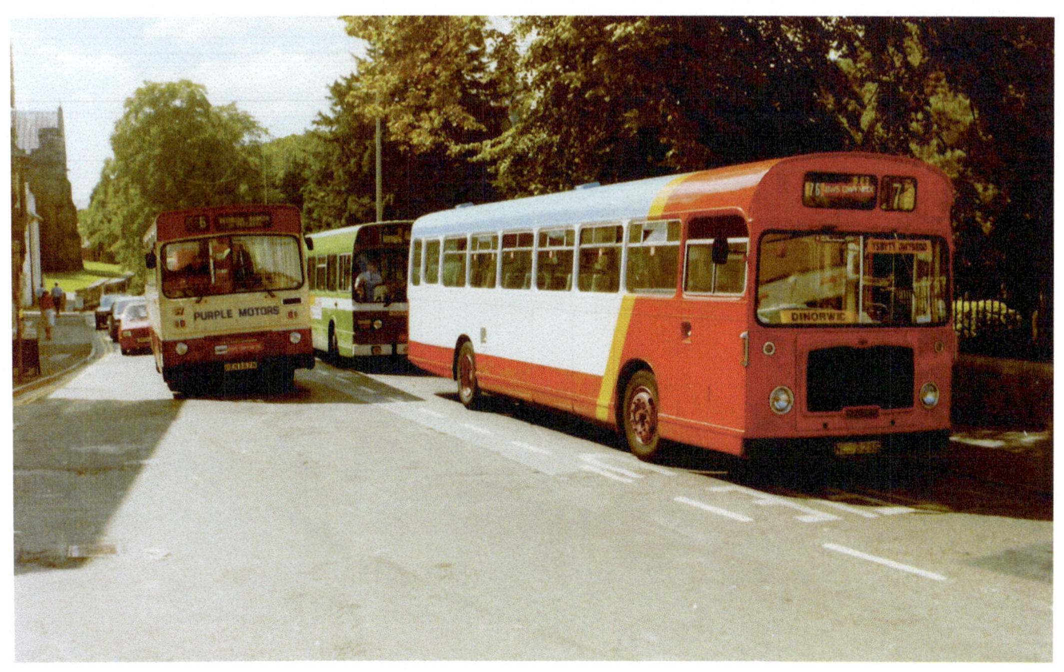

Purple Motors at Ffordd Garth, Bangor, *c.* 1985

Purple Motors was a former independent bus company, based in Bethesda and running local services. They were taken over by Arriva. Their headquarters were located at the old station yard in Bethesda. The company was established by Thomas John Roberts in 1914, running services from Bethesda into Bangor. The 'Castle Garage' and workshop was situated on the south side of the approach road to the old railway station. Limited space meant that buses were often left parked in the open around the station yard.

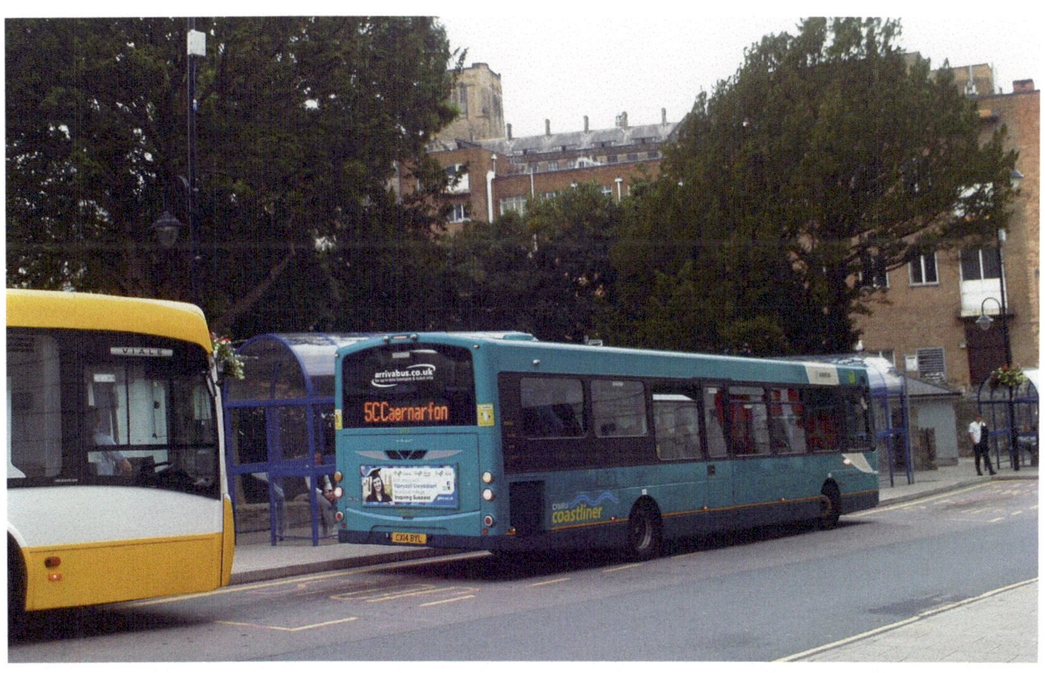

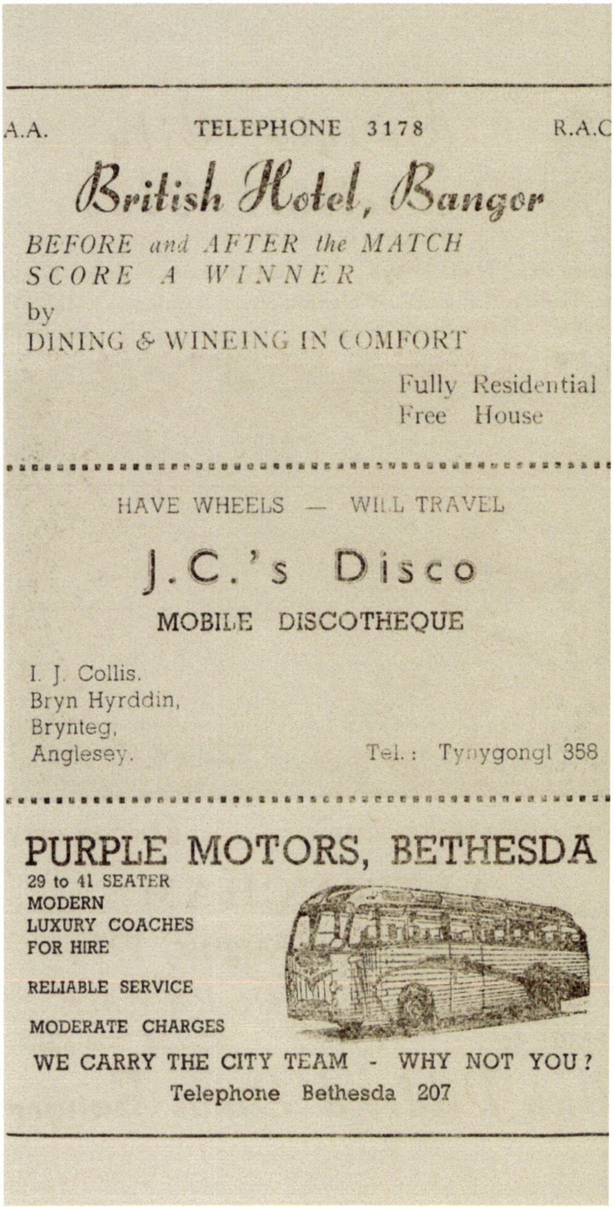

A.A. TELEPHONE 3178 R.A.C

British Hotel, Bangor

BEFORE and AFTER the MATCH
SCORE A WINNER

by
DINING & WINEING IN COMFORT

Fully Residential
Free House

HAVE WHEELS — WILL TRAVEL

J.C.'s Disco

MOBILE DISCOTHEQUE

I. J. Collis.
Bryn Hyrddin,
Brynteg,
Anglesey.

Tel.: Tynygongl 358

PURPLE MOTORS, BETHESDA

29 to 41 SEATER
MODERN
LUXURY COACHES
FOR HIRE

RELIABLE SERVICE

MODERATE CHARGES

WE CARRY THE CITY TEAM - WHY NOT YOU?

Telephone Bethesda 207

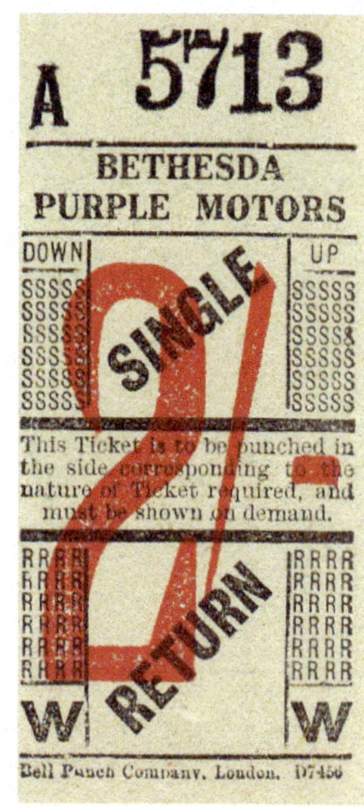

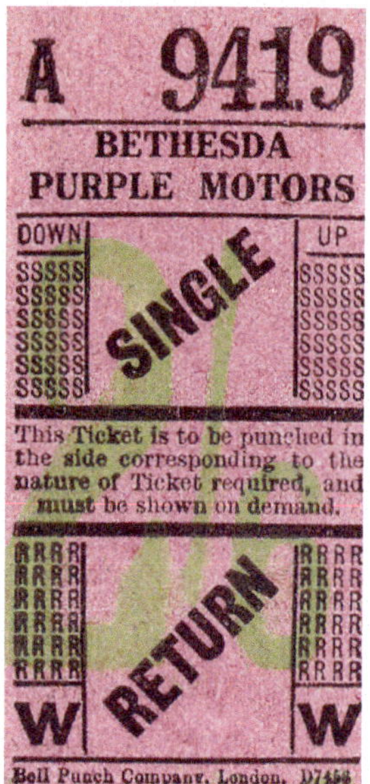

Purple Motors Advertisement and Bus Tickets, Bethesda, *c.* 1970

Purple Motors bus livery was ruby red, maroon and cream in various combinations, sometimes with red relief, but never purple. In 1952 the management and day-to-day running of the fleet was entrusted to Deiniolen Motors. In return the latter company was able to use Purple Motors' well-equipped Bethesda workshop facilities in order to maintain its own fleet. From 1952 to approximately 1977 the single-decker fleet comprised three to four buses and five to six coaches. They ceased trading in 1998.

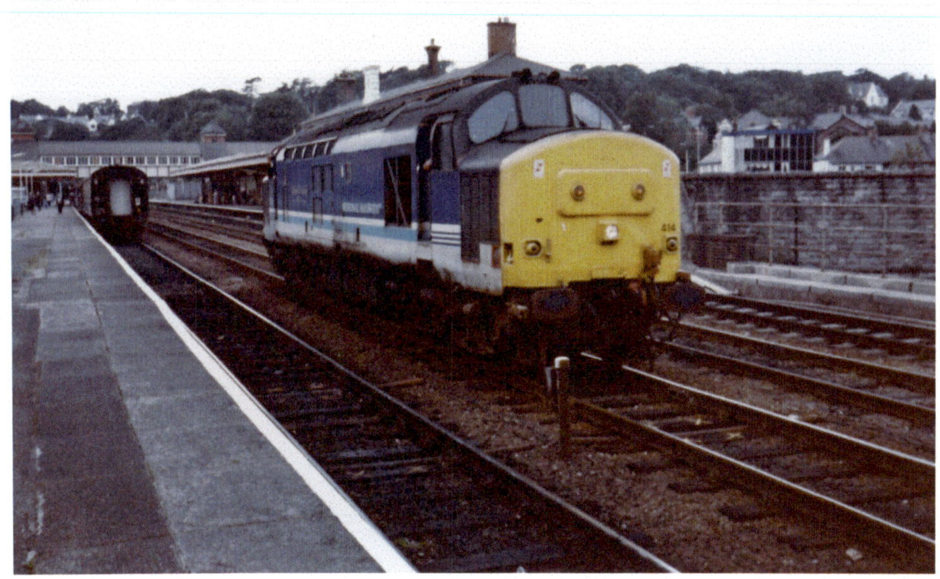

Bangor Railway Station, Ffordd Caergybi (Holyhead Road), *c.* 1985

For two years, from May 1848, Bangor was the terminus of the Chester & Holyhead Railway. Completion of the Britannia Bridge in 1850 then allowed the *Irish Mail* and passenger trains to continue to the port of Holyhead. The main station building, east of the current entrance, was designed by Francis Thompson, the railway's architect. The current booking hall at Bangor and the entrance to the footbridge were built by the LMS Railway in 1927, improving and expanding station facilities at the time.

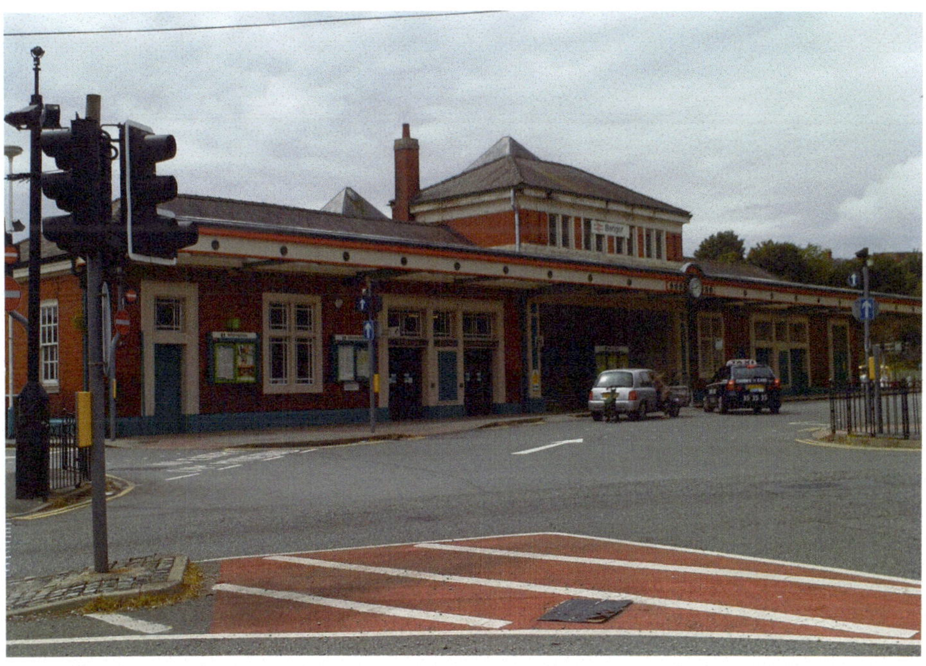

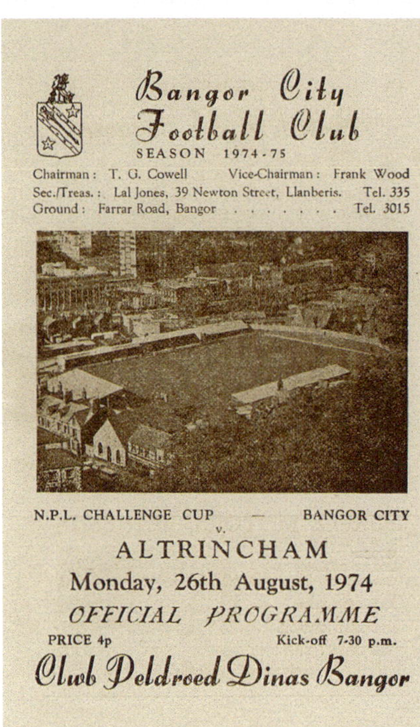
Bangor City Football Club

SEASON 1974-75

Chairman: T. G. Cowell   Vice-Chairman: Frank Wood

Sec./Treas.: Lal Jones, 39 Newton Street, Llanberis. Tel. 335

Ground: Farrar Road, Bangor . . . . Tel. 3015

N.P.L. CHALLENGE CUP — BANGOR CITY

v.

ALTRINCHAM

Monday, 26th August, 1974

OFFICIAL PROGRAMME

PRICE 4p   Kick-off 7-30 p.m.

Club Peldroed Dinas Bangor

Bangor City v Altrincham, Ffordd Farrar, Monday 26 August 1974

Founded in 1876, Bangor City FC is one of Wales' oldest football clubs, ever-present in the League of Wales and former equivalent leagues. When first formed the club played at Maes Y Dref, in the Hirael area of the city. They were eventually evicted from this playing field in favour of the establishment of allotments. Until 2011 they were based at the old cricket ground on Farrar Road, shown above in 1974, before moving to a new stadium at Nant-Porth (*below and inset*).

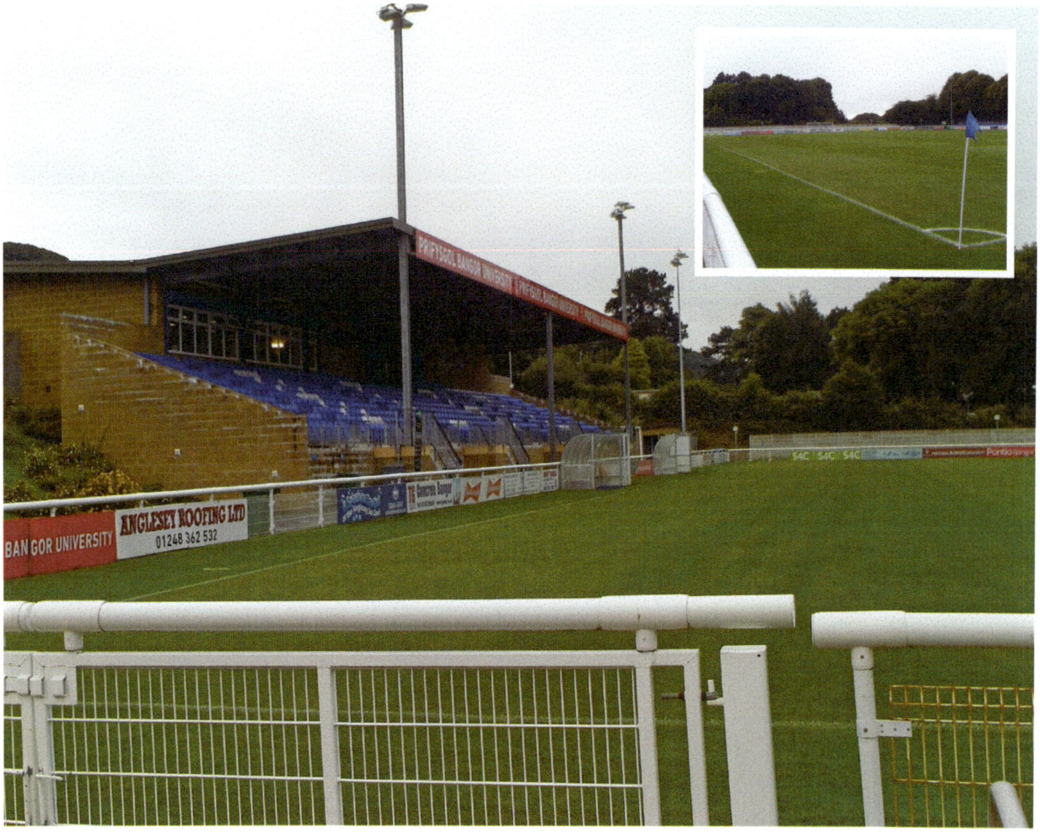

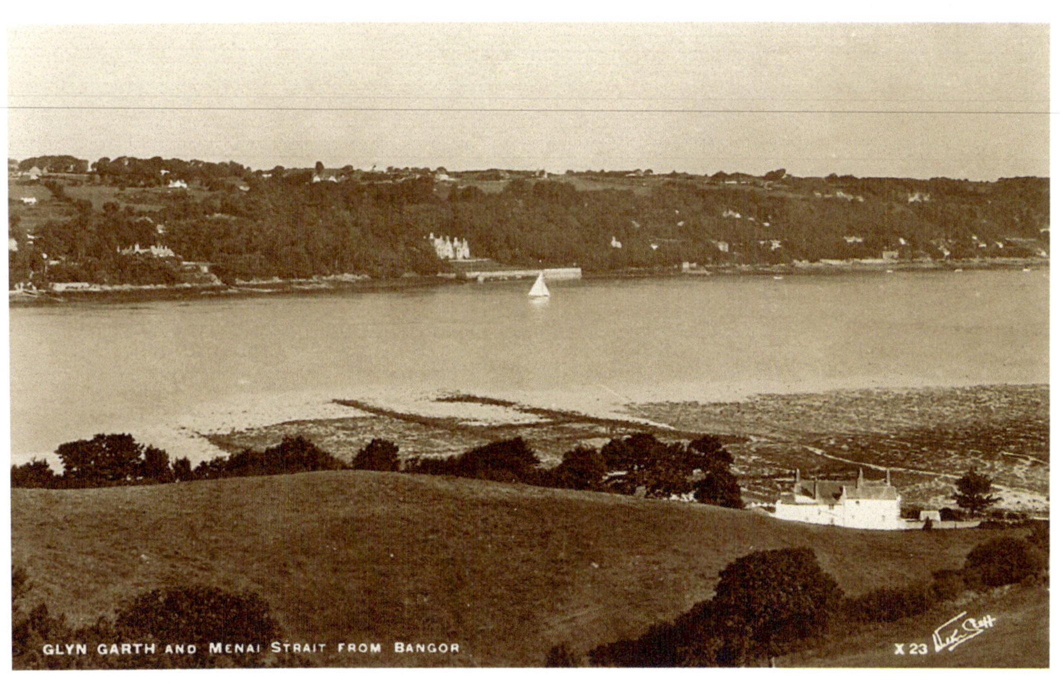

Glyn Garth and Afon Menai (Menai Strait) from Bangor, 1935

The town of Menai Bridge (Porthaethwy), on Anglesey, includes the development along Ffordd Biwmares, known as Glyn Garth. This was a favoured location for holiday homes of the wealthy from the Manchester and Liverpool areas in the nineteenth century, with many of these period dwellings remaining today. This was also where the Bishop of Bangor had his palace. The palace was demolished in the early 1960s and replaced by a block of flats overlooking the Strait, Glyn Garth Court, and completed in 1966.

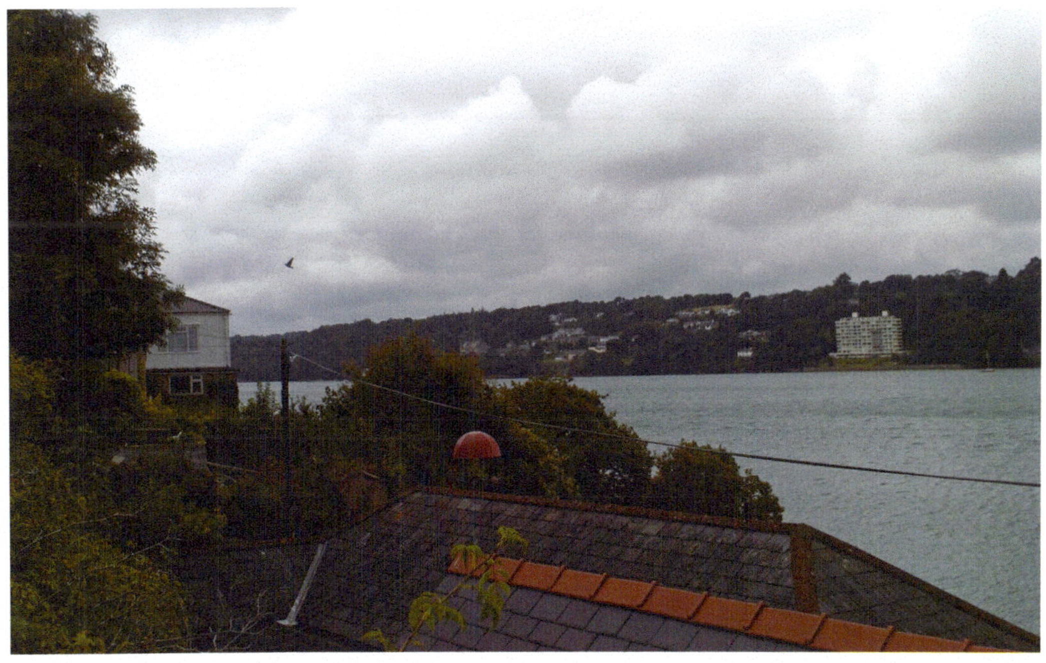

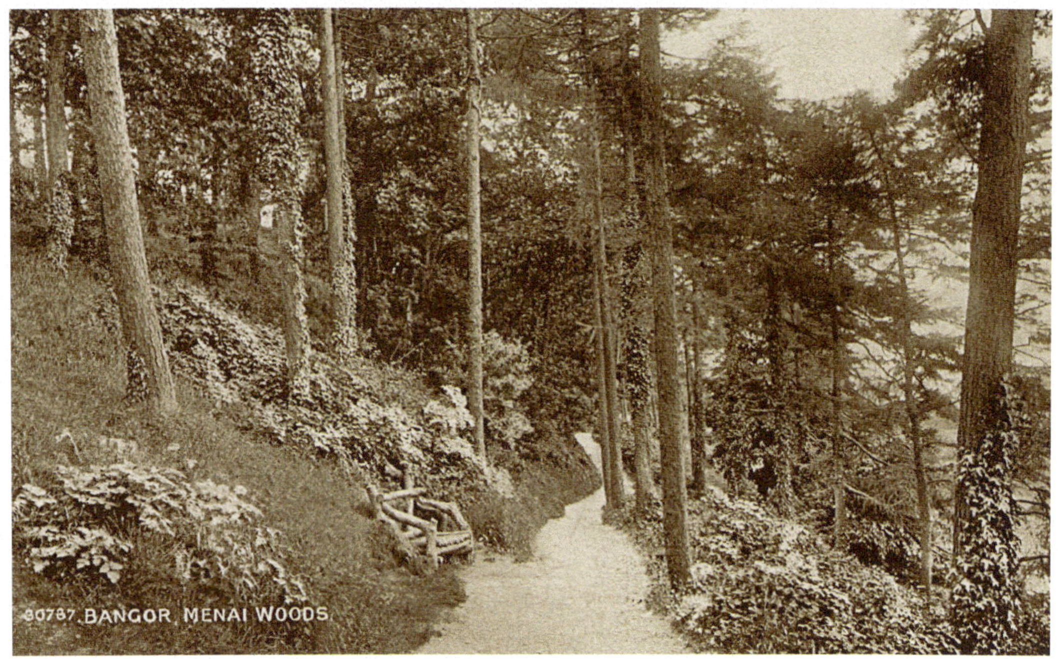

Coed Menai (Menai Woods), Bangor, *c.* 1955, and woodland viewed from Afon Menai, 2016
The tablet at the entrance to the wood, overlooking the Menai Strait at the Bangor end of the Holyhead Road (Ffordd Caergybi), reads,

> Menai Woods Coronation Gift 1953. The freehold of the land occupied by these woods was conveyed to the City of Bangor by Sir Michael Duff of Vaynol Park to commemorate the Coronation of Her Majesty Queen Elizabeth II on 2nd June 1953. This tablet was unveiled by his Worship the Mayor of Bangor Alderman Hugh J. Jones J.P. October 1953.

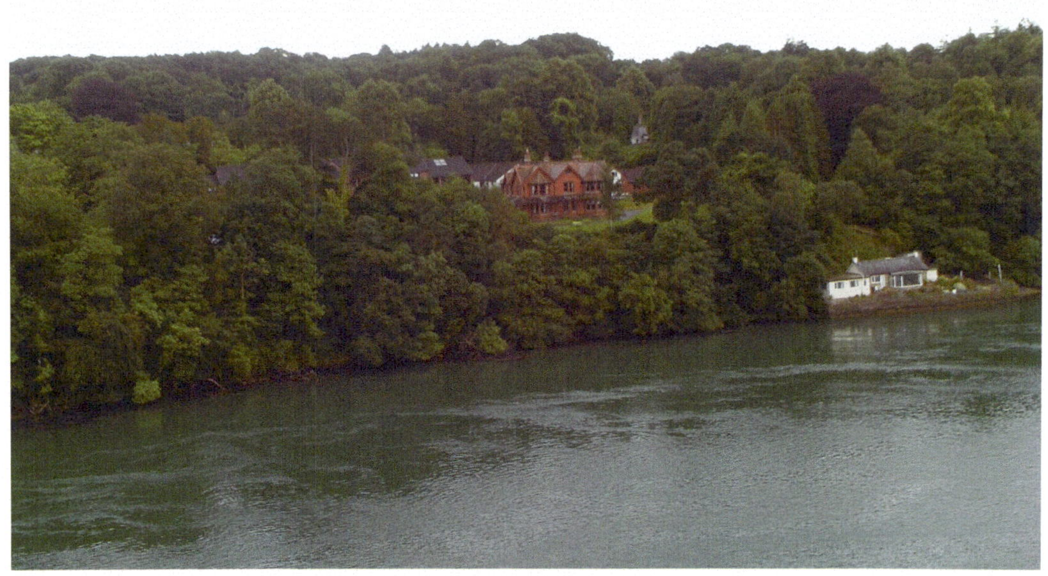

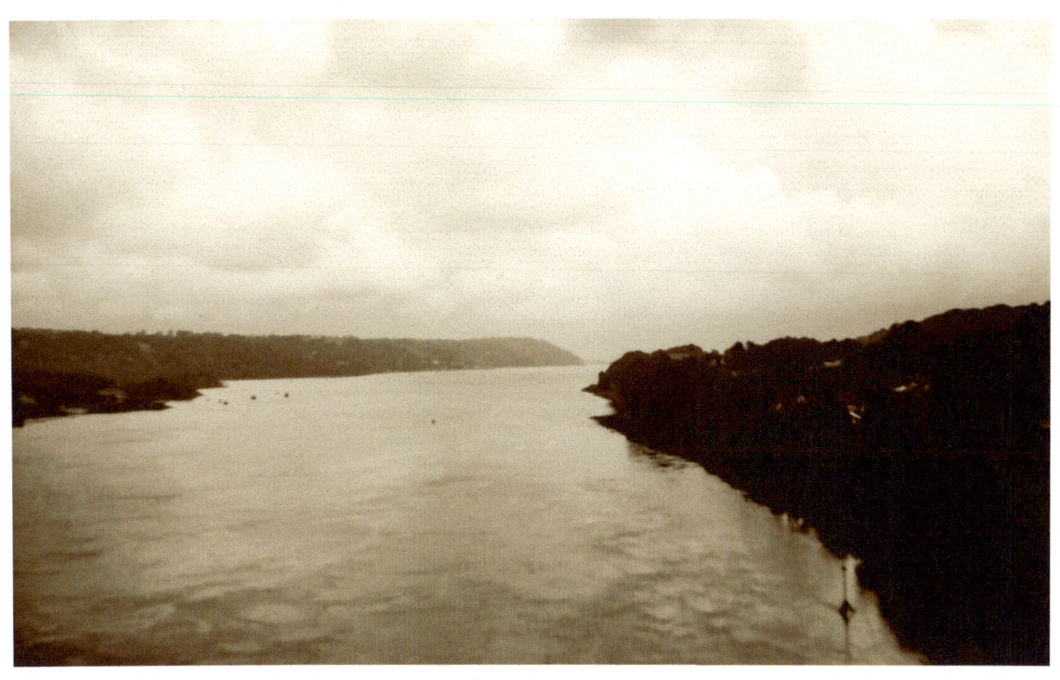

Afon Menai (Menai Strait), 1961

Geologically, the Menai Strait was formed by glacial erosion. It is a narrow stretch of tidal water, which can be extremely treacherous to negotiate depending upon the prevailing tide. One of the most dangerous areas is known as the Swellies, between the two bridges where very strong whirlpools occur. The training ship HMS *Conway* was lost here in 1953. Caernarfon Bar's shifting sandbanks are also dangerous, at the other end of the Strait.

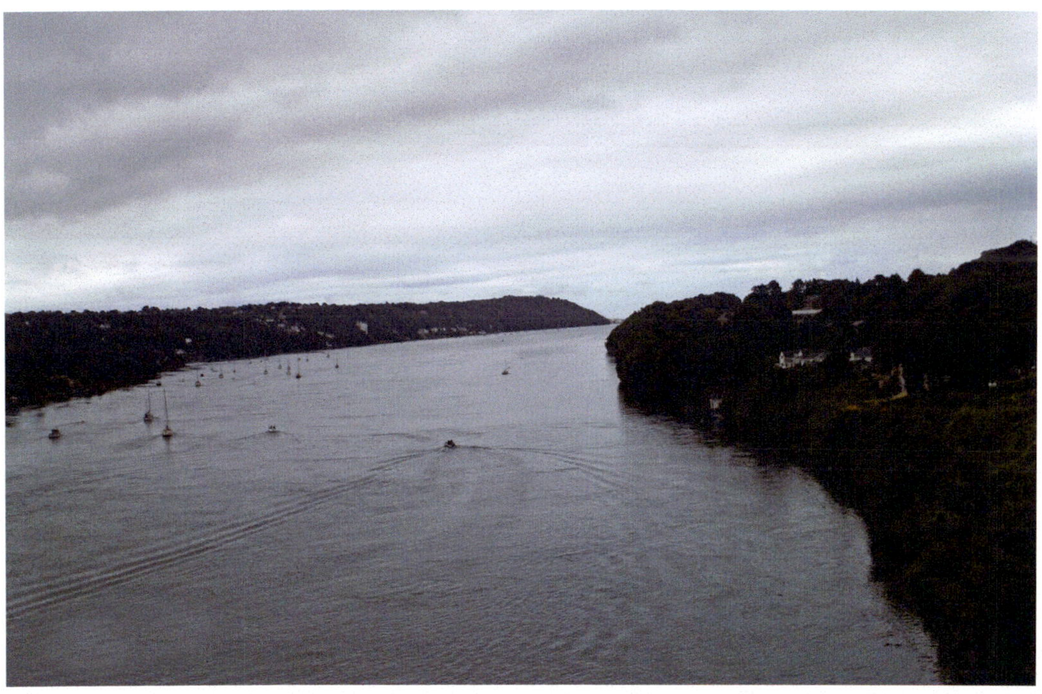

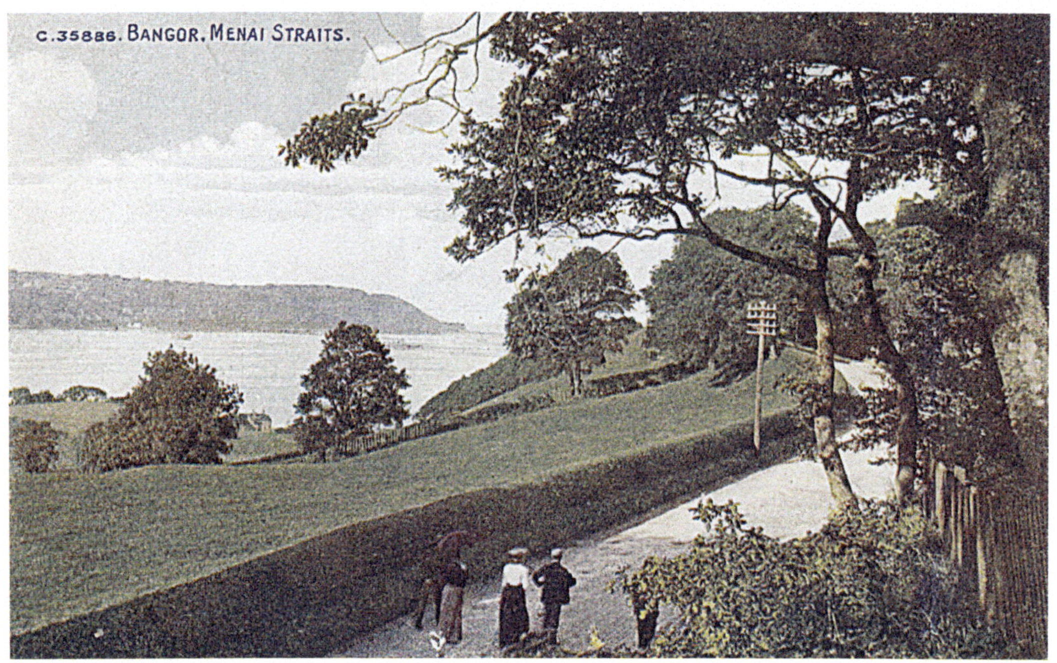

Afon Menai (Menai Strait), *c.* 1910

From the 1890s until 1963 the pleasure steamers of the Liverpool & North Wales Steamship Co. would work their main route from Liverpool to Llandudno, along the Menai Strait and around Anglesey. The company went into voluntary liquidation in 1962 and P & A Campbell took over operations for a while. However, due to the rise of the 'package holiday' in this decade, changing holiday habits in the 1960s and ageing steamships needing refurbishment, the demise of this type of venture was almost inevitable.

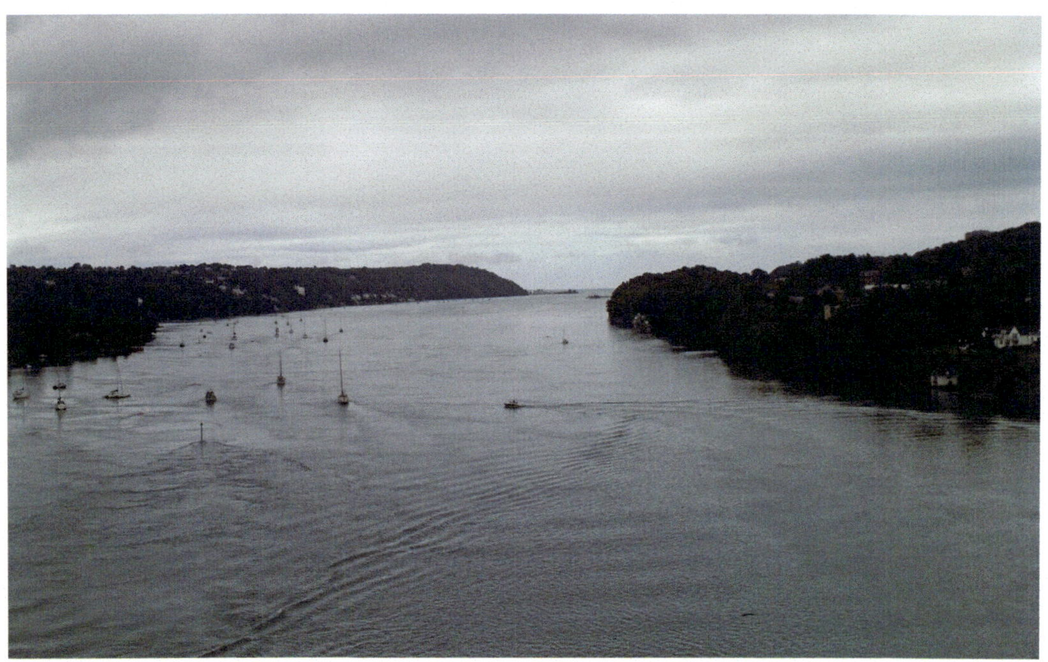

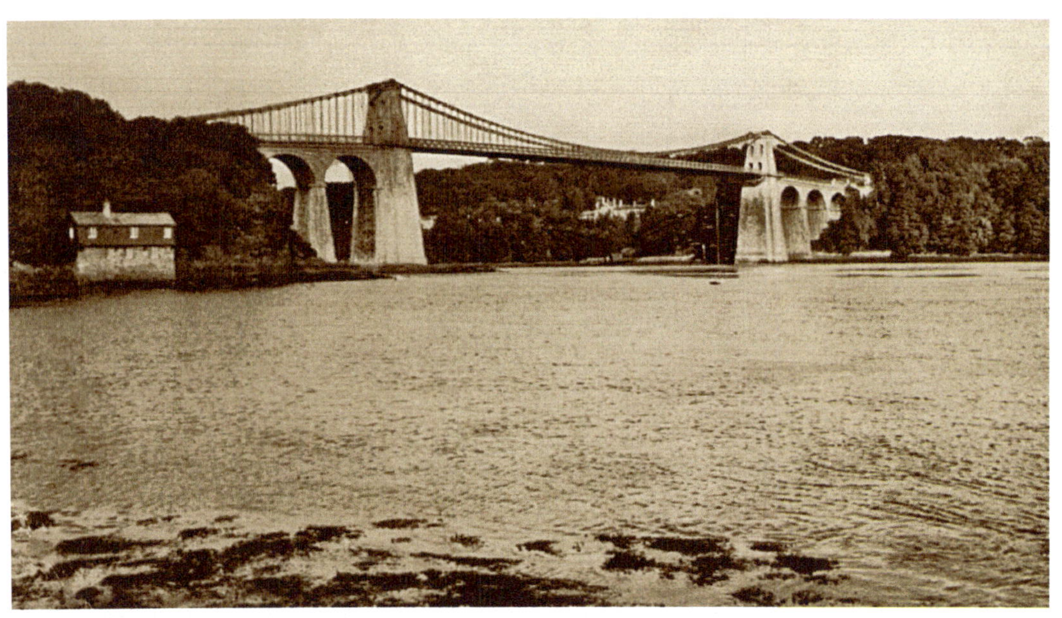

Menai Suspension Bridge, *c.* 1930

Thomas Telford's plan was to improve the route from London to Holyhead by including a bridge over the Menai Strait. It was built with 30.48 metres (100 feet) of clearance under the main span, sixteen chains holding up a 176.47 metre (579 feet) road between the bridge's towers, and block and tackle used to haul the chains into place. Construction began in 1819. Stone quarried at Penmon was used in the arches and piers, with the stonework completed in 1824. The bridge opened on 30 January 1826.

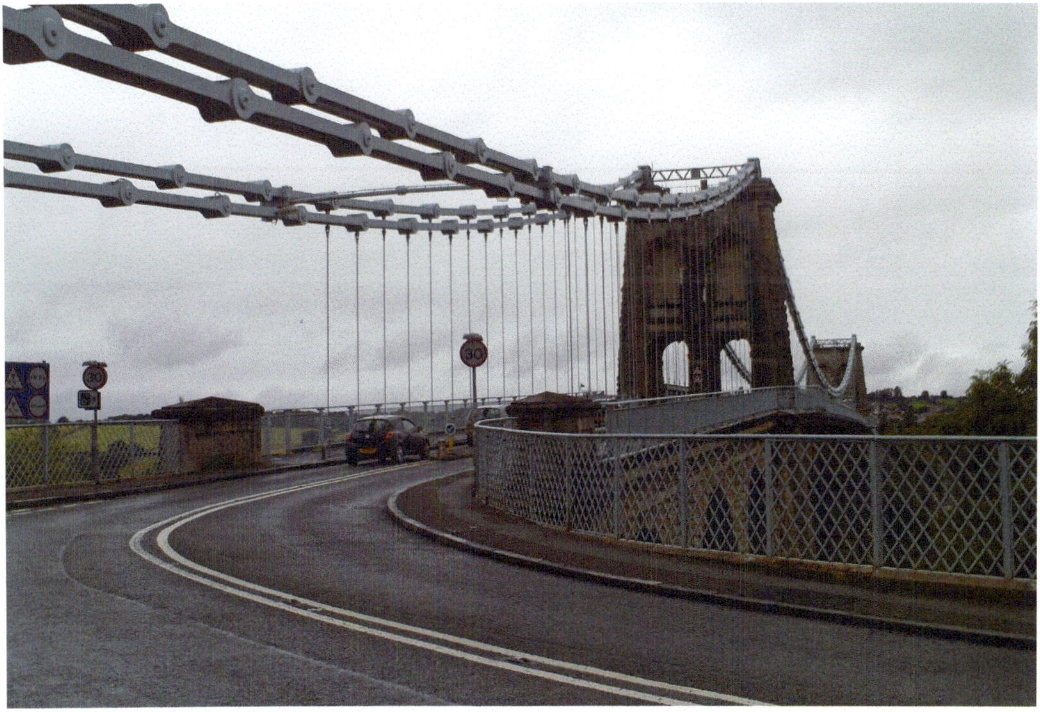

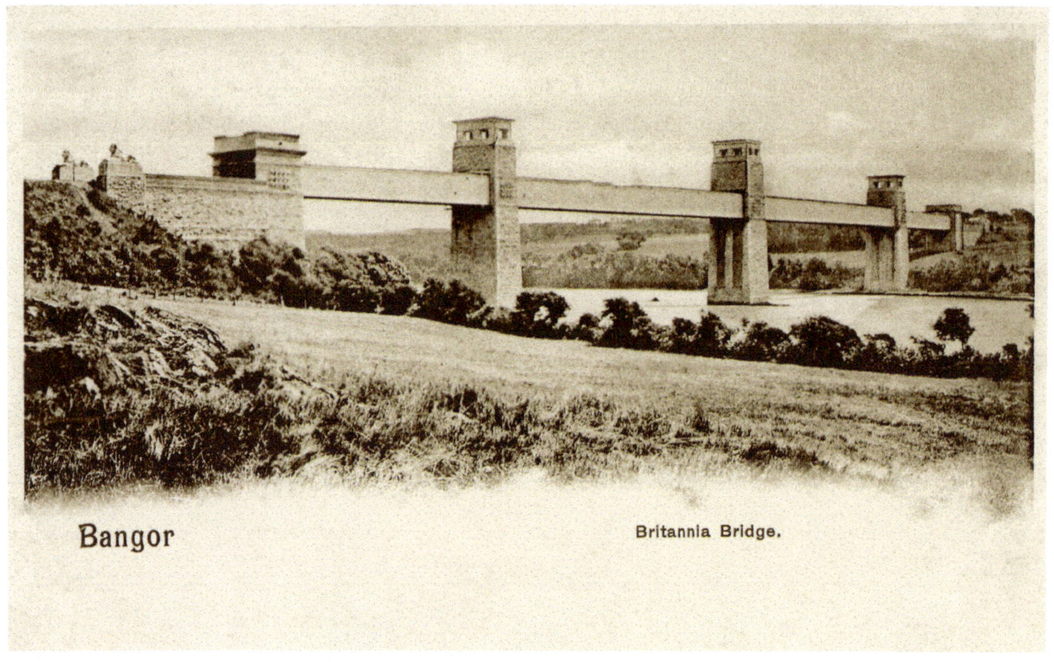

Britannia Bridge, *c.* 1900 *Inset*: the Anglesey Column, *c.* 1960
Plans were formulated by Robert Stephenson, son of George Stephenson. To make the bridge strong enough, it was constructed out of two long iron tubes, rectangular in shape. Limestone from Penmon was used for the stonework. The tubes were constructed on the banks of the strait and weighed 1,524 tonnes. They were put in place by the use of hydraulic pumps, with supporting piers. The bridge opened on 5 March 1850 and was reconstructed on two levels in the 1970s, after an accidental fire.

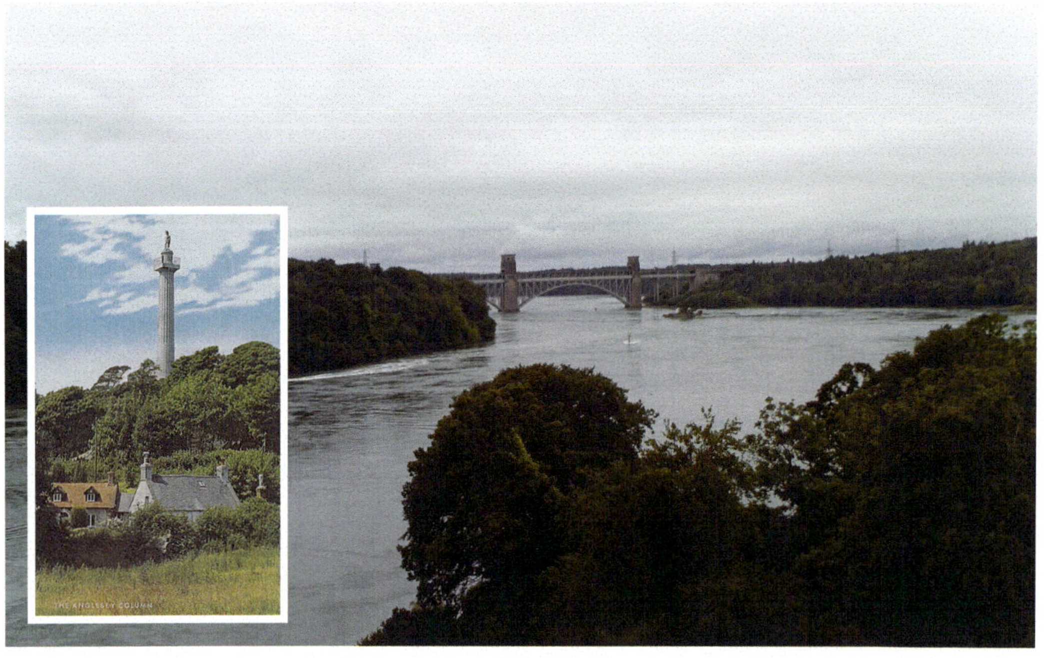

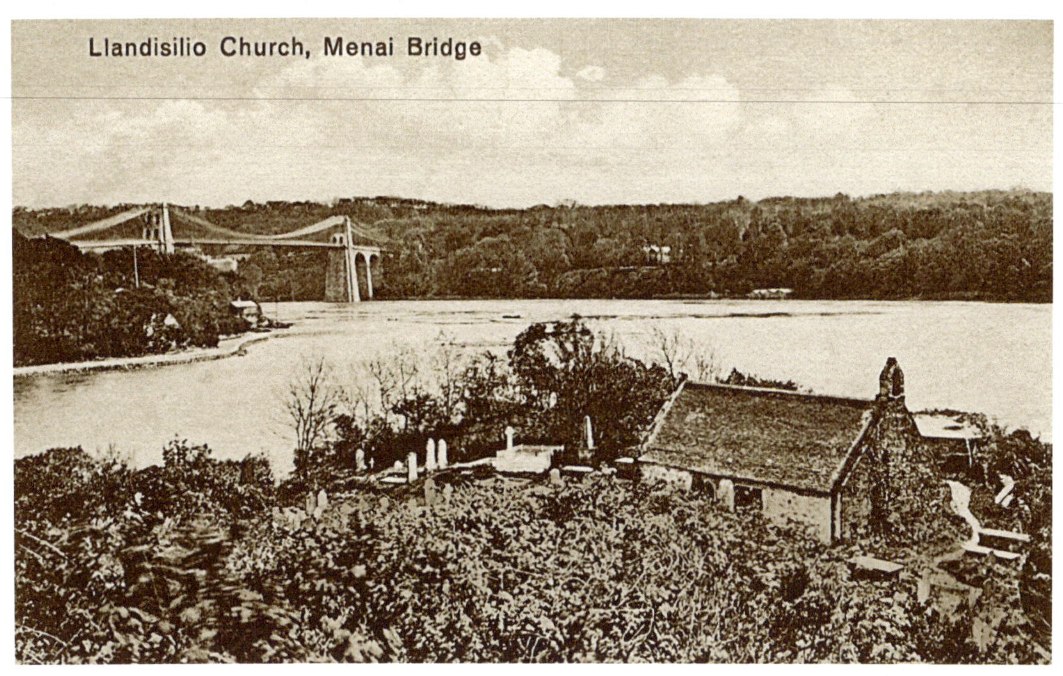

Llandisilio Church, Church Island, 1943

The church is dedicated to St Tysilio, the son of Brochfael Ysgythrog, King of Powys. He had fled court following a strong religious conviction and founded a hermitage on an island in the Menai Strait, around AD 630. The current church dates from the early fifteenth century, with restoration undertaken in the 1890s, which included a reproduction of the original fifteenth-century window at the east end of the church. The original wooden roof trusses were preserved and the octagonal baptismal font is from the fourteenth century.

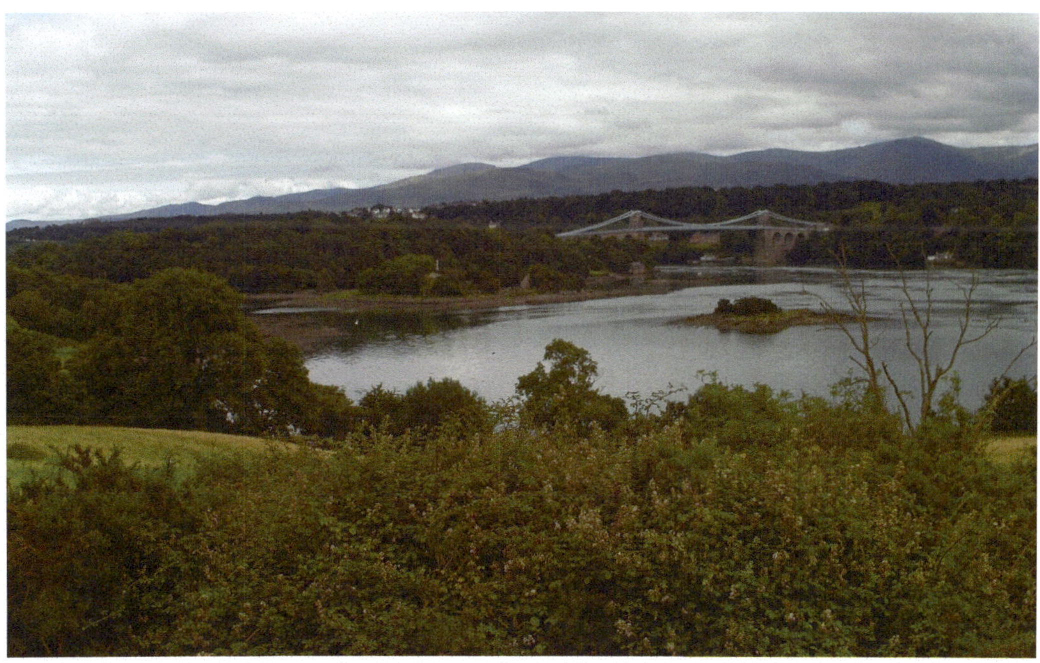

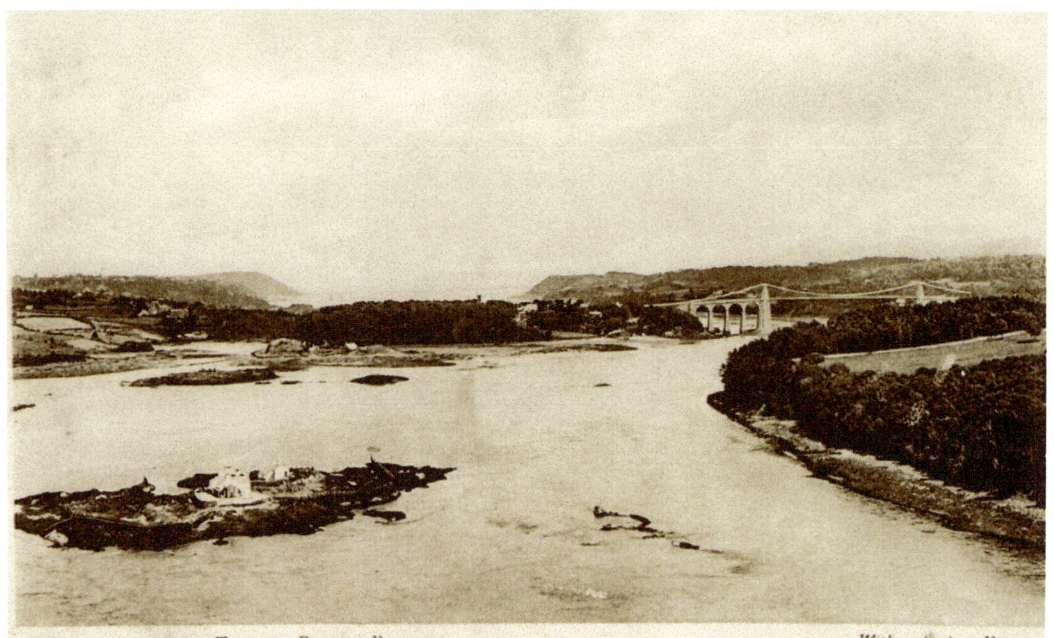

Afon Menai (Menai Strait) from the Tubular Bridge (Britannia Bridge), Bangor, 1906
On 23 May 1970 Britannia Bridge was accidentally destroyed when a group of teenagers, carrying lit paper as a torch, dropped it and set fire to wood and tar inside the structure. The fire burned for nine hours, spreading quickly through the wooden sections of the bridge, which acted like a huge horizontal chimney, aided by the wind. Trains were running between Anglesey and the mainland within eighteen months. However, it was ten years before the new road deck above the railway opened.

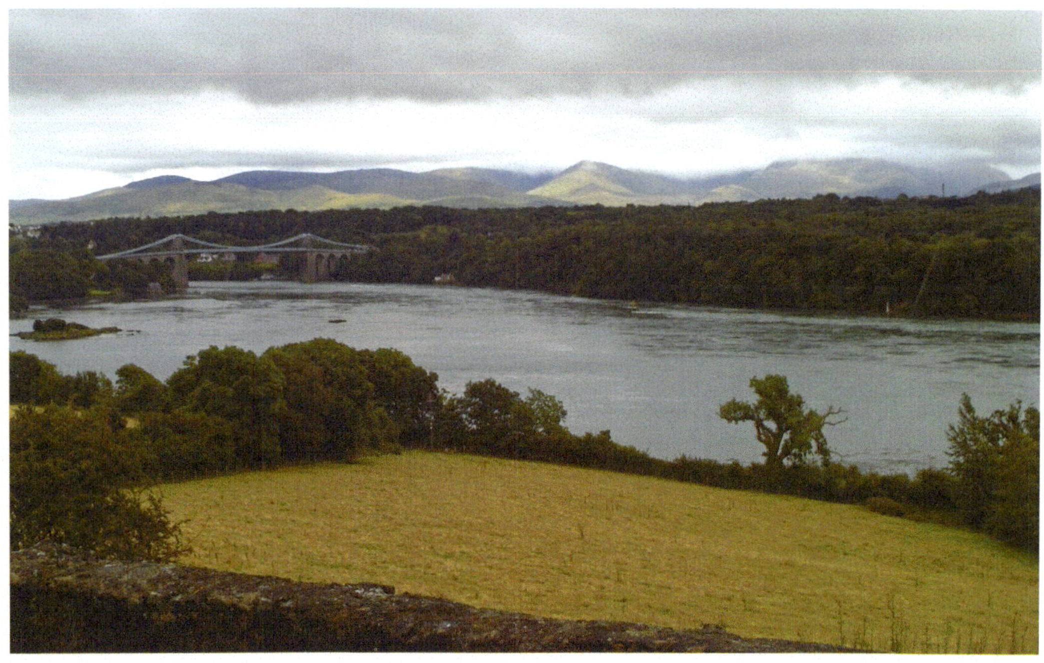

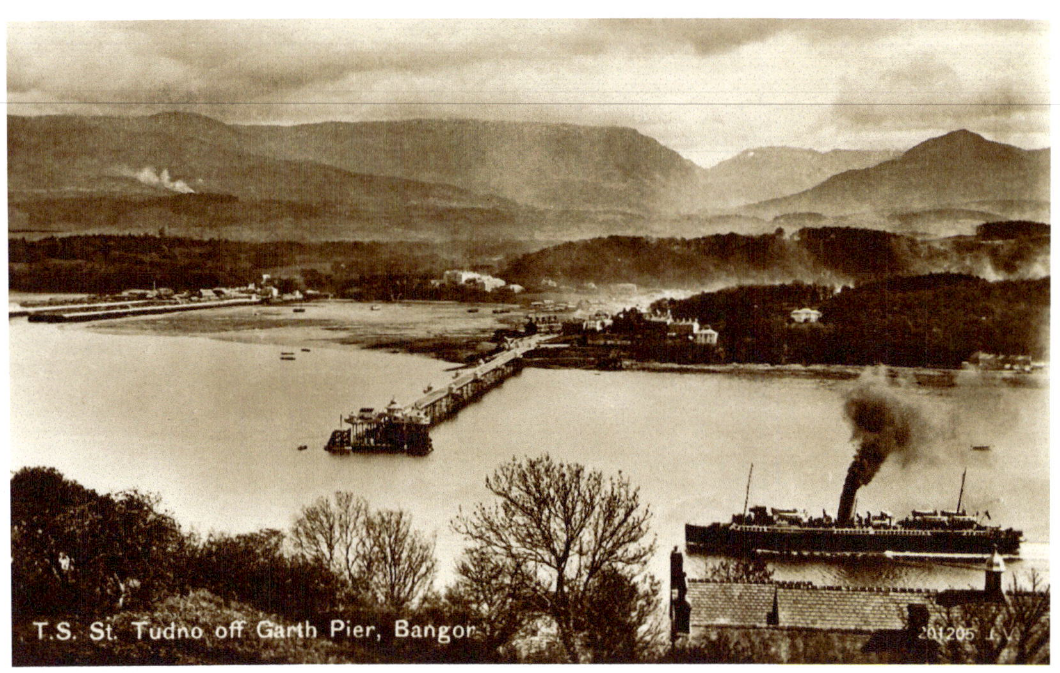

St Tudno, off Garth Pier, Bangor, _c._ 1930

St Tudno was built by Fairfield Govan in 1926 and was launched on Tuesday 2 February 1926, by Fairfield Govan, for the Liverpool & North Wales Steamship Co. The ships main engines were built by Fairfield Co. (Glasgow) and power was provided by four steam turbines. *St Tudno* arrived back at the yard for scrapping on 19 April 1963. In the Second World War the ship was an armed boarding vessel, then between 1940 and 1947 it became a depot ship for minesweepers in the Medway.

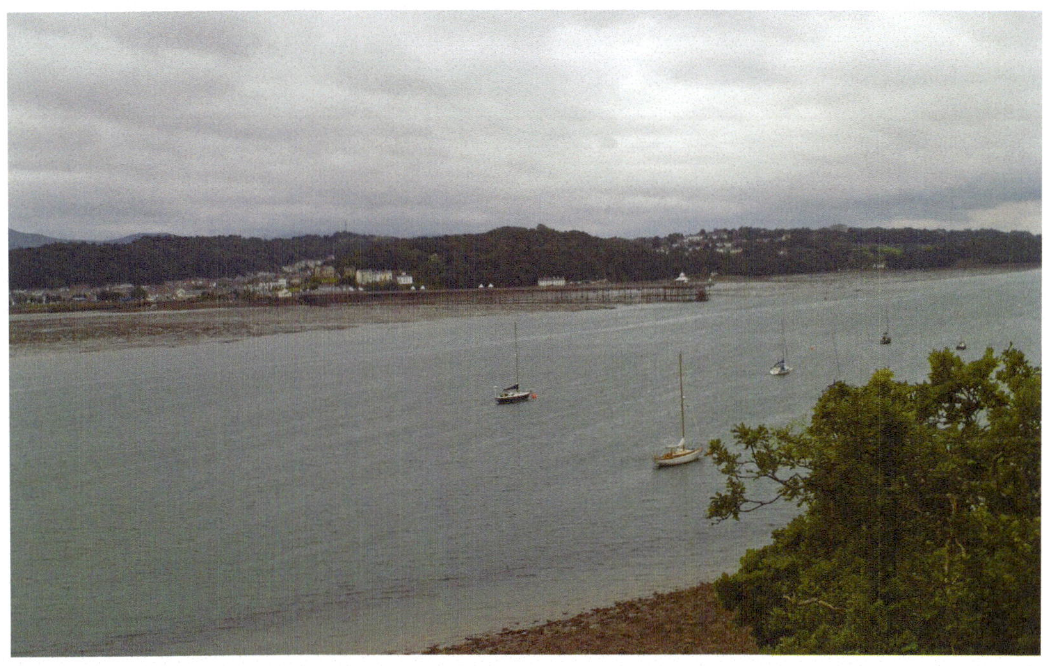

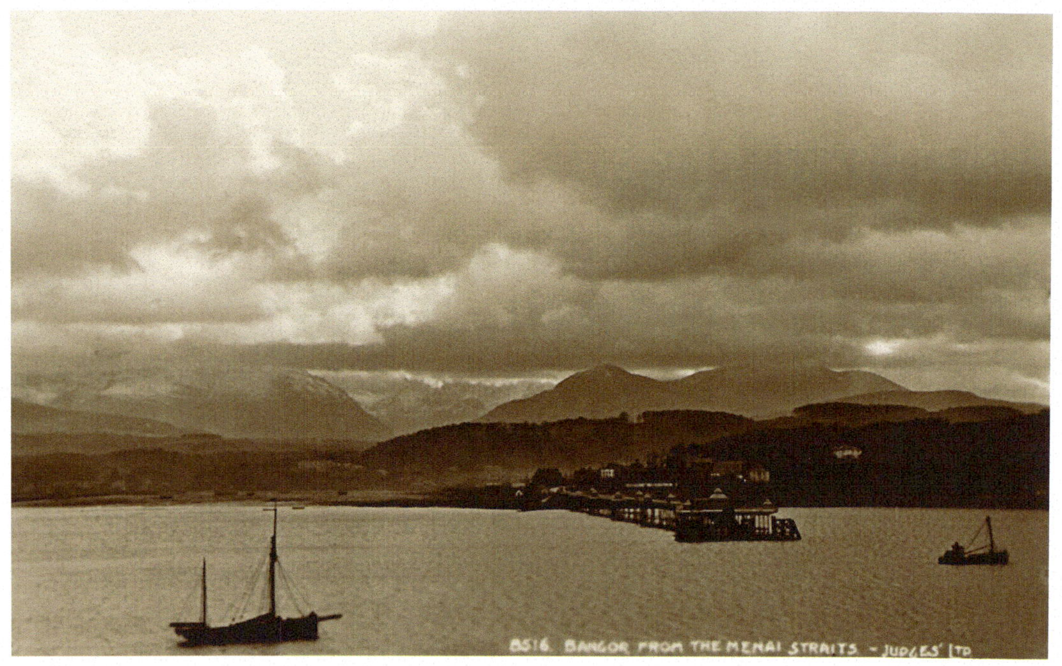

Bangor from Afon Menai (Menai Strait), 1939

Bangor is historically in the county of Caernarfonshire. Its population was 18,808 in 2011, including more than 10,000 students at Bangor University. Bangor Mountain lies east of Bangor and casts a shadow across High Street (Stryd Fawr), Glan Adda and Hirael, so that from November to March some parts of High Street receive no direct sunlight. There is another ridge to the north of High Street, called Upper Bangor (Bangor Uchaf). Port Penrhyn was important in the nineteenth-century slate export trade.

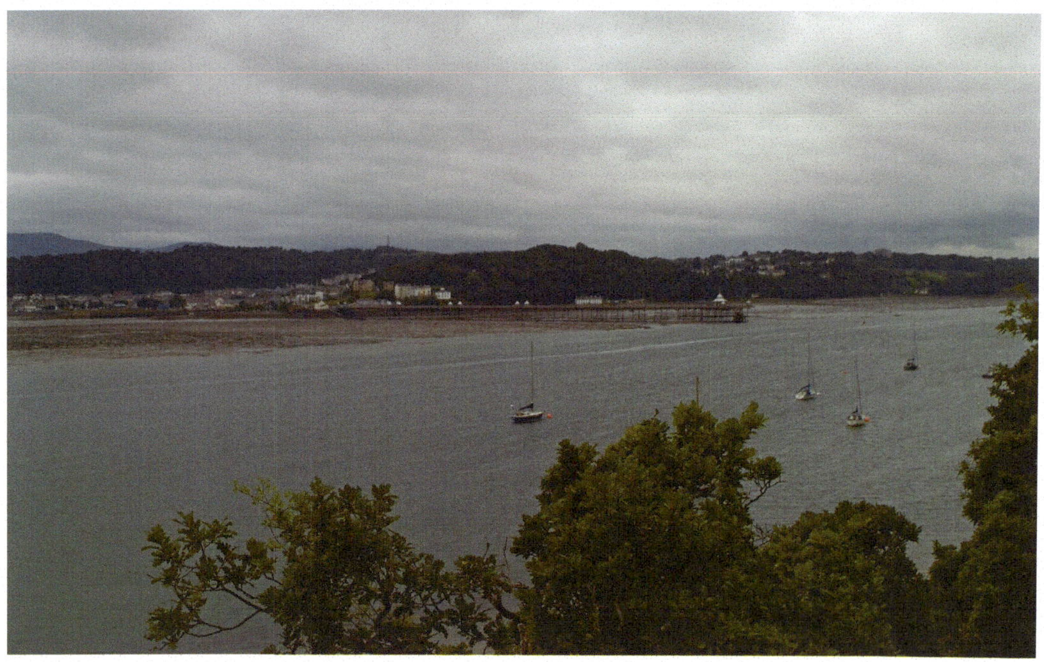

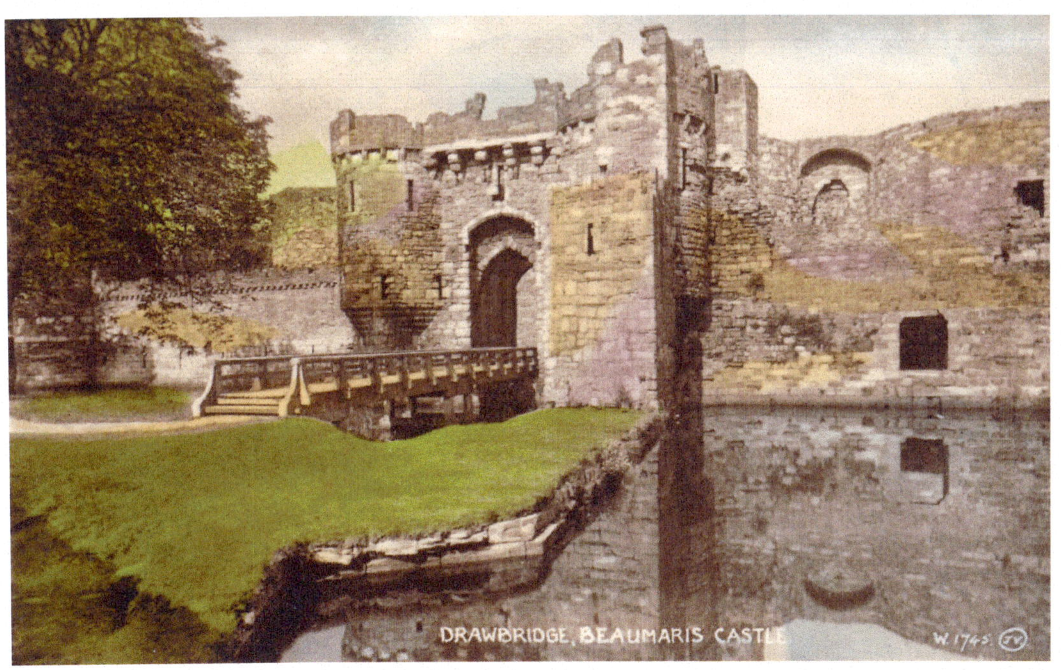

Biwmares (Beaumaris) Castle, 1905

Buildings in the town include a courthouse, built in 1614; the fourteenth-century St Mary's and St Nicholas's Church; the fourteenth-century Tudor Rose, one of the oldest original timber-framed buildings in Britain; and the Bull's Head Inn, 1472, which General Thomas Mytton made his headquarters during the 'Siege of Beaumaris', 1648. Red Hill, north of Beaumaris, was named in memory of the siege. Dewi (David) Hughes of Anglesey founded Beaumaris Grammar School in 1603, but only the ancient hall of the original building survives.

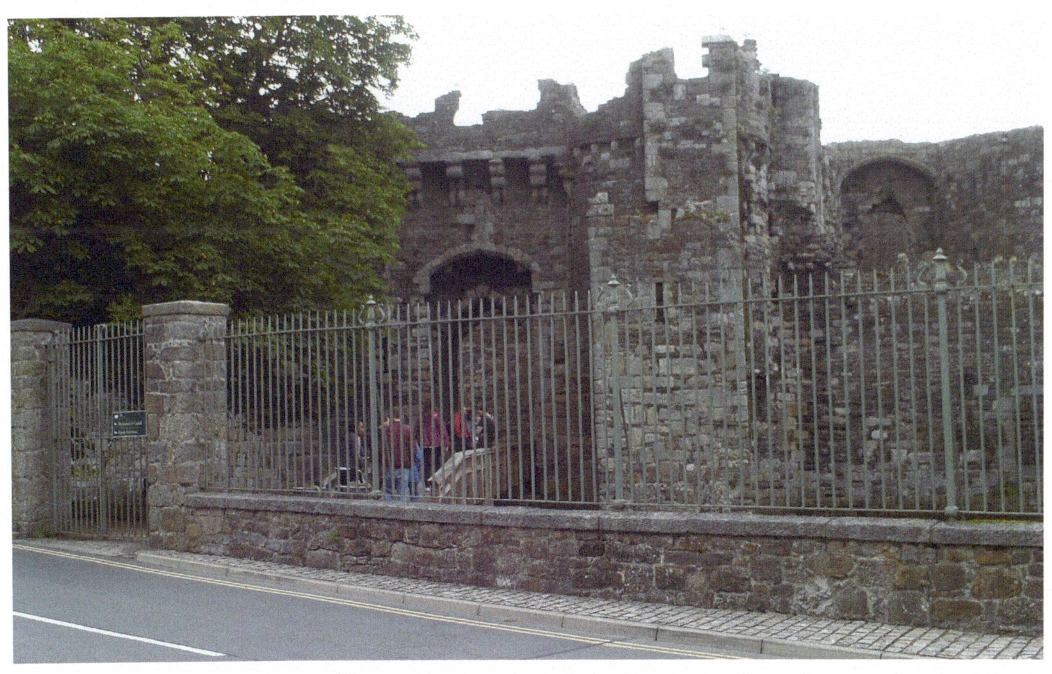

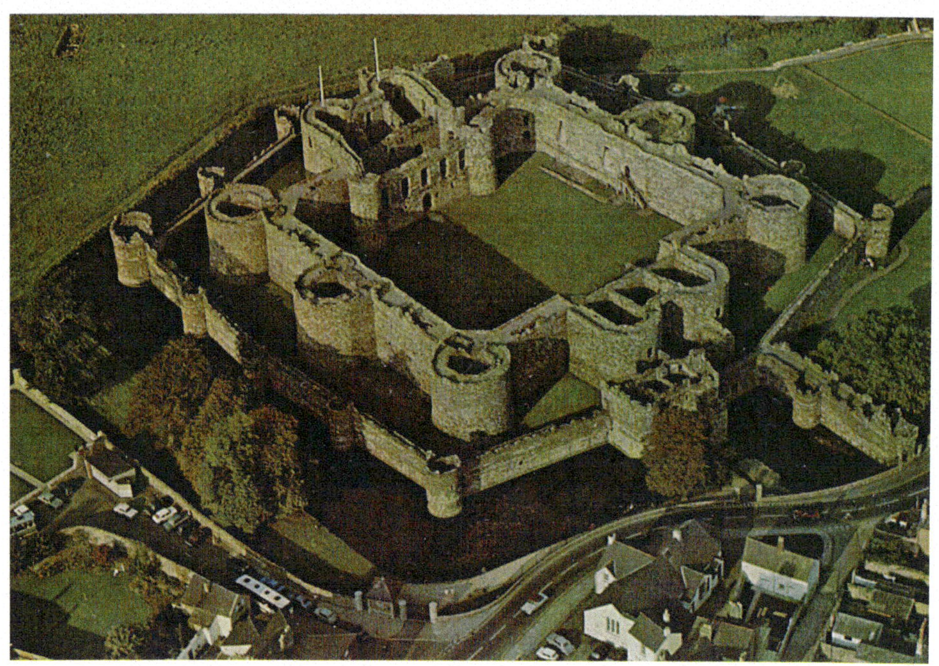

Biwmares (Beaumaris) Castle Aerial View, *c.* 1970

Edward I never got to complete Beaumaris Castle because his finances were stretched to their limit. There were also other threats to the kingdom, such as the Scots' increasingly effective resistance, which diverted his attention away from Wales. Despite these problems Beaumaris Castle was technically defensively perfect, constructed on a 'walls within walls' plan. The population of Llanfaes was forcibly moved to Newborough, a distance of 19 kilometres (12 miles), in order to allow for the castle's construction. The new town of Beaumaris became a borough.

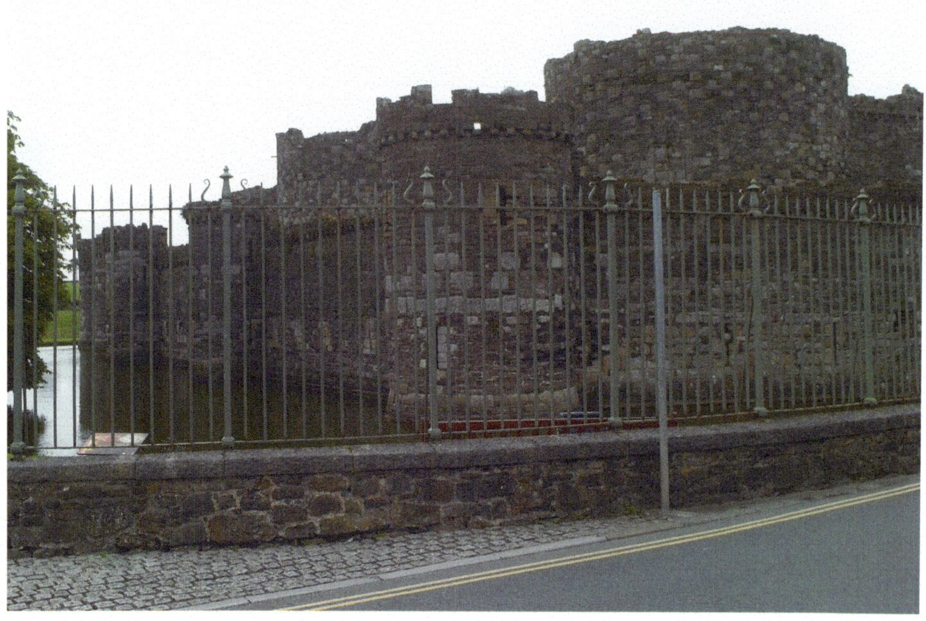

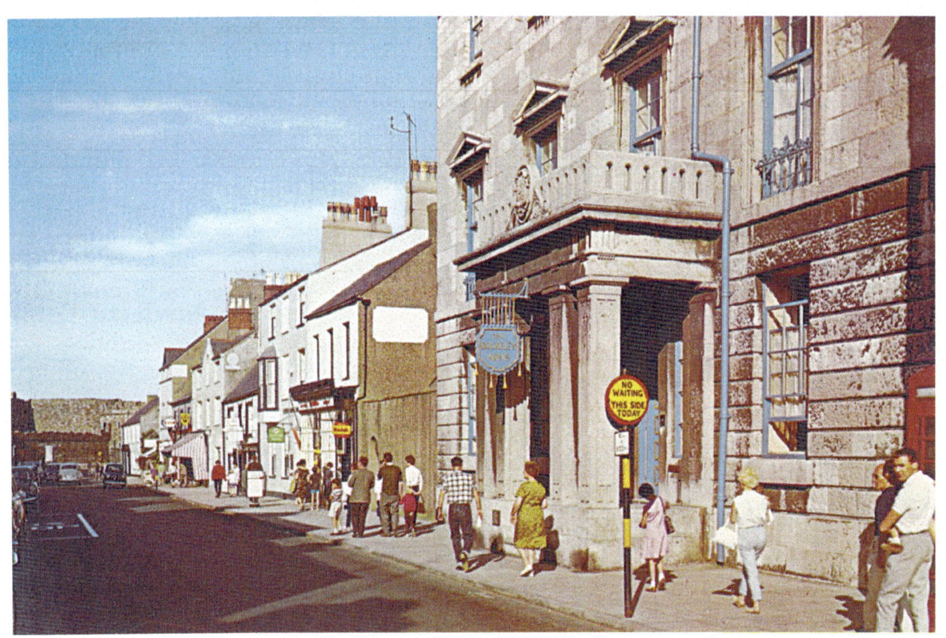

The Bulkeley Arms Hotel, Stryd Castell (Castle Street), Biwmares (Beaumaris), *c.* 1960

The Bulkeley family was the most influential family on Anglesey (Ynys Mon) in the seventeenth century. The hotel was designed by the architect Joseph Aloysius Hansom, in conjunction with Sir Richard Bulkeley. A total of 450 houses were demolished for its construction. Building began in 1829, and the hotel, which today is Grade I listed, was completed in 1832 as a 'Georgian showpiece'. Princess Victoria stayed at the hotel that year when she visited Wales for the opening ceremony of the Britannia Bridge, which linked Anglesey with the mainland.

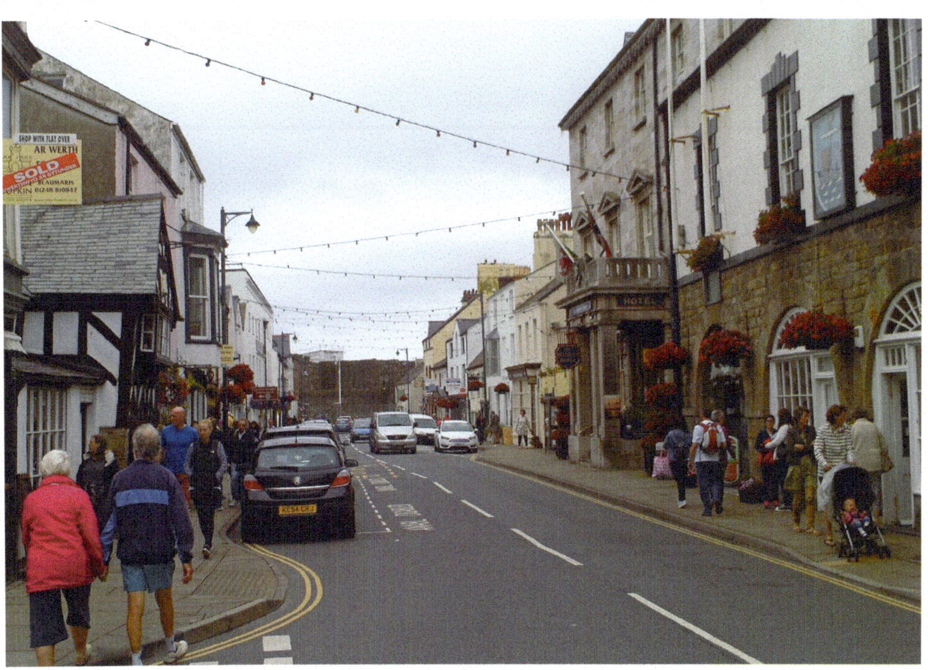

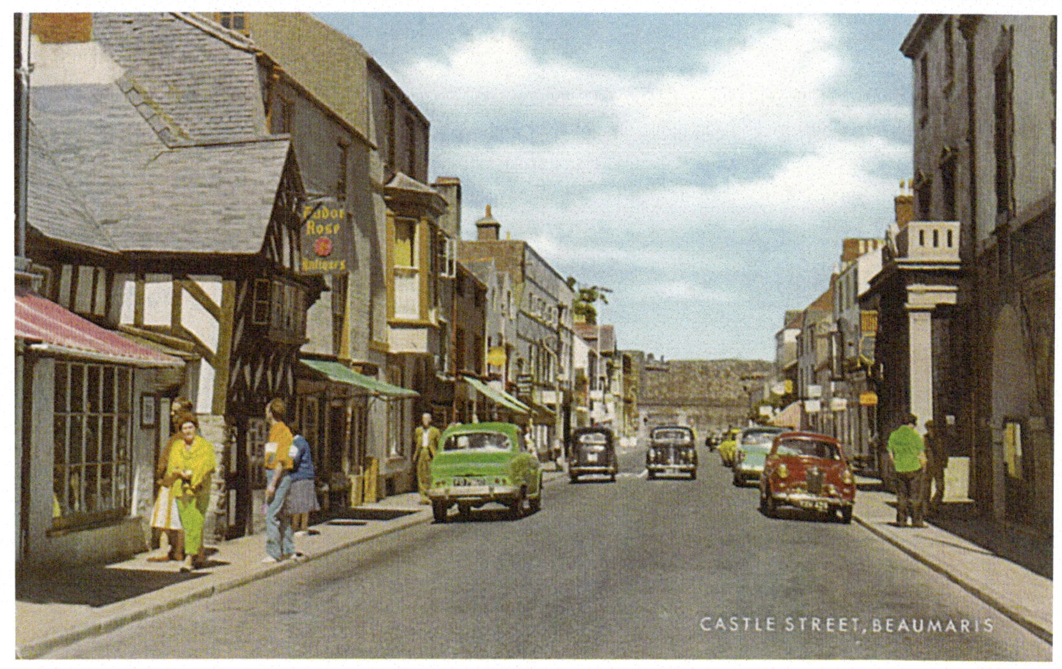

Tudor Rose, Stryd Castell (Castle Street), Biwmares (Beaumaris), *c.* 1960

The building dates from the 1480s. When constructed, most of the other dwellings along Castle Street were of similar design. It was originally a hall house, larger than the frontage suggests, the centre being a high room with no ceiling. A two-storey solar wing on the south side, seen from the street, consisted of family living accommodation and storage. The hall survives behind this wing. A floor was added in the sixteenth century and there was probably a north wing at one time.

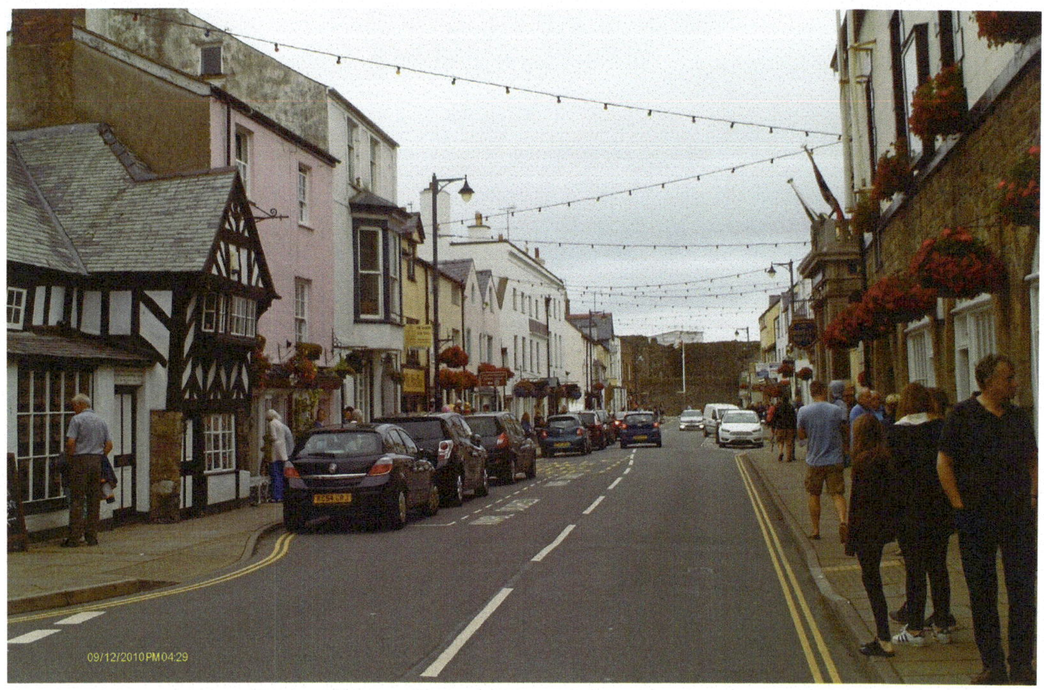

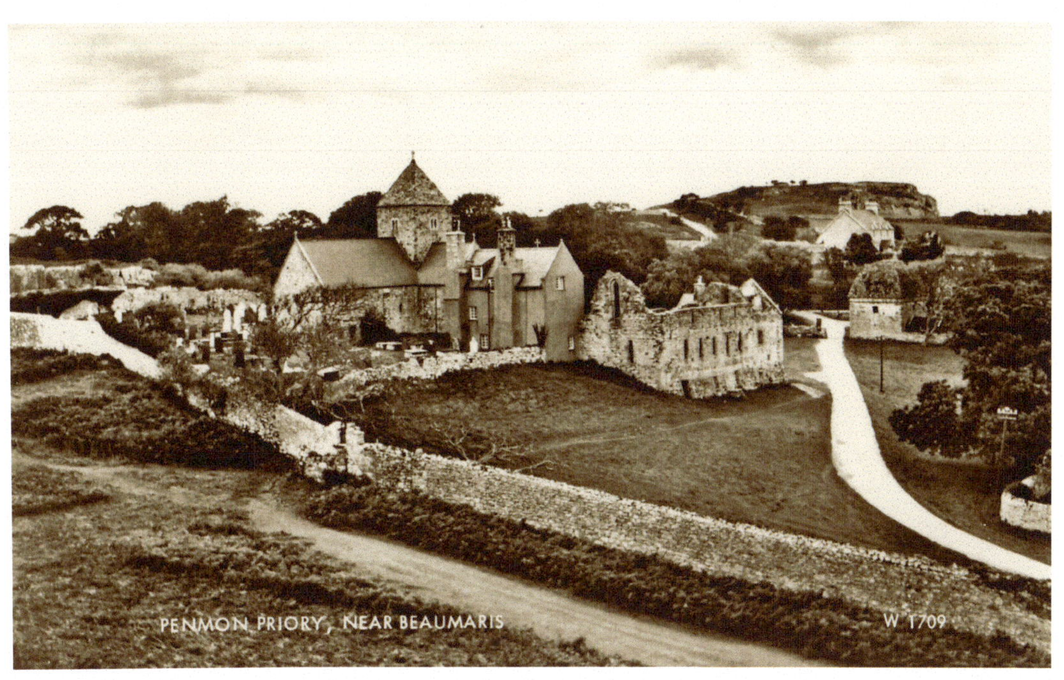

Penmon Priory, near Biwmares (Beaumaris), Anglesey, *c.* 1950

The origins of the site date back to St Seiriol in the sixth century. The remains of the present priory date from the thirteenth century, when the house became part of the Augustinian order and was enlarged. This is now the parish church. The priory was dissolved in 1538 and the buildings passed into the ownership of the Bulkeley family of Beaumaris. The priory church is still used as a place of worship today and is a well-known landmark, visible from the Strait.

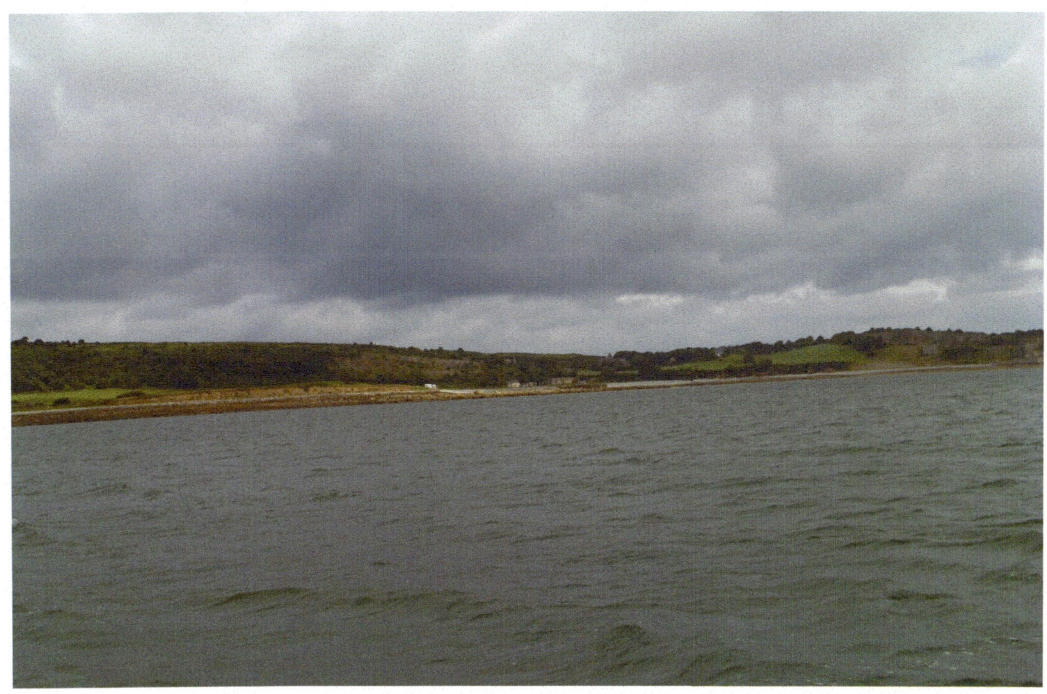

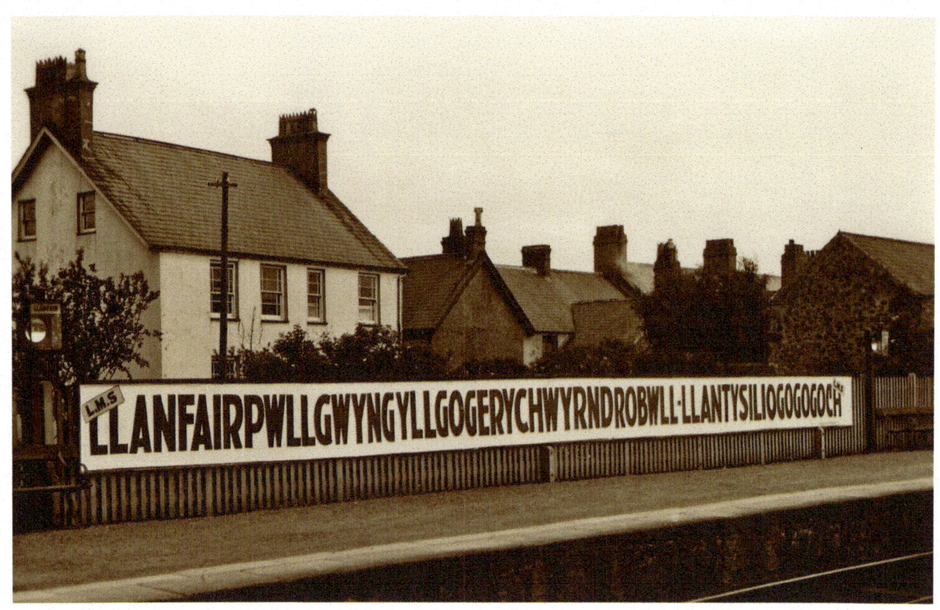

Llanfairpwllgwyngyllgogerychwyrndrobwllllantysiliogogogoch Railway Station, Anglesey, c. 1930. *Inset*: Station Sign

'Saint Mary's church in the hollow of the white hazel near a rapid whirlpool and the church of Saint Tysilio of the red cave', in English. This village has the longest name in Britain, which was devised in the 1860s to showcase its tourist potential. With fifty-eight characters it is the longest place name in Europe and the second longest official one-word place name in the world. Nearby is the Marquess of Anglesey's column, celebrating his heroism at the Battle of Waterloo.

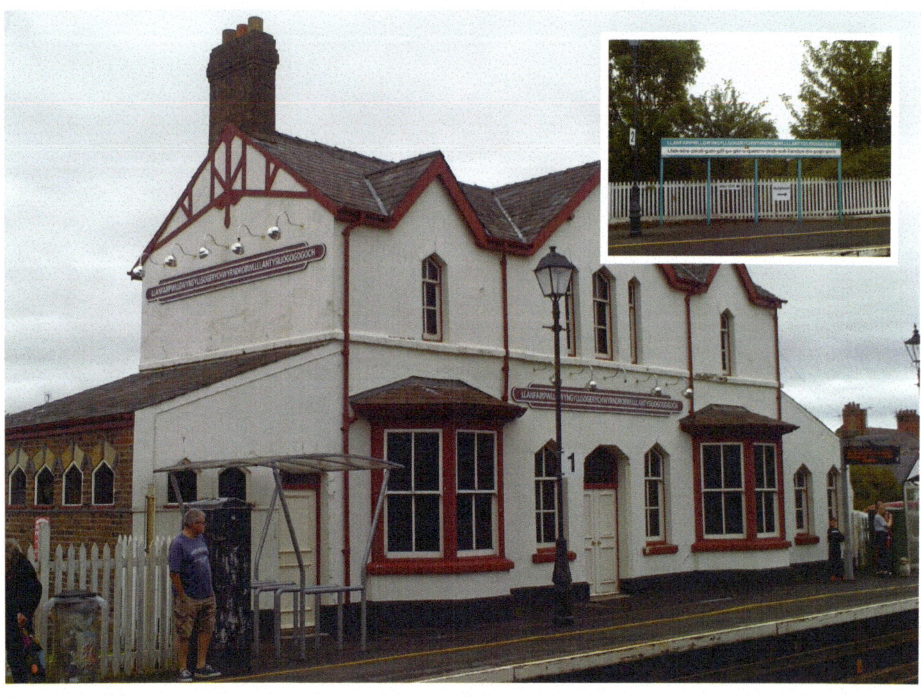

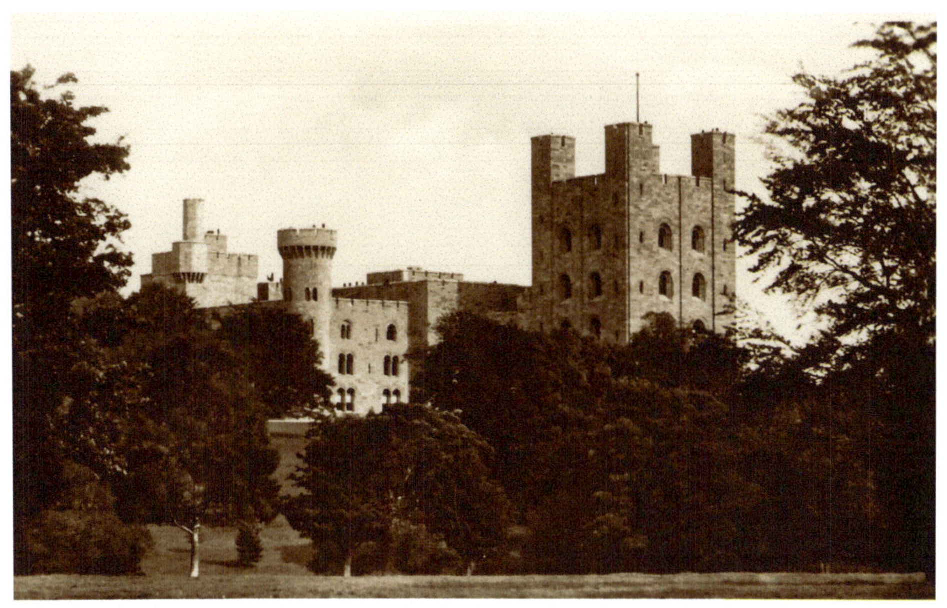

Castell Penrhyn (Penrhyn Castle), c. 1930

The present castle was built between 1820 and 1833 for George Hay Dawkins Pennant, by the famous architect Thomas Hopper, who chose a Neo-Norman design (*inset,* gateway), rather than an in-vogue Gothic one. Hopper oversaw the whole construction process, including furniture selection made by local craftsmen. In 1840 George died and his daughter inherited Penrhyn, marrying Edward Gordon Douglas, First Lord Penrhyn of Llandygai. In 1949 the Fourth Lord Penrhyn died and by 1951 Penrhyn Castle came under the care of the National Trust.

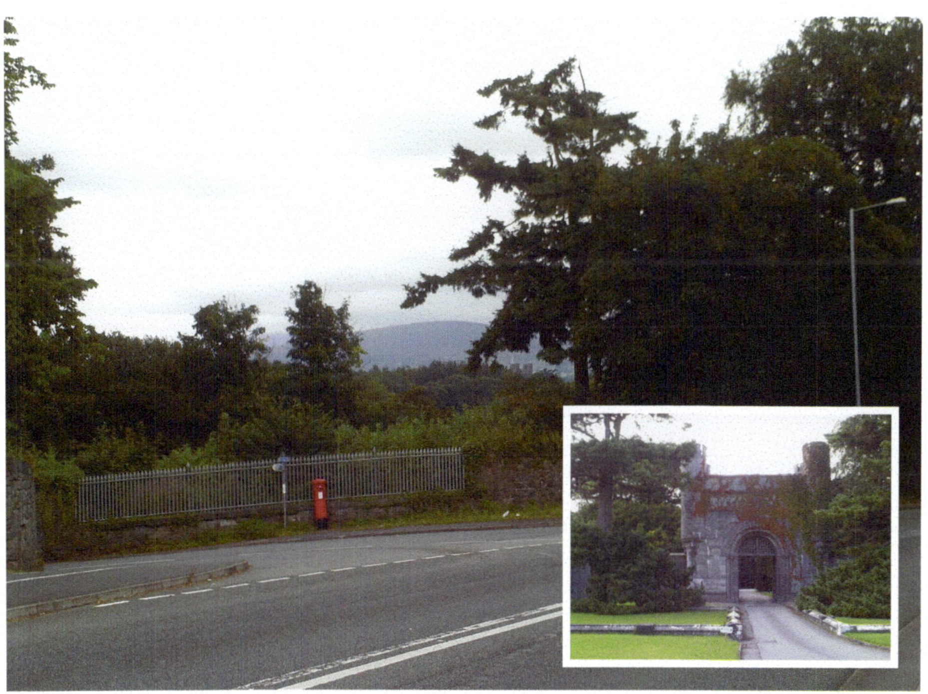

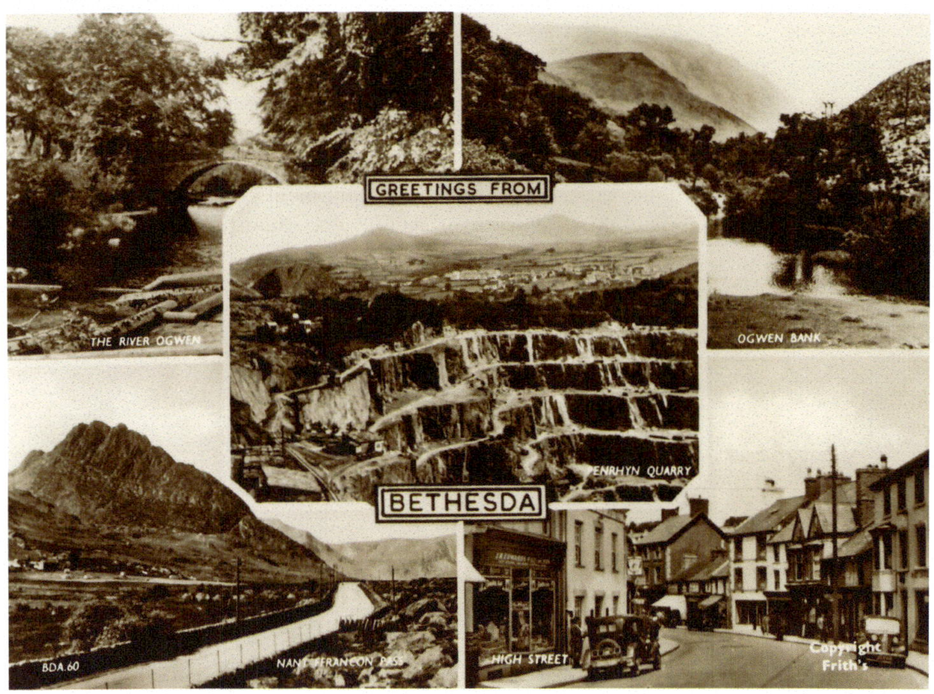

Penrhyn Slate Quarry, Bethesda, *c.* 1930

At the end of the nineteenth century it was the world's largest slate quarry. The main pit is nearly 1.6 kilometres (1 mile) long, 370 metres (1,200 feet) deep, and is now flooded. It was worked by nearly 3,000 quarrymen. First developed in the 1770s by Richard Pennant, later Baron Penrhyn, it is likely there was earlier slate extraction here. In 1798 the narrow gauge Penrhyn Quarry Railway was built, meaning slate could be transported to the sea at Port Penrhyn for export.

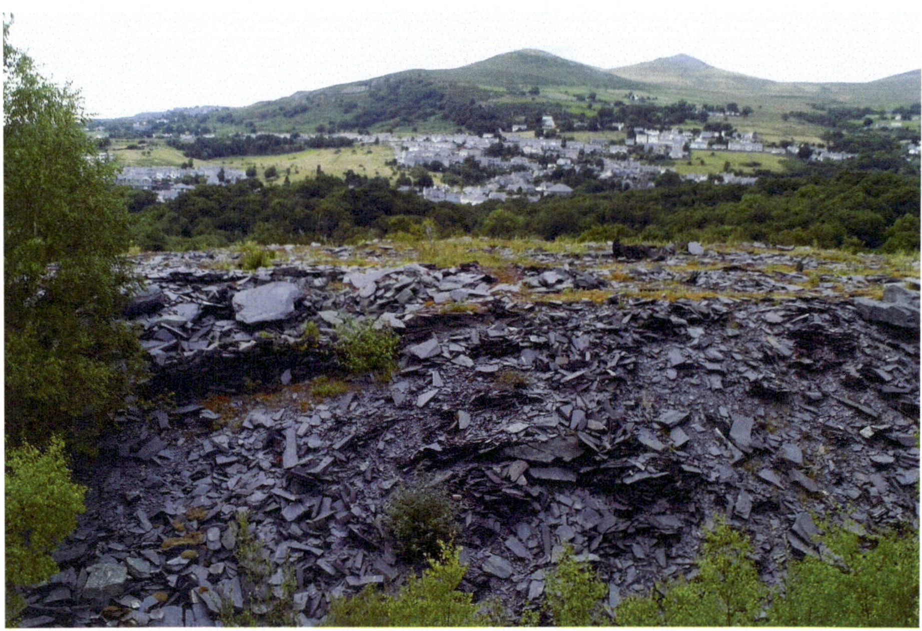

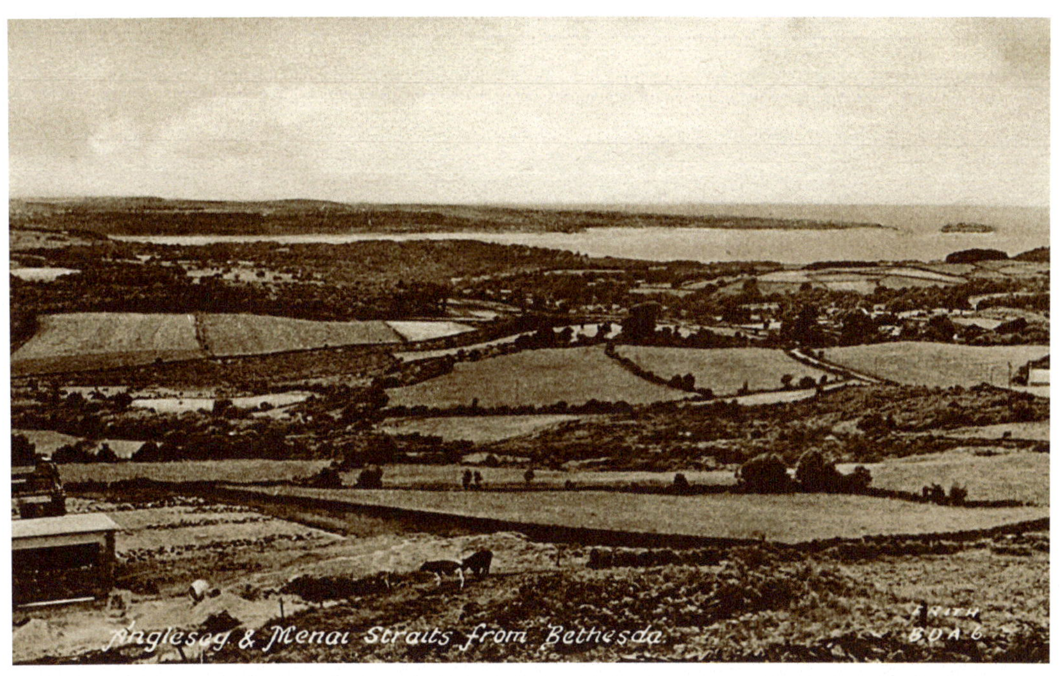

Anglesey and Afon Menai (Menai Strait) from Bethesda, *c.* 1930
When I was a resident of Rachub, a number of years ago, Anglesey and the Menai Strait were just about visible from my front bedroom window on a clear day. This view was probably taken from a much closer vantage point and when the weather had not 'closed in', as it did on my particular visit. The modern photograph has been taken from the top of Braichmelyn (Yellow Arm) and looks across Bethesda and Llanllechid in the direction of Bangor and Anglesey.

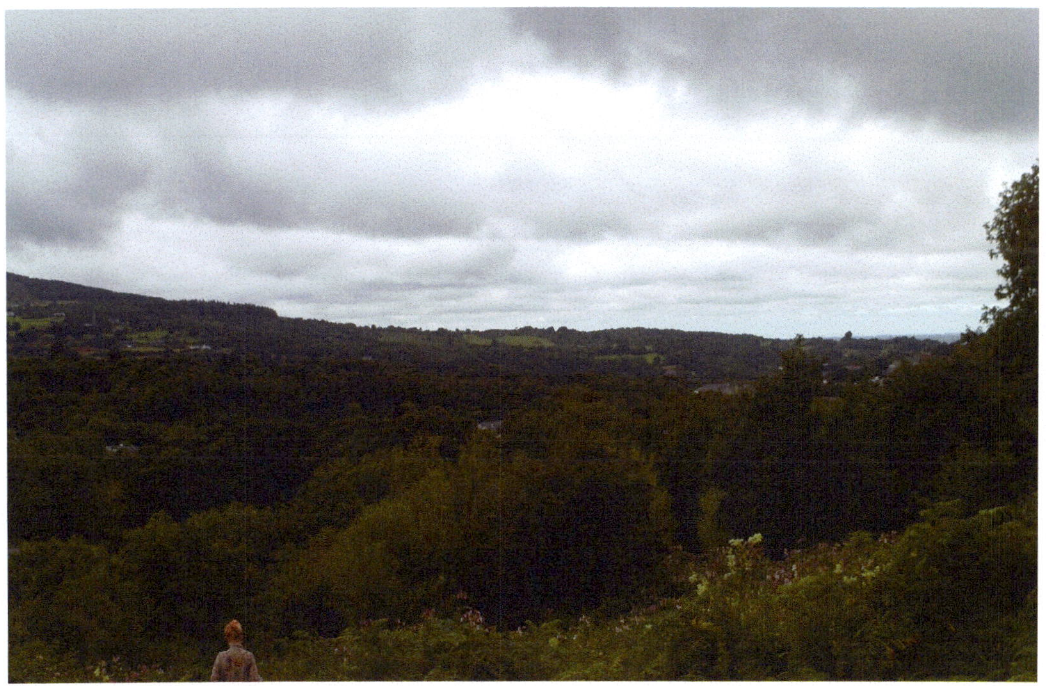

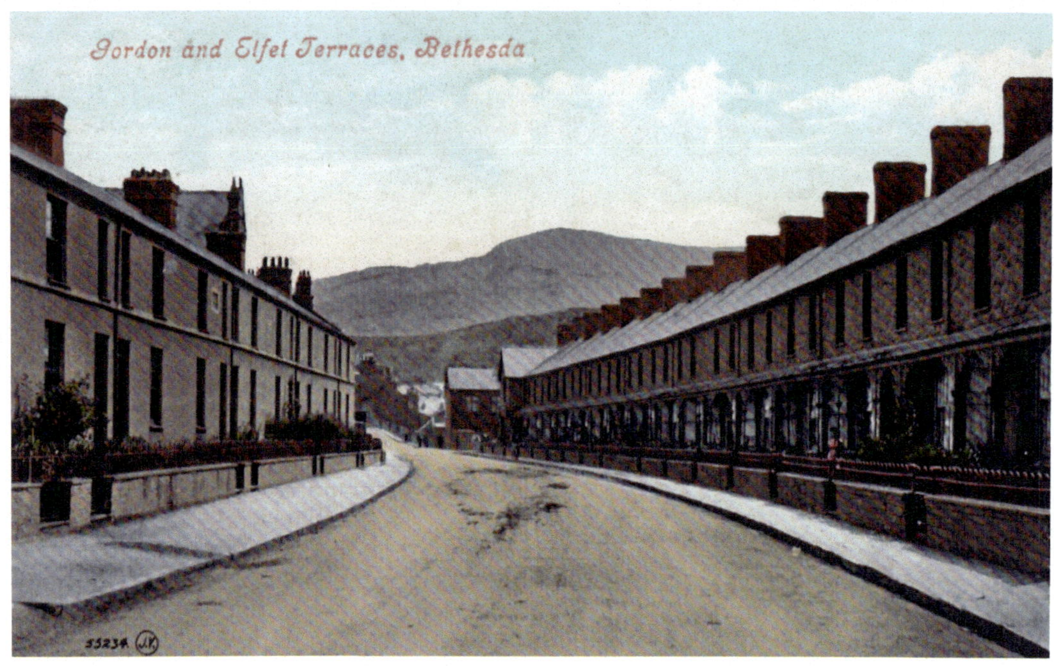

Gordon and Elfed Terraces, Ffordd Bangor, Bethesda, 1908

Elfed Terrace (*inset*) has a date stone of 1898 set into it and it is probable that Gordon Terrace – on the opposite side of Bethesda's A5 Bangor Road – was built in the same period. Both terraces make use of local stone and slate in their construction and are substantially built. The modern photograph has been taken further back to accommodate the 'curve' in the A5, which creates a 'blind corner' here. In 1908 the Roberts family were resident at No. 17 Gordon Terrace.

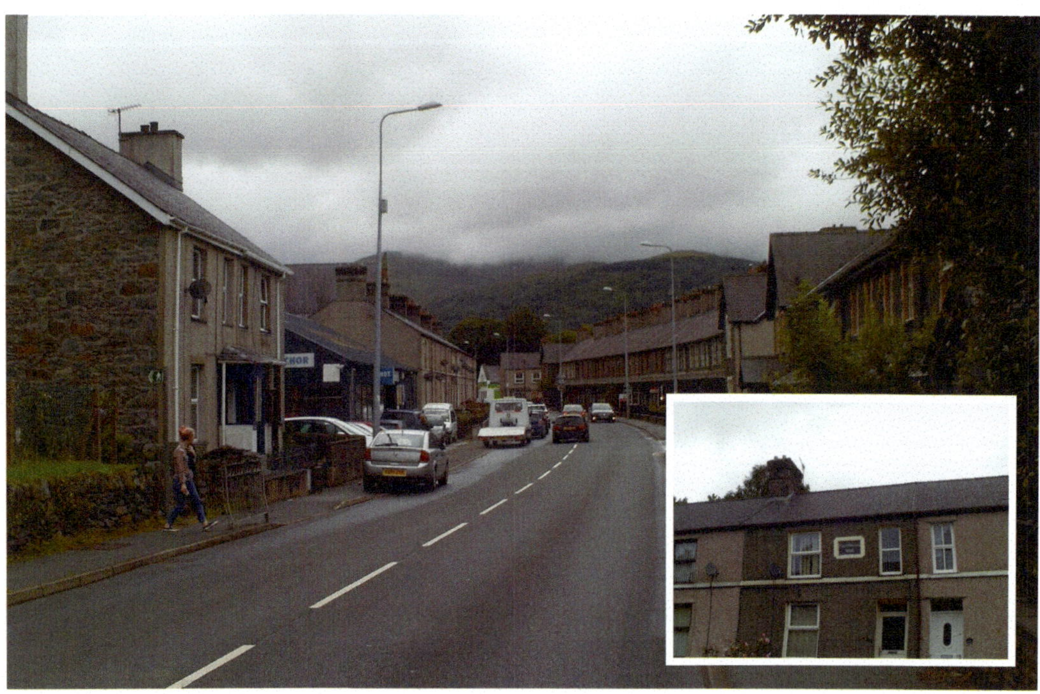

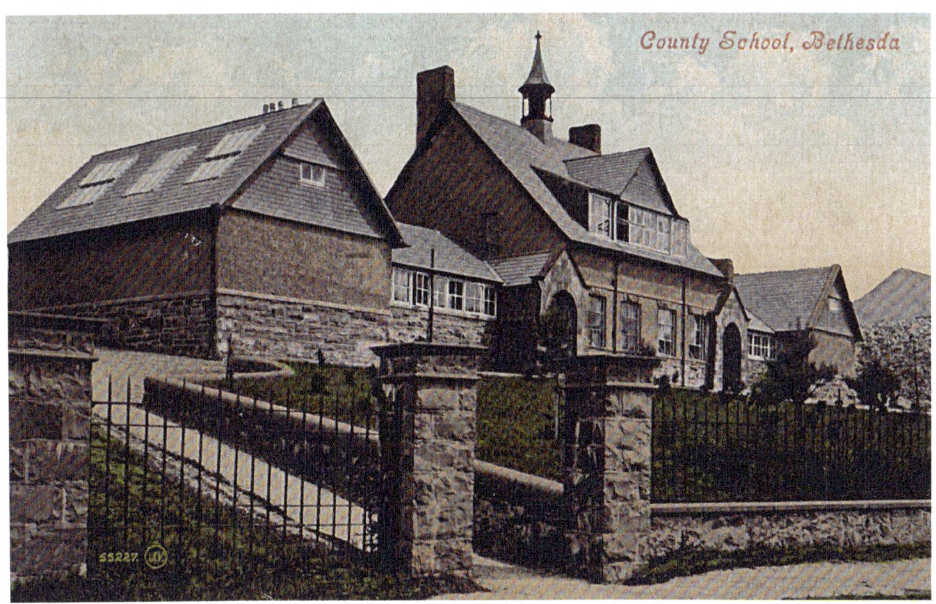

Bethesda County School, Ffordd Coetmor, c. 1905

The school is now named Ysgol Dyffryn Ogwen (Ogwen Valley School) and has approximately 400 pupils. Some of the buildings date from 1895 when a county school (grammar school) was established here. My father remembers taking his 'eleven-plus', or equivalent, examination here in the 1940s. The present comprehensive school dates from 1951 and it is fed by primary schools from the surrounding villages. An extension to the school was opened by Professor Sir Idris Foster.

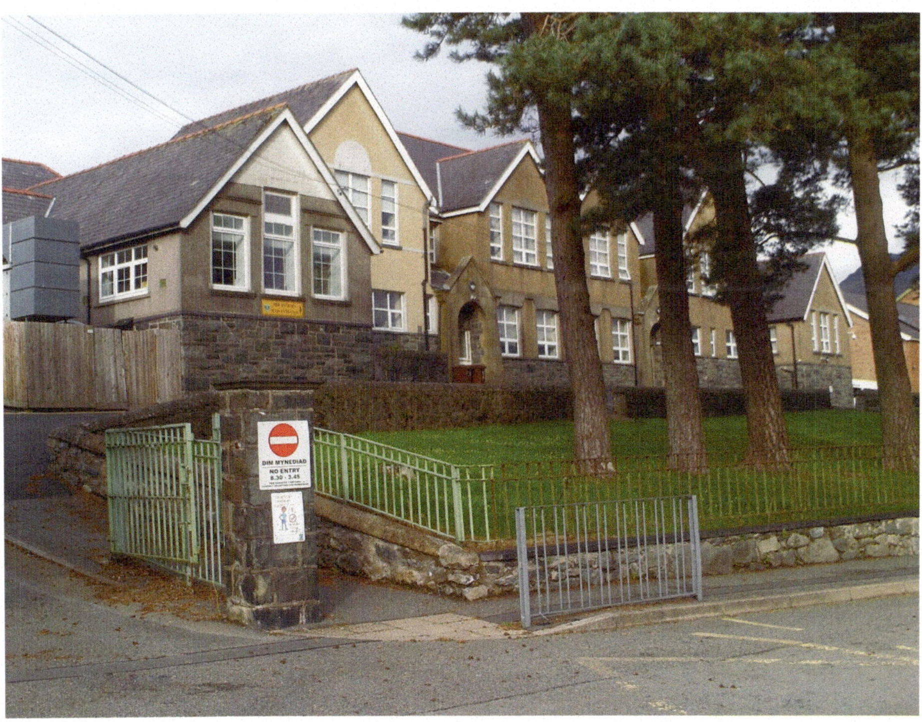

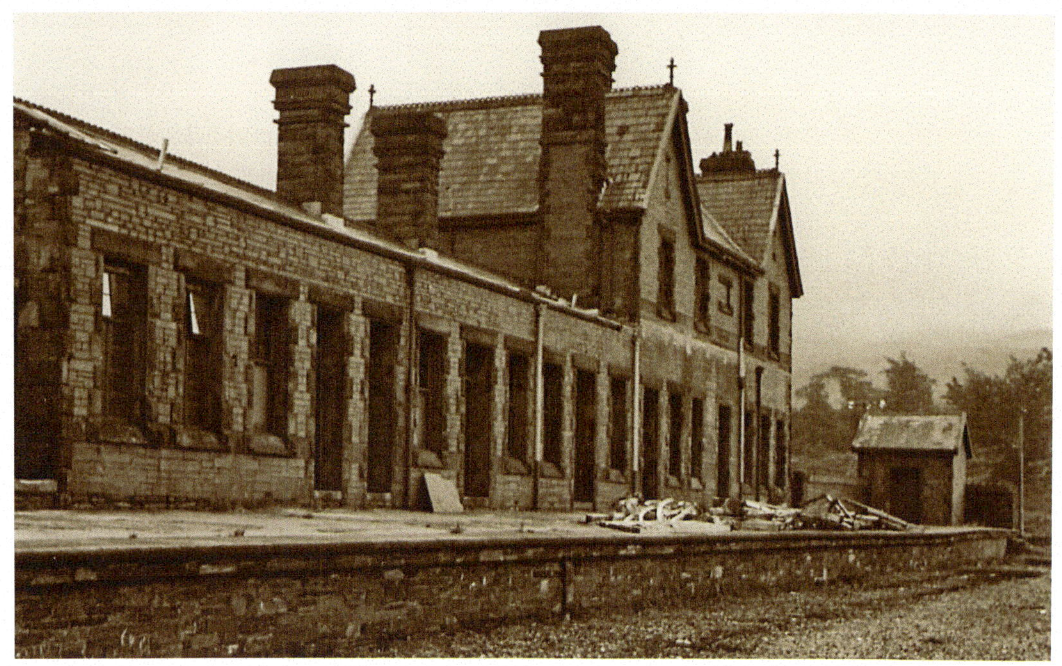

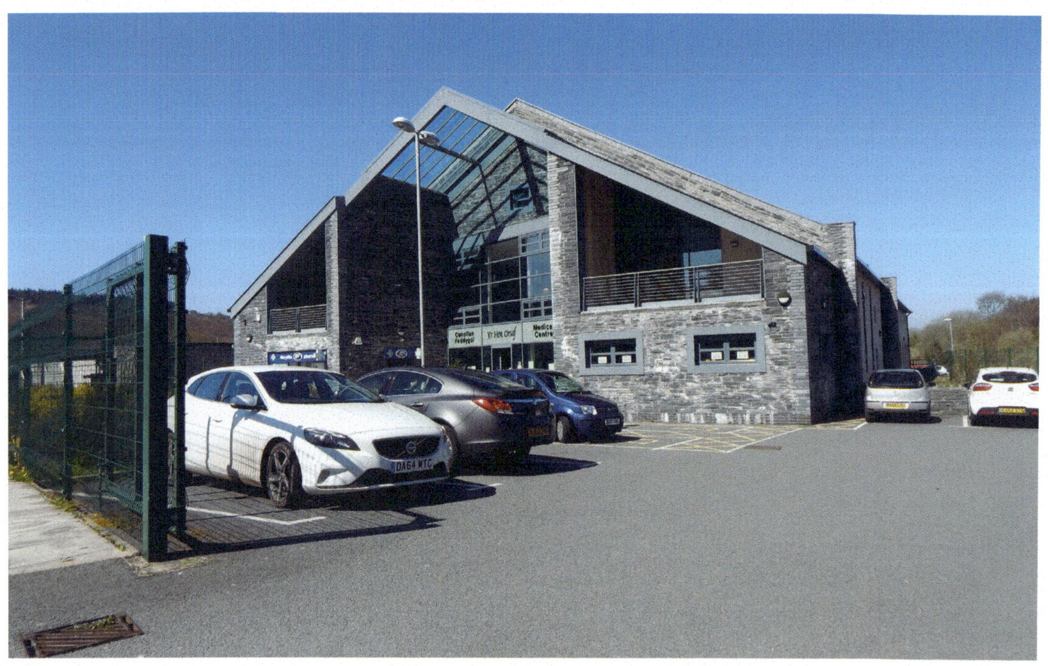

Bethesda Railway Station, Ffordd Orsaf (Station Road), Bethesda, *c.* 1965
Now demolished, the station was opened on 1 August 1884, on the north side of Station Road, by the LNWR. It closed to passengers on 3 December 1951 and shut down completely on 20 October 1963. Its single-track branch line linked Bethesda to the Chester and Holyhead main line at Bethesda Junction. It rose over 91.44 metres (300 feet) towards Bethesda. Engineered by Edward Walter Nealor Wood, it opened to passengers on 1 July 1884 and to goods services on 1 September 1885. The line operated push-pull trains.

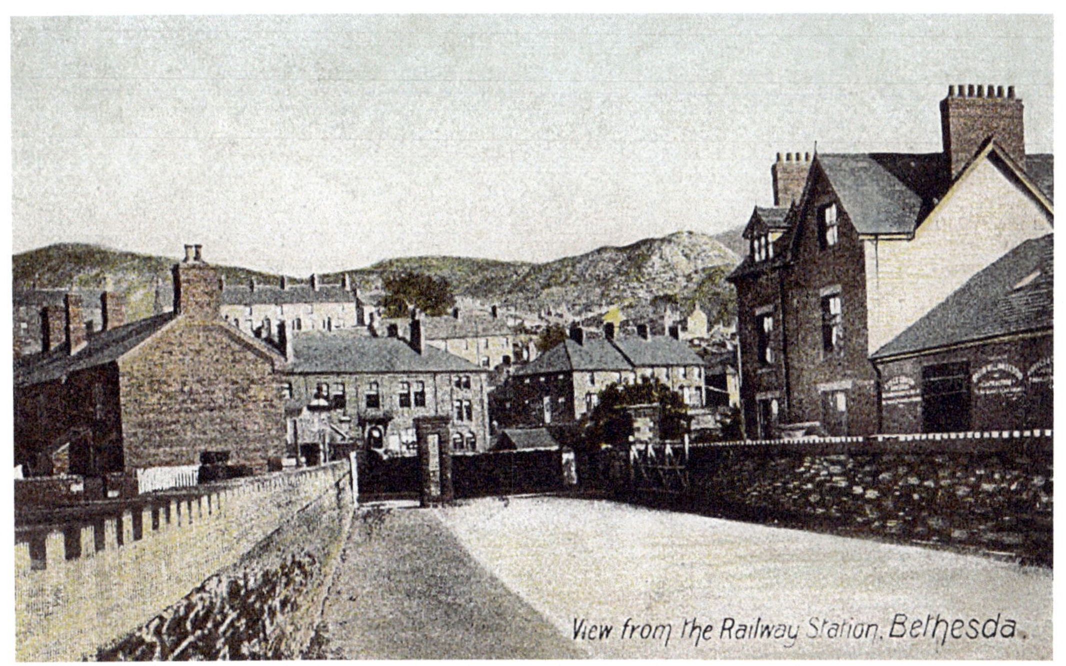

View from the Railway Station, Ffordd Orsaf (Station Road), Bethesda, 1908

Bethesda station was located north of the town, west of the A5 and north of Station Road. The station was on the west side of the line and had a single 131-metre (430-feet) platform, with the building towards its southern end. There was a goods yard west of the station. The station building was demolished in the 1970s and a social club built. In 2010 the Old Station Medical Centre (Yr Hen Orsaf) was built on part of the former station's goods yard.

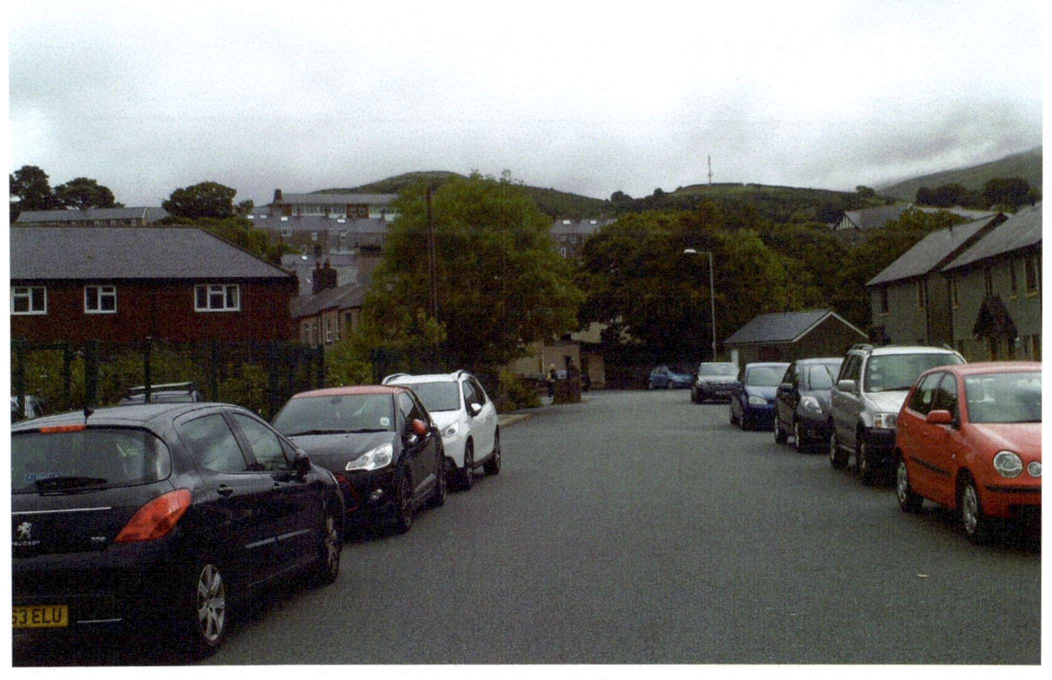

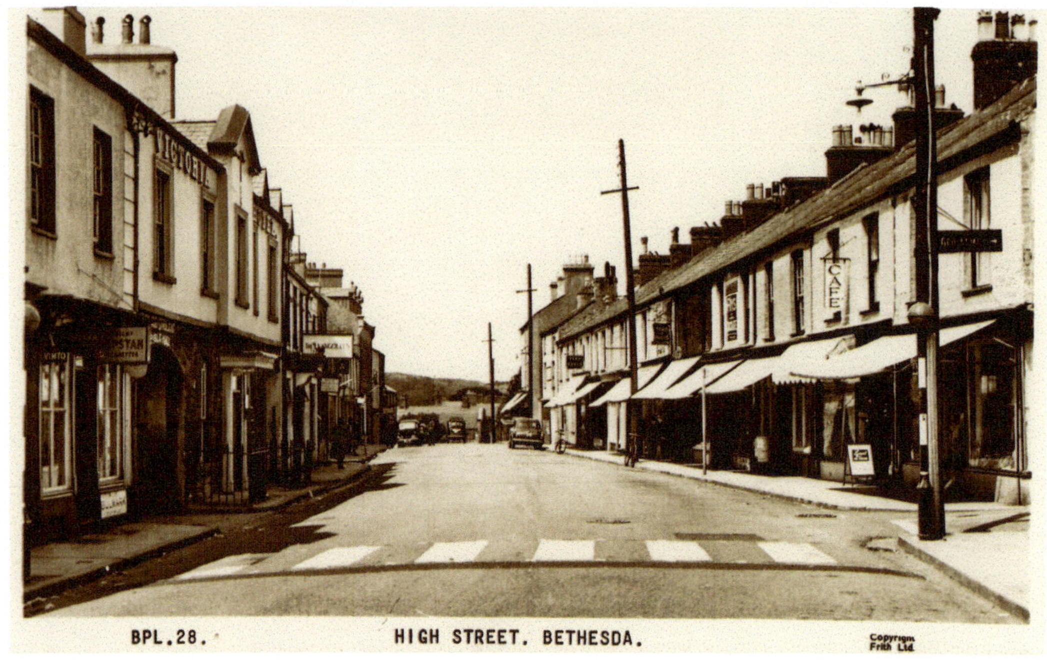

Victoria Hotel, Stryd Fawr (High Street), Bethesda, *c.* 1950

The Victoria Hotel was Grade II listed on 25 April 1997, as an early to mid-nineteenth-century public house. The inn fronts the modern Neuadd Ogwen performance venue (*inset,* interior), replacing the old market hall, built by Lord Penrhyn around 1796, according to Thomas Pennant. The inn was listed as an example of an earlier nineteenth-century inn, with good Victorian lettering to the façade, showing Bethesda's importance as a coaching establishment on the Holyhead Road.

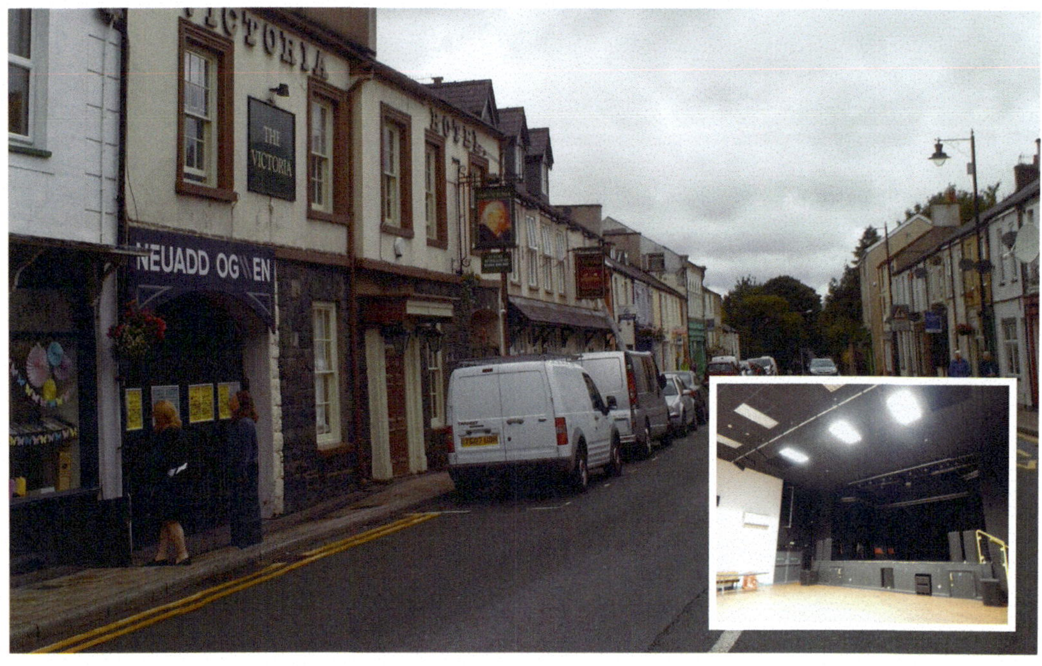

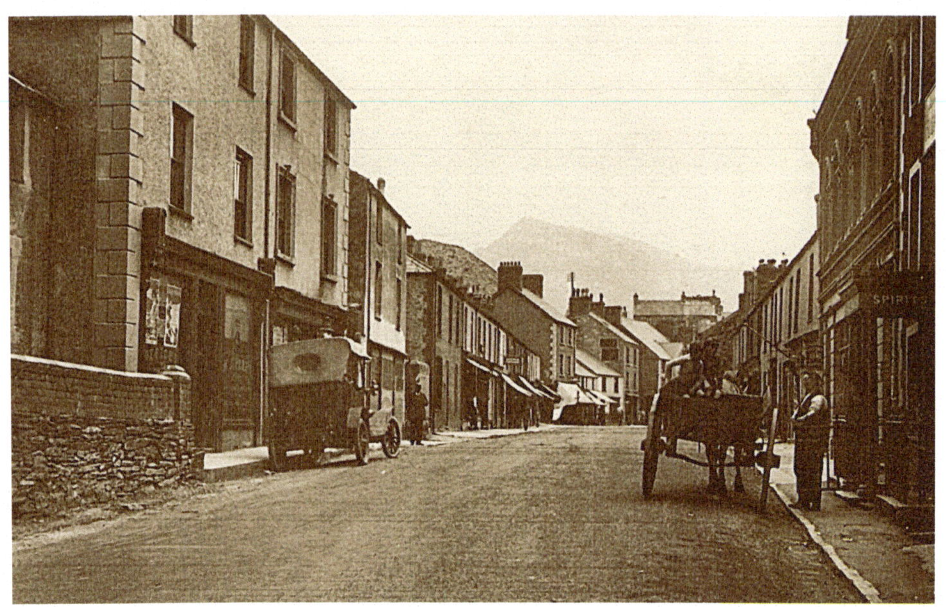

Stryd Fawr (High Street), Bethesda, *c.* 1922

The main A5 road through the town heads towards Bangor and the coast in a westerly direction, or the Snowdonia National Park in an easterly direction. At its peak the population of Bethesda was more than 10,000, but by 2001 it was only 4,327. The decline of slate quarrying is the main reason for this and there are now only around 200 employed at Penrhyn Quarry, in a much-reduced operation. Most residents commute along the coast, or into Cheshire, or have relocated to the cities.

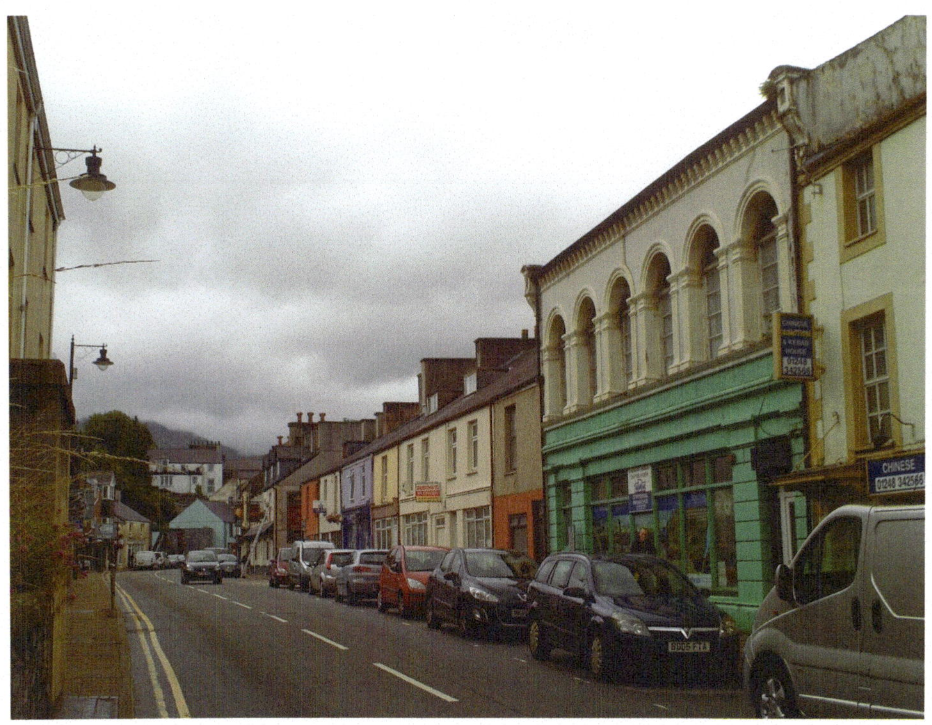

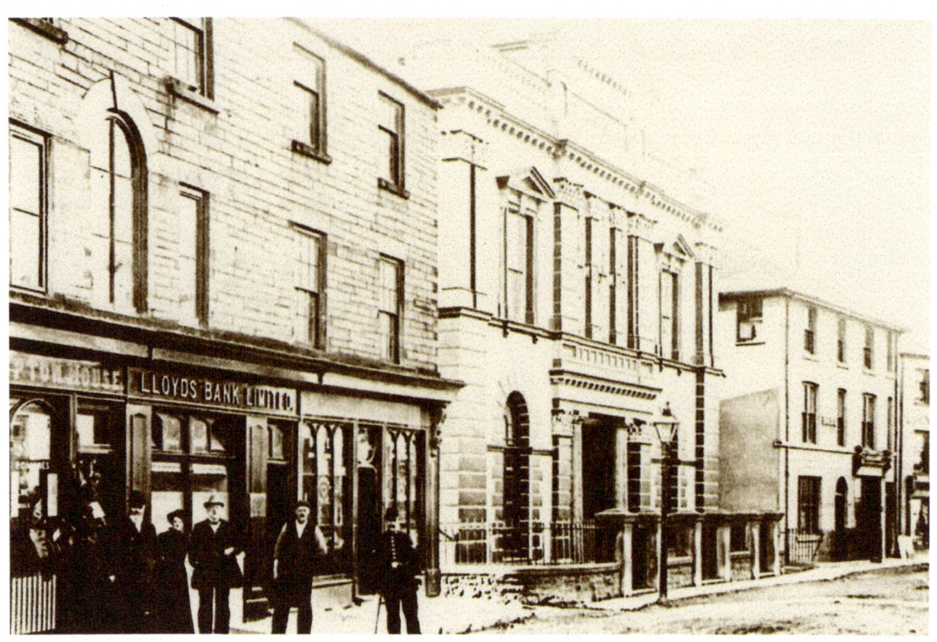

Bethesda Chapel, Stryd Fawr (High Street), Bethesda, *c.* 1890

Bethesda is noted for its chapels, mostly dating from the 1904/05 'Welsh Revival' period. The town is named after the Bethesda Chapel, which has now been converted into residential flats. Bethesda is also noted for the Grade I-listed Calvinistic Methodist Jerusalem Chapel. It also has forty Grade II-listed buildings, including three public houses. The Douglas Arms was named after the family that established the Penrhyn Slate Quarry and was largely responsible for the growth of the settlement in the nineteenth century.

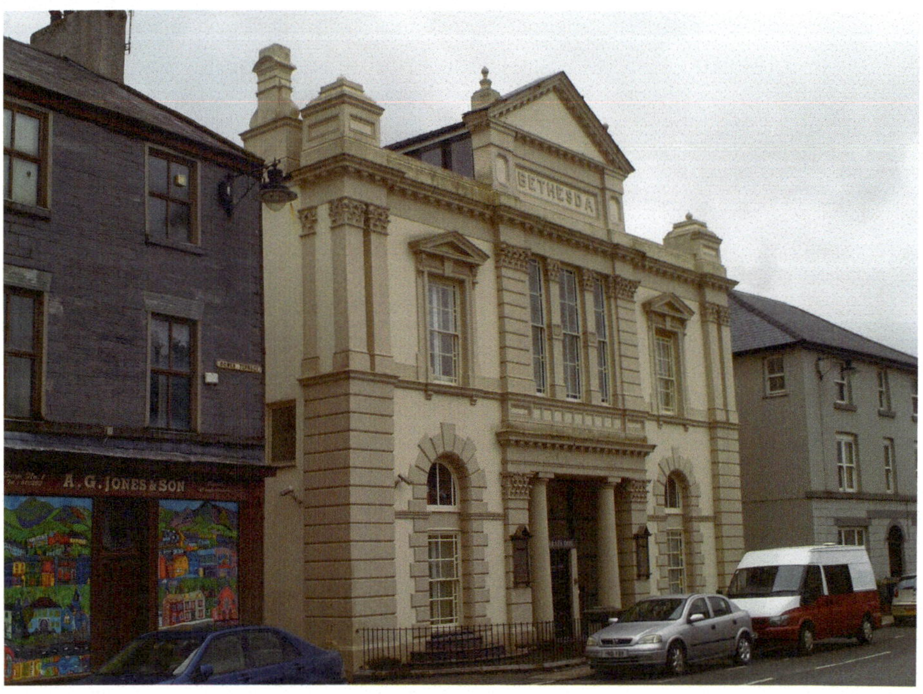

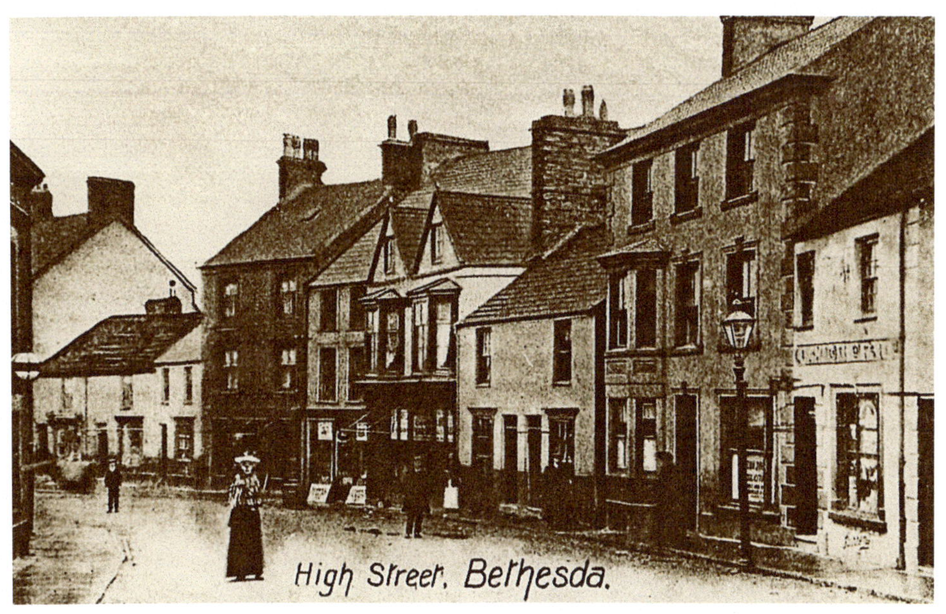

Looking Towards the Victoria Hotel, Stryd Fawr (High Street), Bethesda, *c.* 1890

The A5 main road runs through the town, with most of the settlement to the east and north-east. Housing runs up the hillsides here, around Gerlan, Rachub and Braichmelyn, as the A5 marks the boundary between Lord Penrhyn's former land and the freehold land. The eastern end of Bethesda is bounded by the Carneddau Mountains. The layout of the High Street reflects these boundaries today, with all Bethesda's public houses to be found on one side of the road.

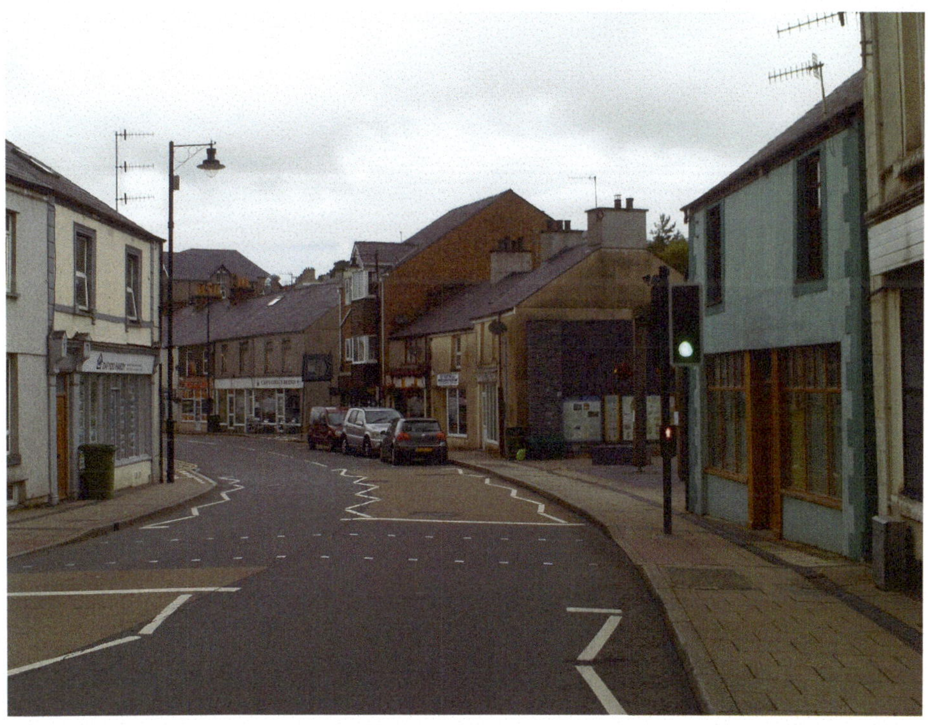

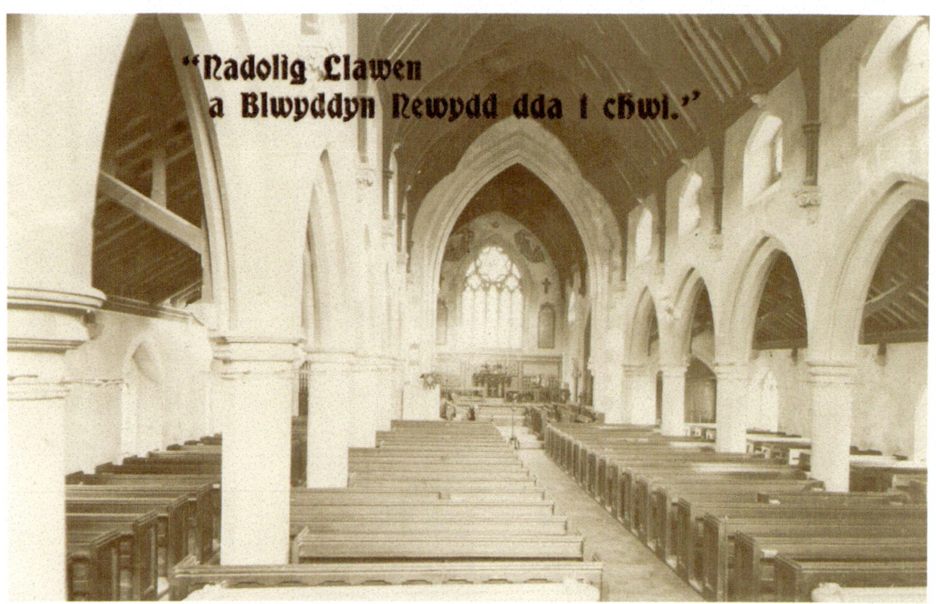

Glanogwen Parish Church (Christchurch), Maes Garnedd (Garnedd Field), Stryd Fawr (High Street), Bethesda, *c.* 1900

Glanogwen Parish Church is situated on a sloping churchyard and is approached through gates on the A5, which are opposite Ogwen Terrace. It was built around 1855/56 by T. H. Wyatt of London, for Lord Penrhyn. There was a limited competition between three firms for the contract and Wyatt, who was related to Lord Penrhyn's agent, got the job. The vicar was sued as a result. This landmark church was Grade II listed on 25 April 1997 as an example of mid-nineteenth-century Gothic's 'more conservative school.'

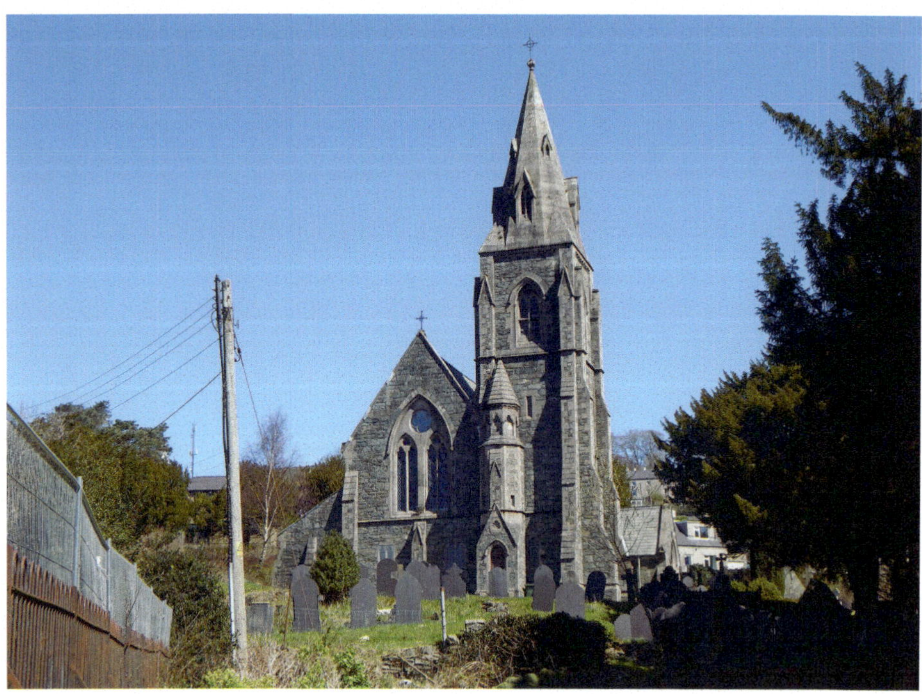

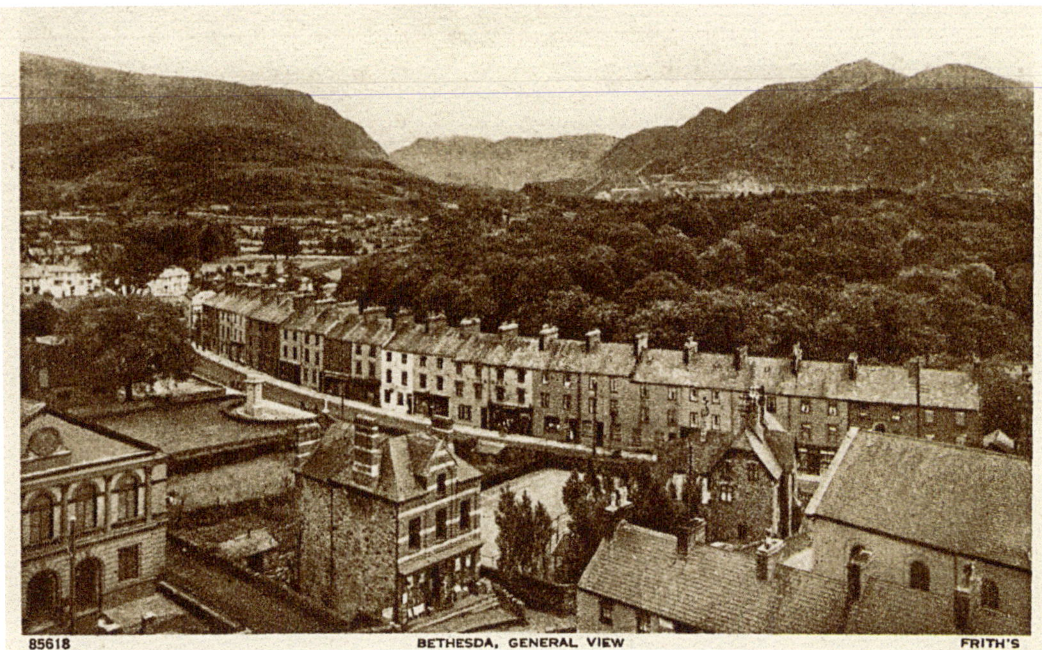

Bethesda, *c.* 1950

This view looks down onto Bethesda High Street, where the war memorial (*inset*) can be seen on the left. Spoil tips of the Penrhyn Quarry are shown behind Bethesda, looking towards Ogwen Valley (Dyffryn Ogwen). Bethesda Cenotaph was erected by Richard Williams in 1923, to a design by R. J. Hughes. It commemorates the people of Ogwen Valley who gave their lives in both world wars. The metal arch (2005) in front of the memorial states 'Er cof am y milwyr' (In memory of the soldiers).

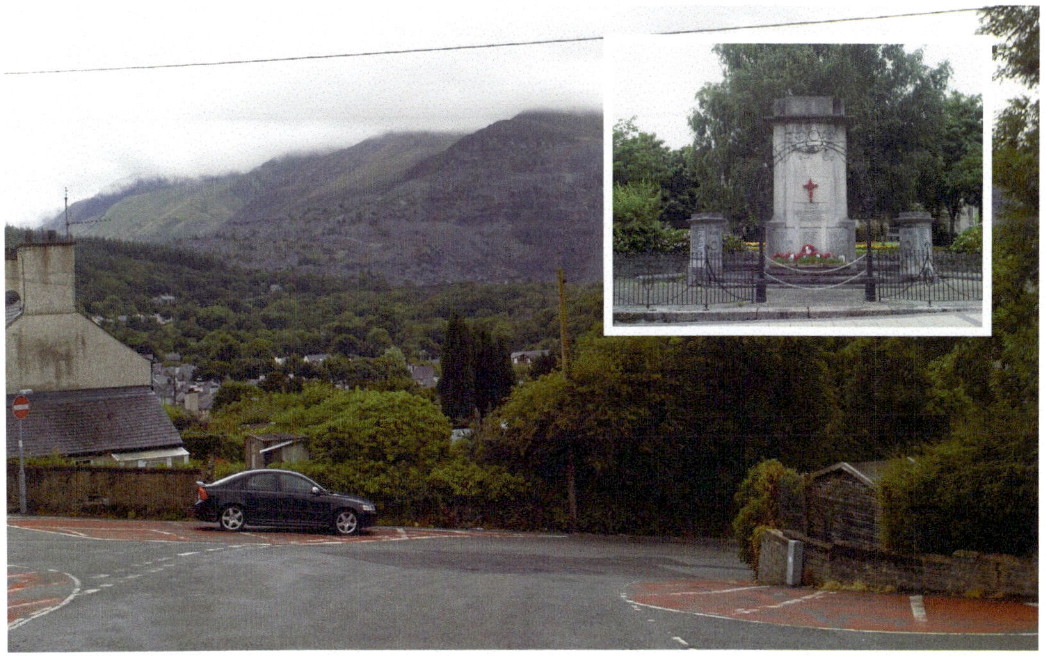

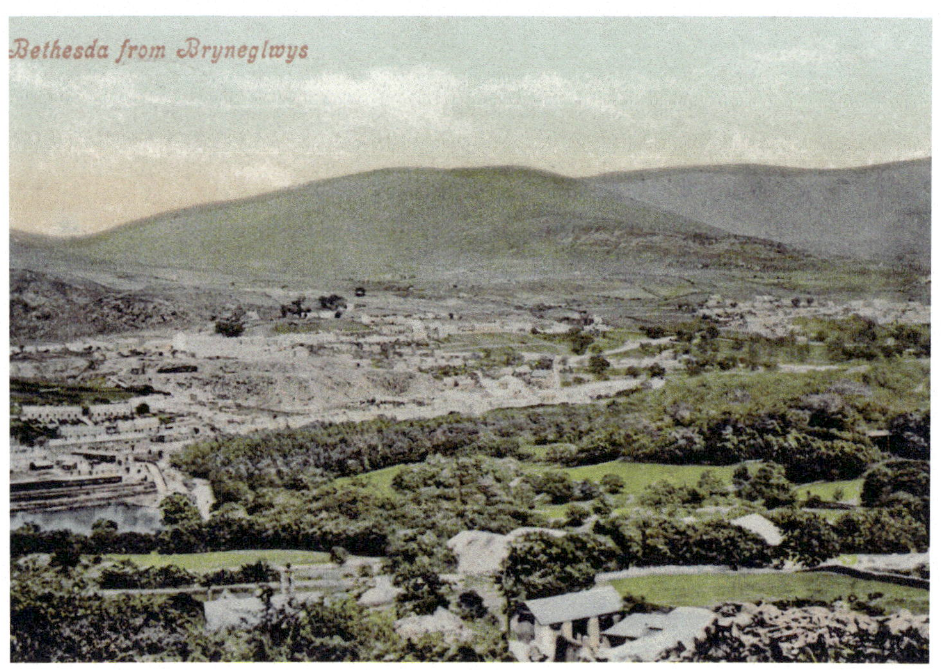

Bethesda from Bryneglwys (Church Hill), 1910

Bryneglwys was constructed around 1850 as part of a small planned community for workers at the nearby Penrhyn Slate Quarry. The cottages were typical of Edward Douglas-Pennant's projected plans for the improvement of the Penrhyn Estate. Cottages in Bryneglwys started to appear slightly earlier than St Ann's Church (*inset*), which was rebuilt by the estate in 1865 after the original church of 1813 had been destroyed by new workings at the quarry. It is now abandoned due to structural defects.

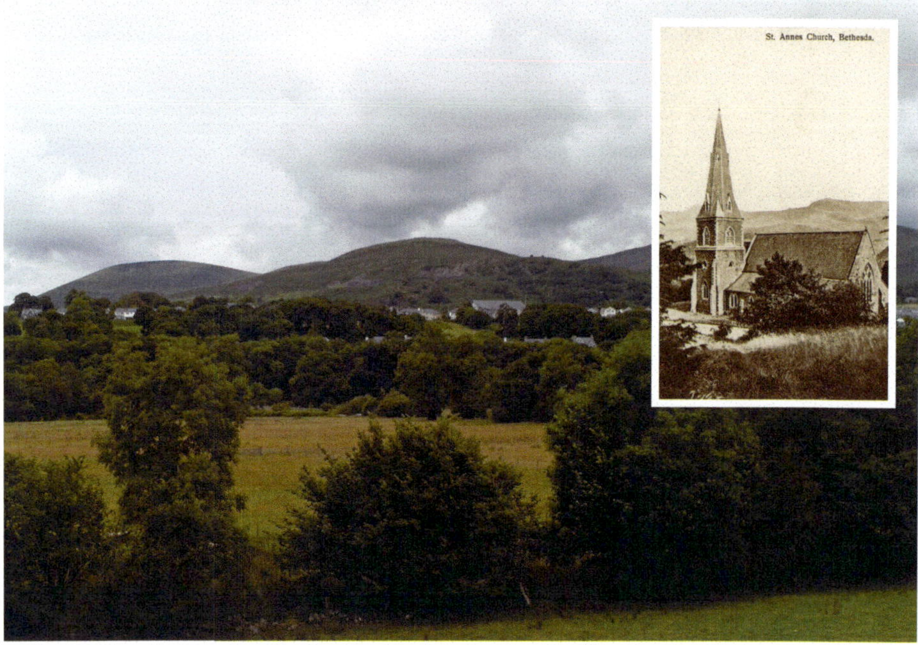

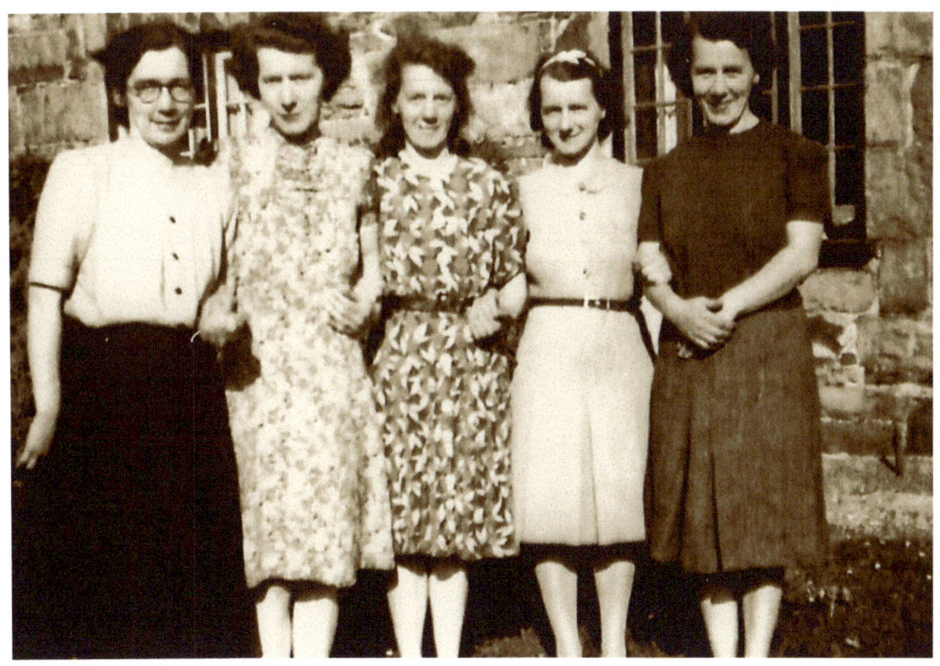

The Williams Family at Braichmelyn (Yellow Arm), *c*. 1940
During the Penrhyn lockout of 1900–03 many quarrymen, including my great grandfather Owen Williams, left Bethesda to seek work in the South Lancashire coalfields at Ashton-in-Makerfield. A census of the time shows whole streets given over to Welsh quarrymen and their families. It was here that Owen married Elizabeth Ann Owens, another Welsh migrant and my great-grandmother. Owen's time at the pit was short-lived, as he lost an eye in an underground explosion. When recovered, he returned to Braichmelyn.

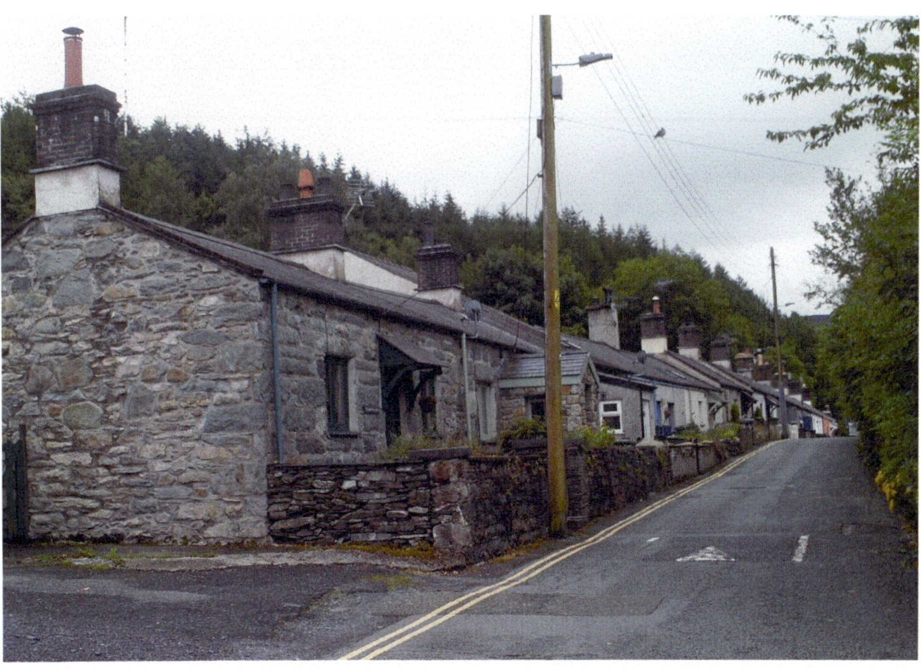

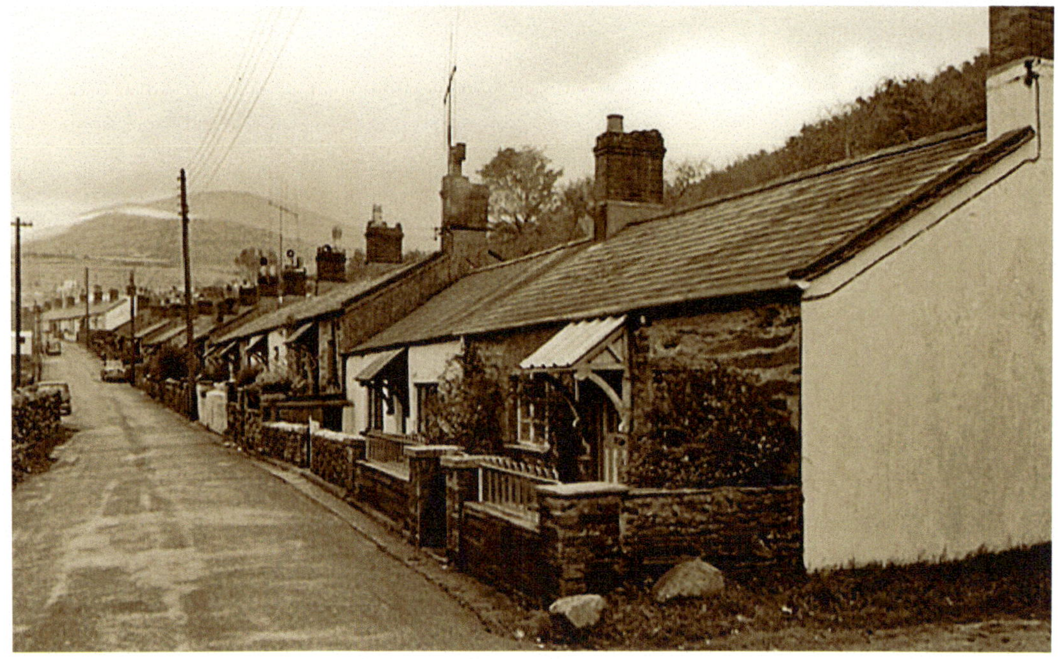

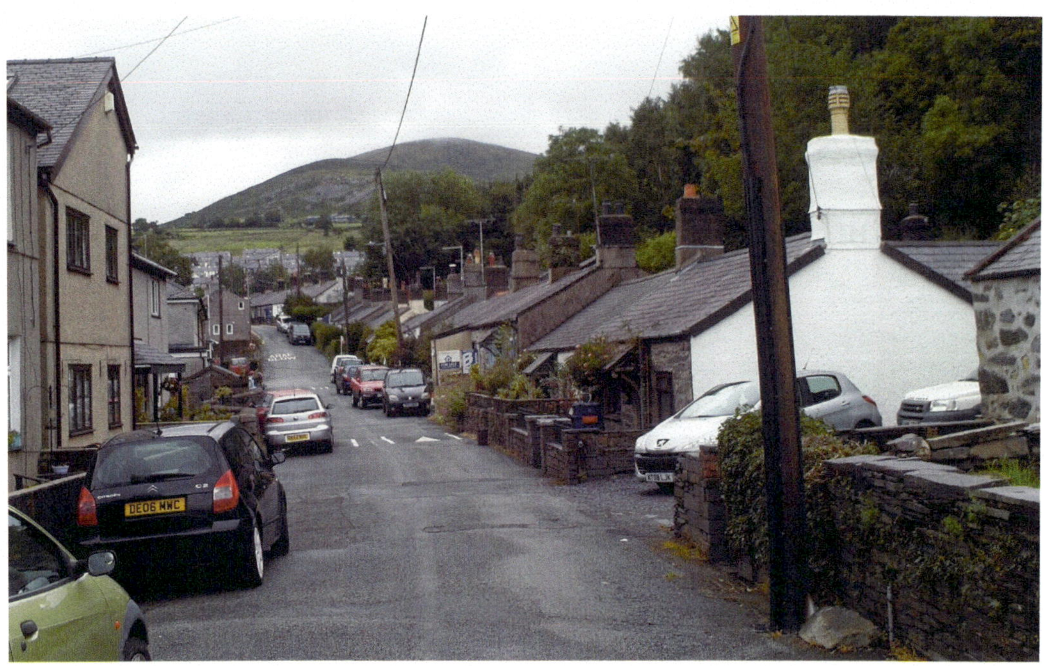

Braichmelyn (Yellow Arm), Bethesda, 1964

This photograph of Braichmelyn in 1964 shows several of the quarrymen's cottages, many of which were inhabited by my grandmother's brothers, who worked at the Penrhyn Slate Quarry all their lives. Today many of these cottages are Grade II listed. They are classic examples of the type of living conditions experienced by quarrymen in the early twentieth century. Their working lives were ones of hard, physical labour and constant exposure to danger and slate dust, which made silicosis commonplace.

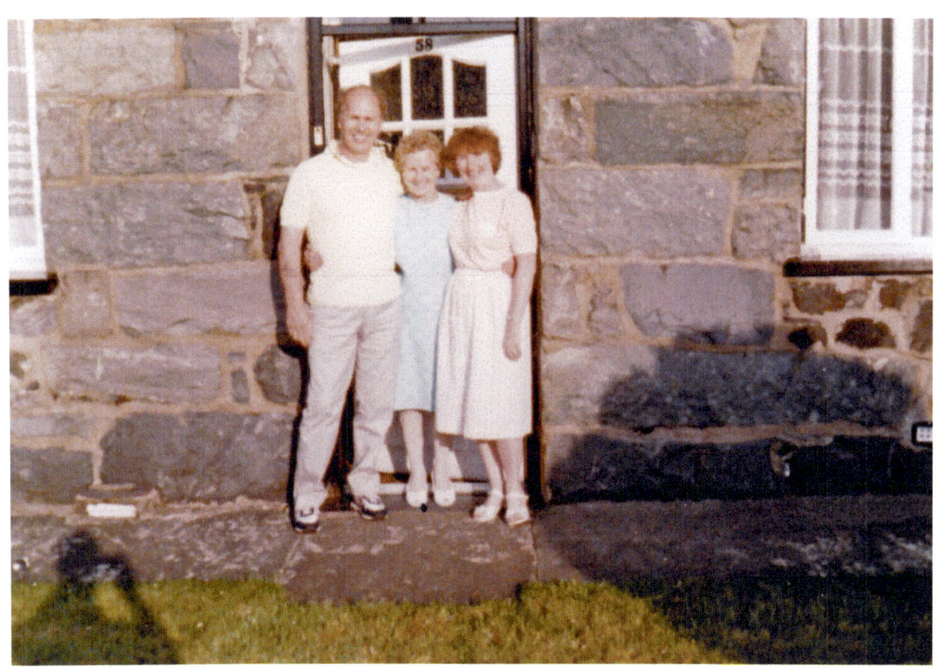

The Williams Family, Bryn Awel (Windy Hill), No. 58 Braichmelyn, Bethesda, May 1990
After my great grandfather's recuperation from his injury he returned to Bethesda and, with his miner's pension, purchased the cottage of Bryn Awel at the top of Braichmelyn. This cottage remained in the family until the early 1990s. When photographed in 1990 it was two separate cottages, which it remains today, with an extended frontage. Owen was to die in 1919 from a combination of complications caused by his injuries and the 'Spanish flu' virus.

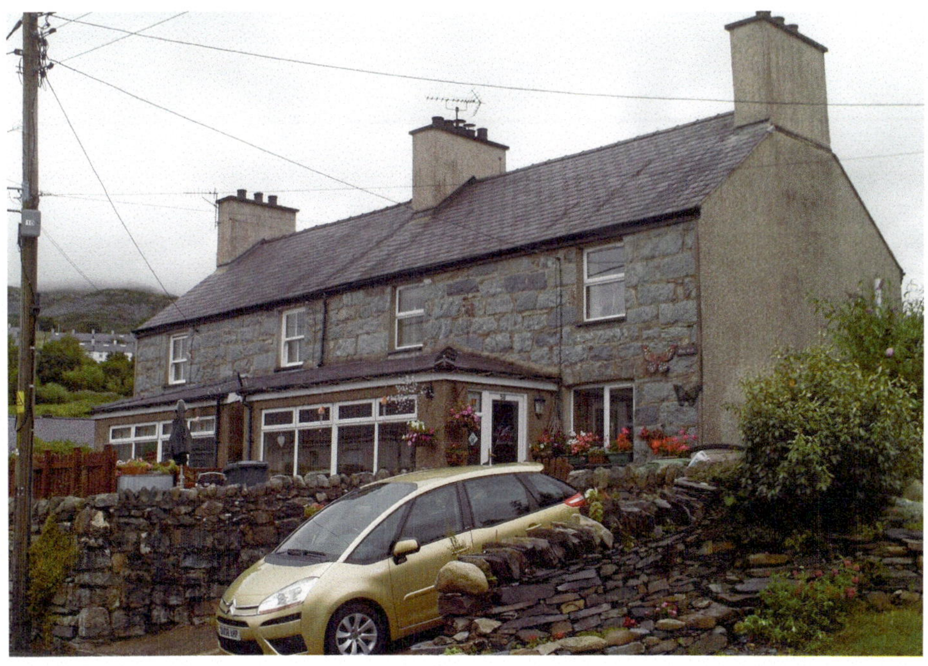

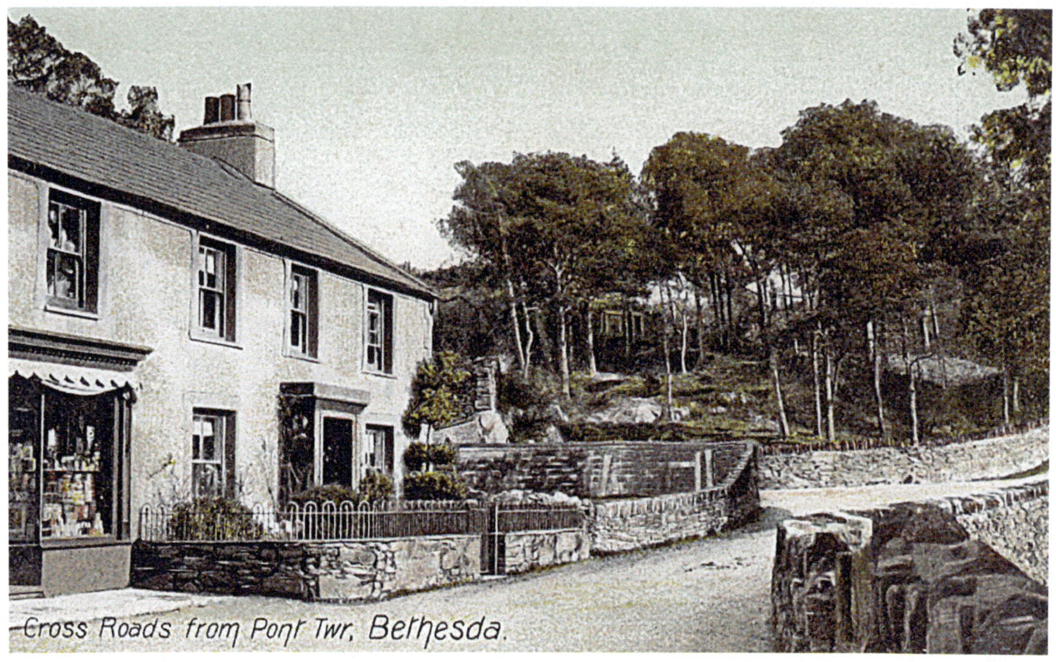

Crossroads from Pont Twr (Tower Bridge), Bethesda, *c.* 1900

Pont Twr is a Grade II-listed road bridge carrying the B4409 over the River Ogwen, by the entrance to Penrhyn Slate Quarry. The road bridge's construction date is unknown but it is likely to have been sometime in the eighteenth century. It was said to have been in a state of ruin in the 1790s, was widened in 1805 and carries the old road to Llandygai and Bangor across the bridge. The cottages on the left included a hardware store – now gone.

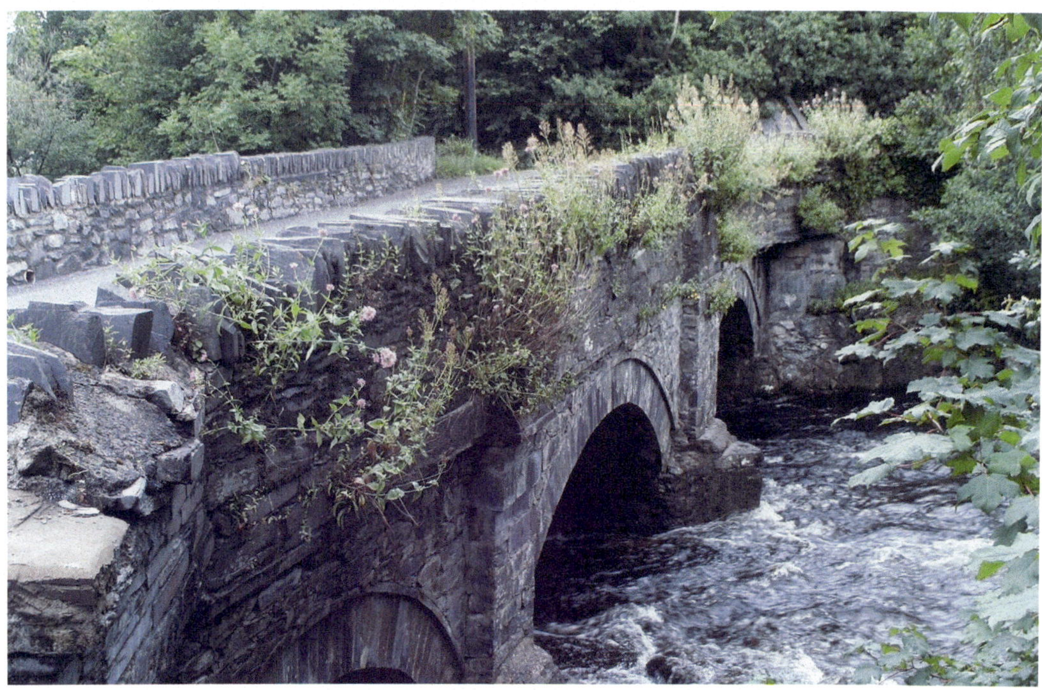

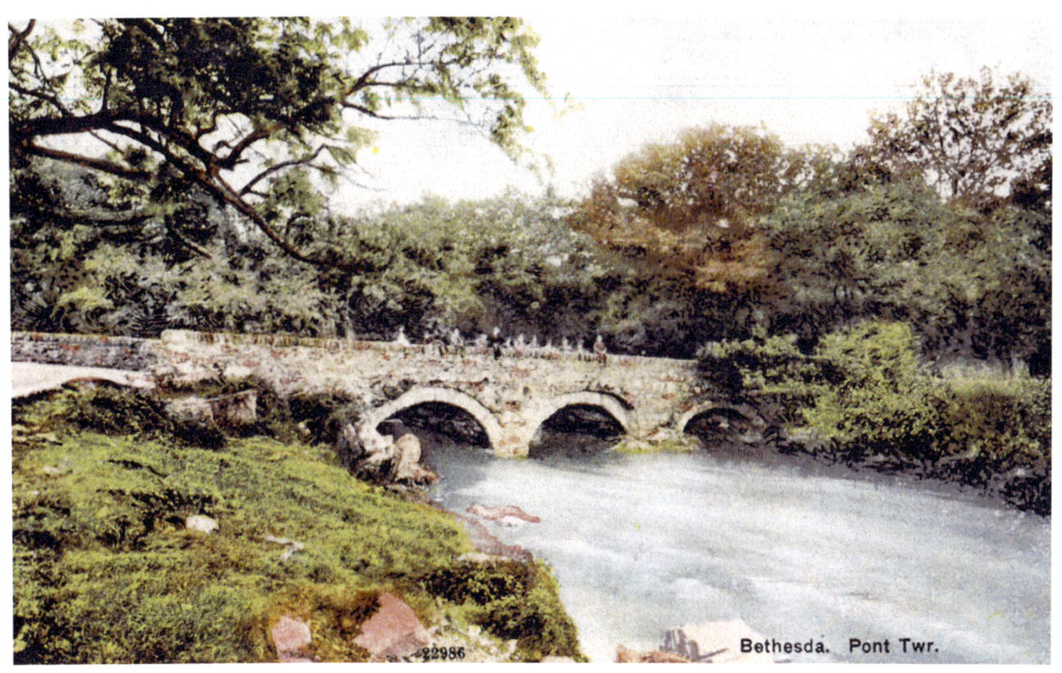

Pont Twr (Tower Bridge), Bethesda, *c.* 1900

A description of its mode of construction reads 'rubble stone, three-arched bridge doubled in width in the early nineteenth century'. The present south side looks of around 1830 construction. The bridge was listed because it is the oldest of the bridges crossing the Afon Ogwen (River Ogwen). The junction with the A5 remains busy, with traffic to and from the slate quarry. It is also next to the Ogwen Bank Caravan Park and is a route often crossed by walkers.

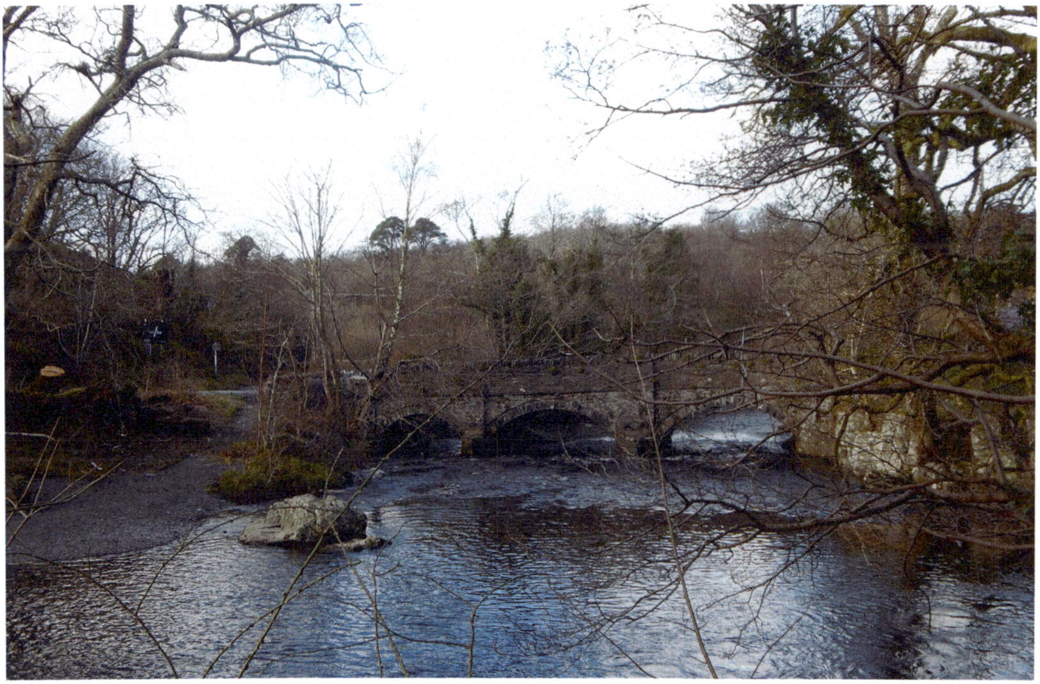

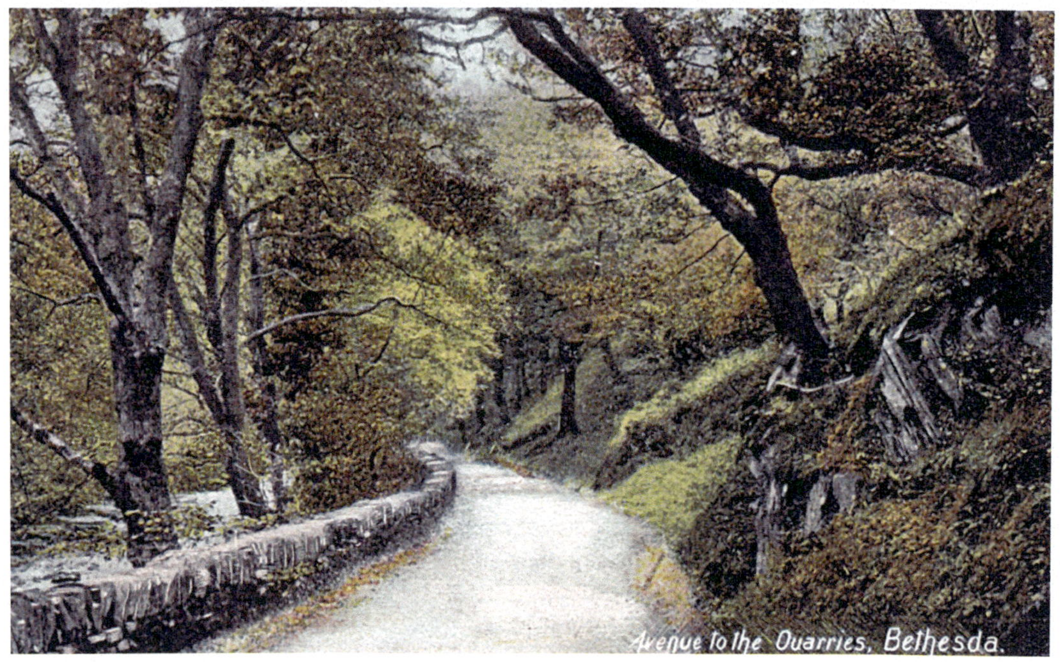

Avenue to the Quarries, Bethesda, *c.* 1906
Once the main entrance and exit for quarrymen at the Penrhyn Slate Quarry. My father remembers lying in bed as a young boy on cold winter mornings at Braichmelyn and listening to the thunder of hob-nail boots from hundreds of quarrymen making their way to Penrhyn Quarry below. He knew when it had been snowing without looking through his bedroom window, as they made no noise when passing. Today it is a quiet country walk with magnificent views.

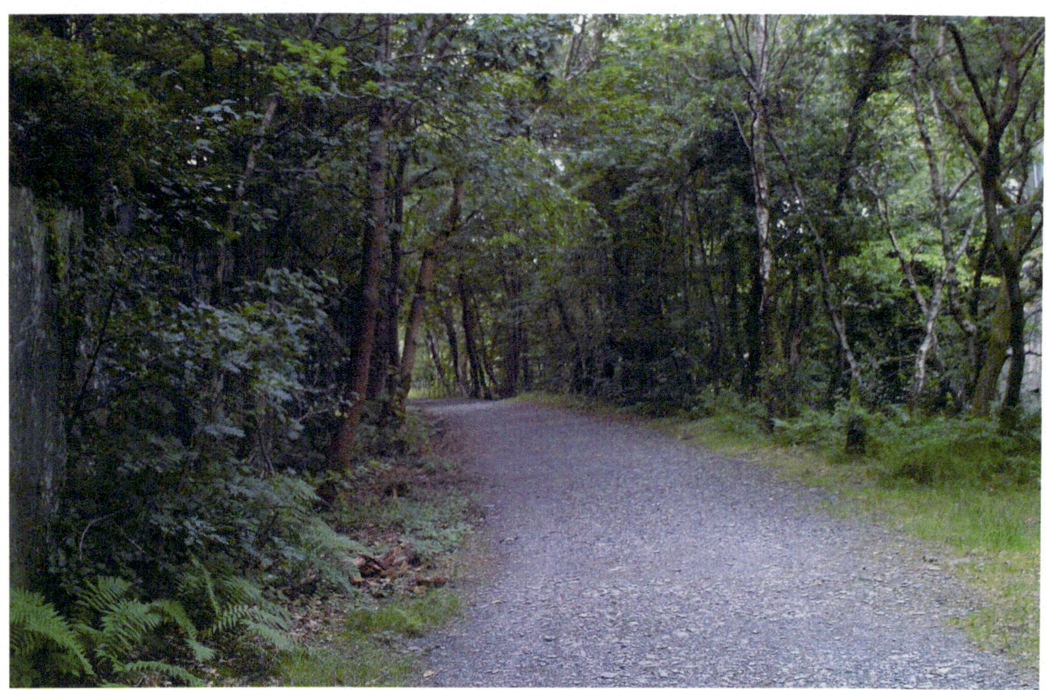

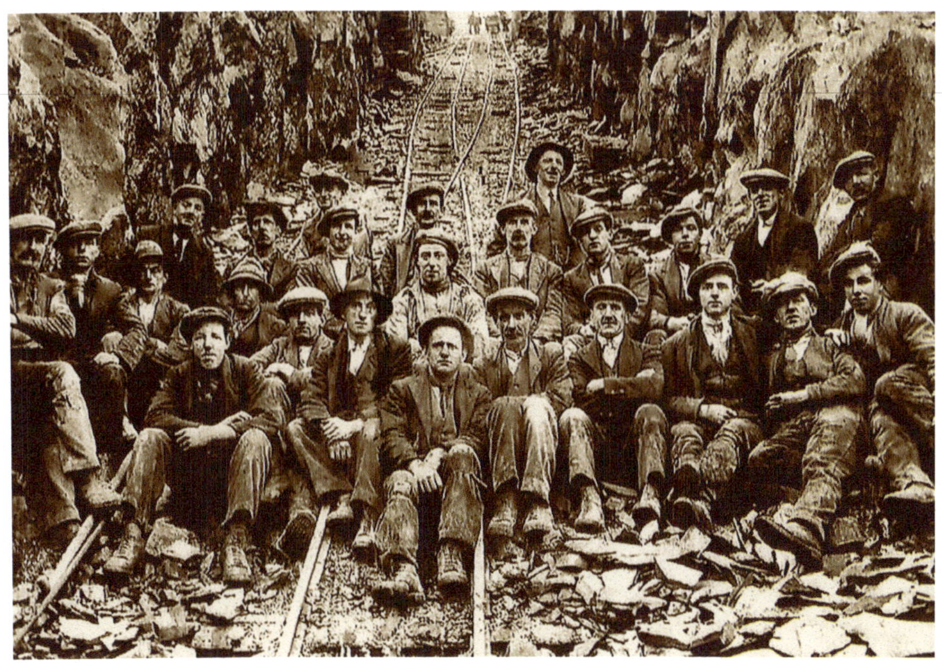

Penrhyn Quarrymen, Bethesda, *c.* 1915, and Streic Fawr Penrhyn, 1900–03 (Great Strike Penrhyn) Memorial

Pictured at Penrhyn Quarry are my grandmother's brothers, William Williams, second from the end (front row, right) and Dewi (David) Williams, (back row, left). Dewi exemplified the danger quarrymen faced on a daily basis – losing a foot, crushed when explosives were accidentally ignited prematurely. The longest dispute in British industrial history took place at Penrhyn Quarry. There were three separate disputes: in 1874, 1896/97 and the longest, 1900–03. The discussions and disputes between the men, union, managers and owners of Penrhyn were very bitter.

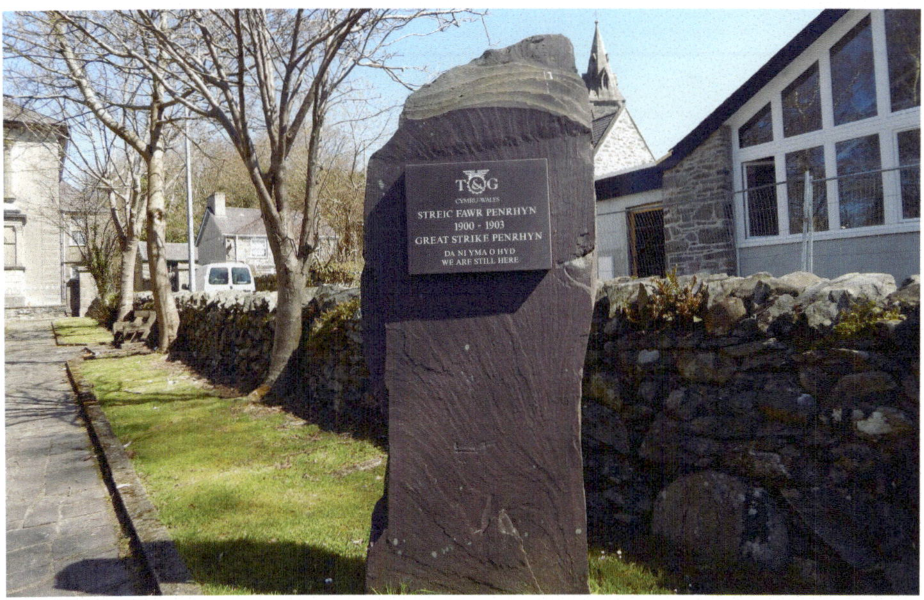

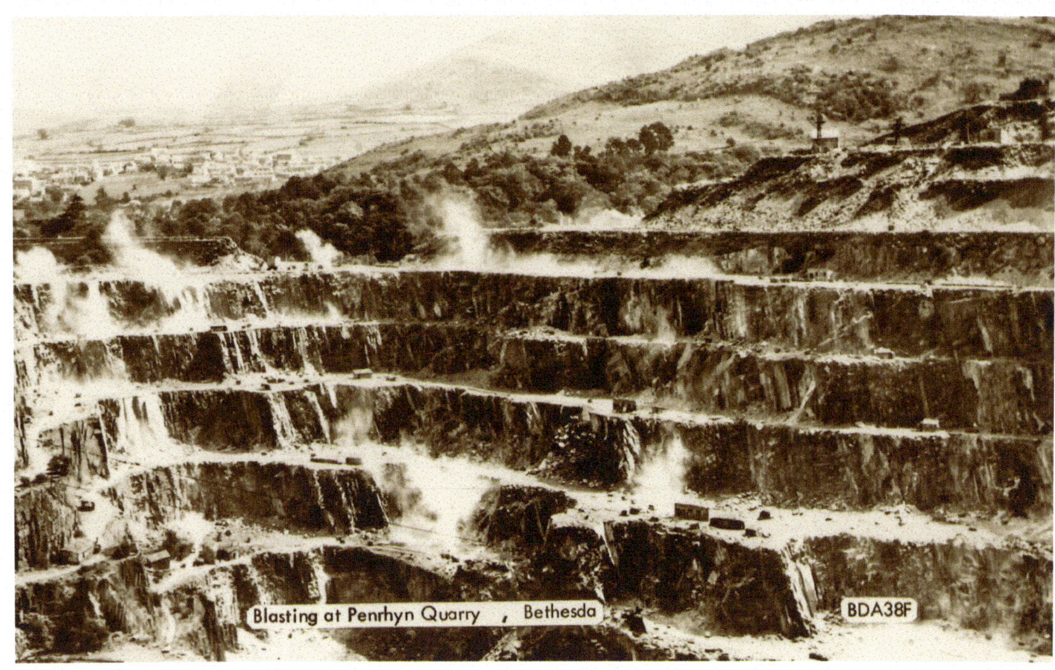

Blasting at Penrhyn Quarry, Bethesda, *c.* 1910. *Inset*: Warning Sign, 2016
The Penrhyn Quarry lockout began on 22 November 1900, when 2,800 men walked out. Lord Penrhyn and his agent, E. A. Young, refused workers readmission, with the dispute lasting three years as a result of this decision. This caused much division and hardship in the local community, with many leaving the area for the South Wales coalfields in order to provide for their families. However, my great grandfather left for the south Lancashire coalfields, and although he eventually returned, many did not.

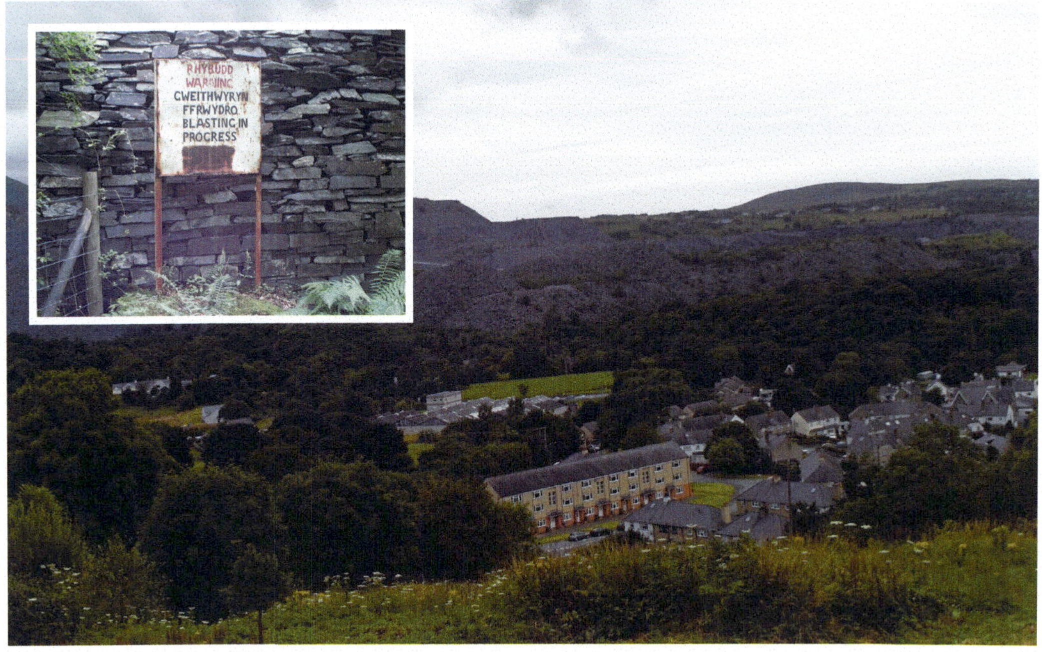

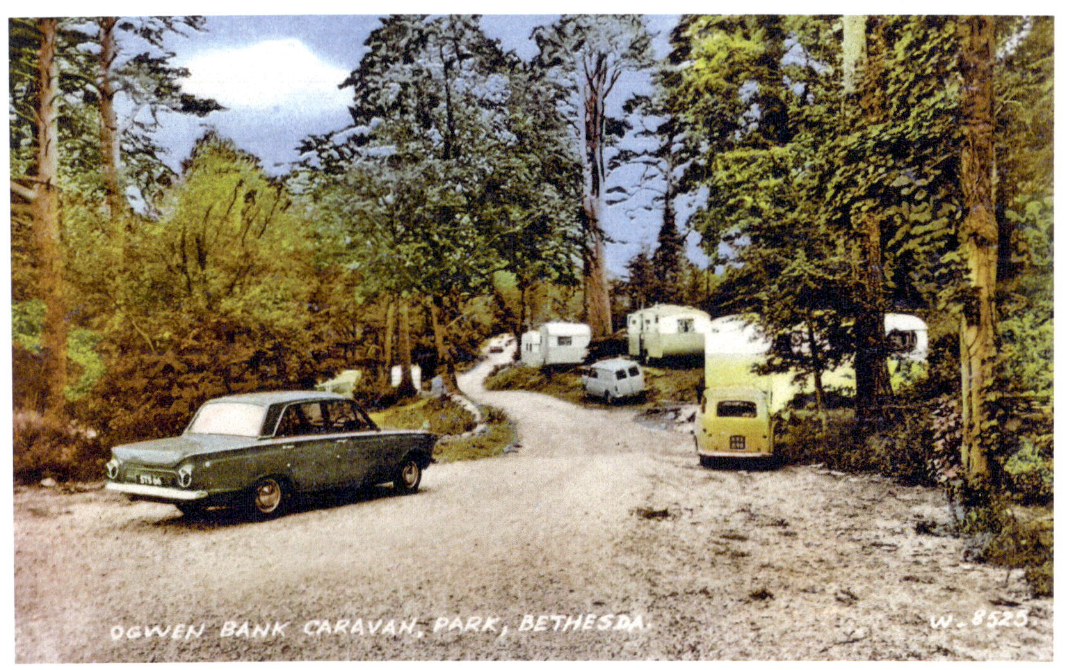

Ogwen Bank Caravan Park, Bethesda, *c.* 1960

Located in the picturesque Ogwen Valley (Dyffryn Ogwen), the caravan park has come a long way since these pictures were taken in the 1960s. The park nestles in quiet woodland, with Ogwen Bank Falls providing some spectacular views of Snowdonia. Activity-based holidays have always been popular in the National Park, with organised fishing, climbing and hiking trips, as well as the 'zip-wire' at the now disused Penrhyn Quarry. The caravan park's 'country club' was formerly Penrhyn Castle's hunting lodge.

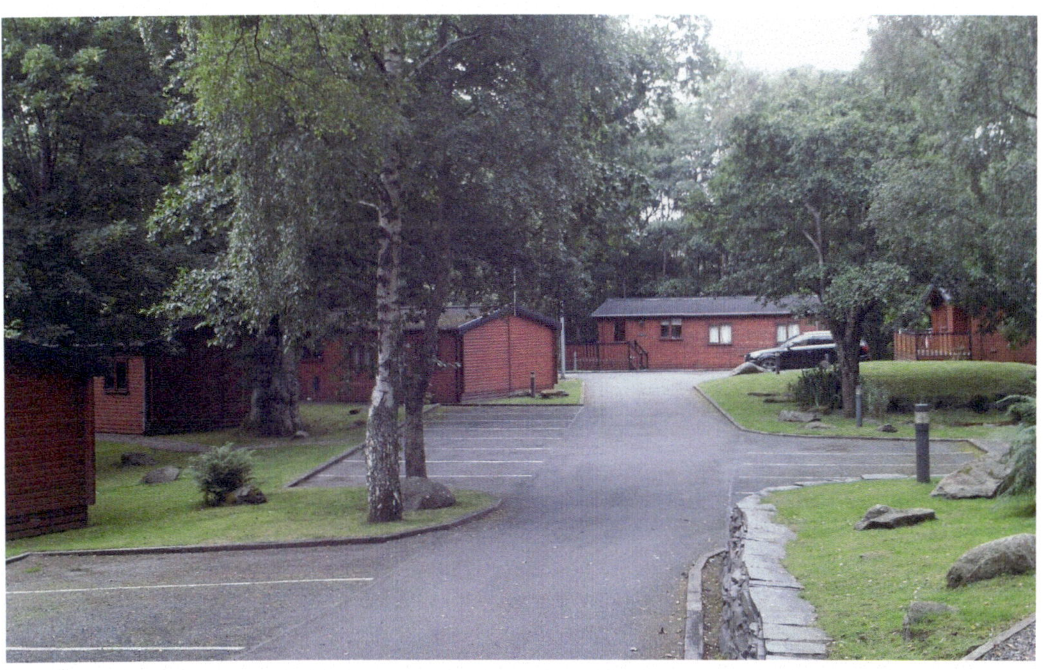

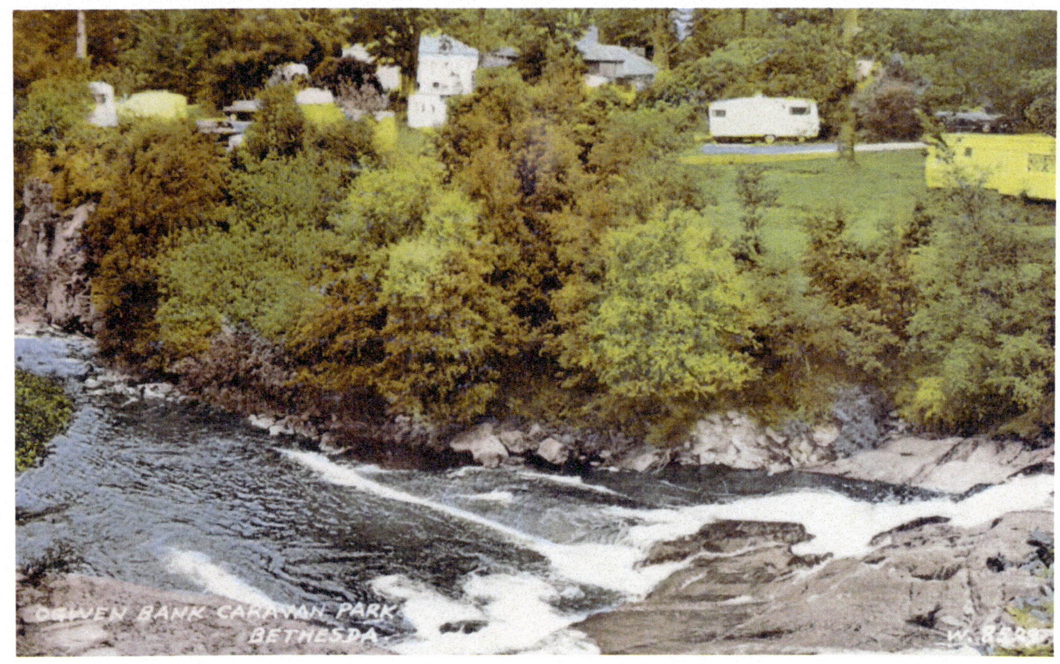

Ogwen Bank Caravan Park, Bethesda, *c.* 1960

The caravan park has long been a popular spot for holidaymakers due to its central location and access for the north Wales coast and the National Park of Snowdonia. It is also popular with walkers and those who wish to pursue outdoor activities, for the same reasons. The location is along the banks of the River Ogwen, and with its many waterfalls and tranquil pools, it is an ideal location. On the opposite bank is the former walk to the Penrhyn Quarry.

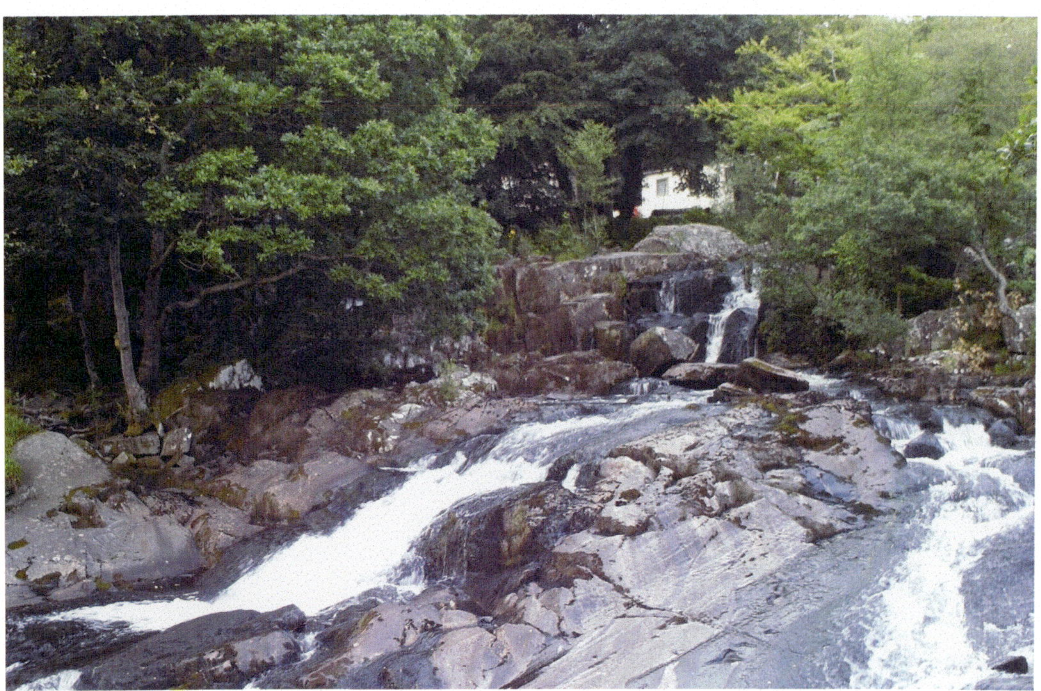

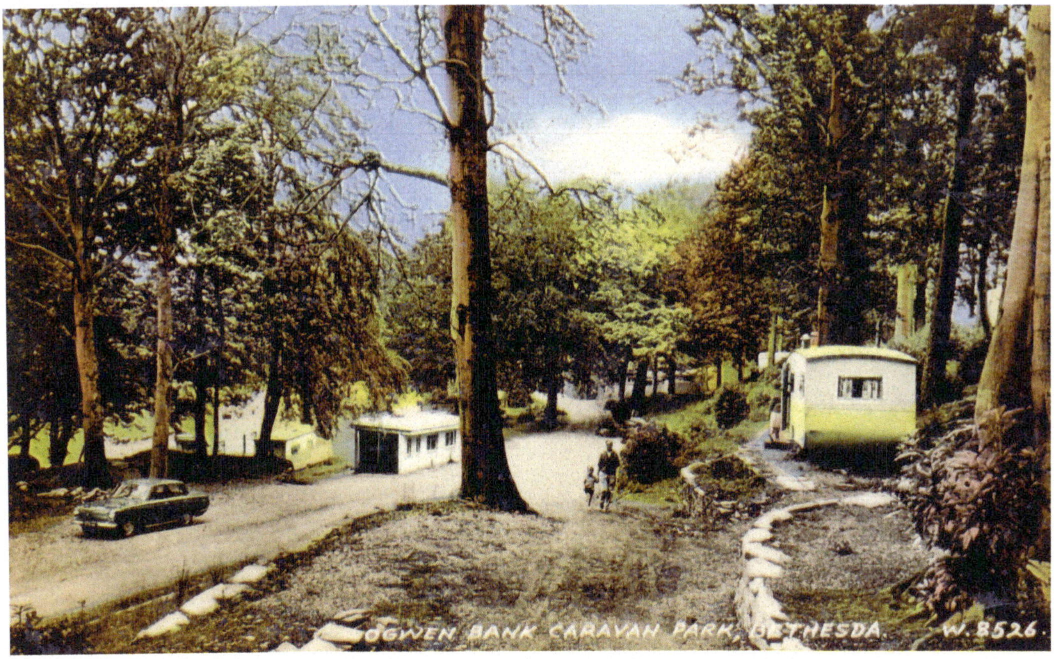

Ogwen Bank Caravan Park, Bethesda, *c.* 1960

The caravan park is bounded by the former walk to the Penrhyn Slate Quarry on one side, and the A5 main road through Bethesda, towards Bangor and the Snowdonia National Park, on the other. There are some spectacular views of the Carneddau Mountain Range and Nant Ffrancon. I also have some personal memories of visiting the location on holiday with my parents as a child, and my young son Sammy playing happily with his holiday friend, Benjamin, this summer.

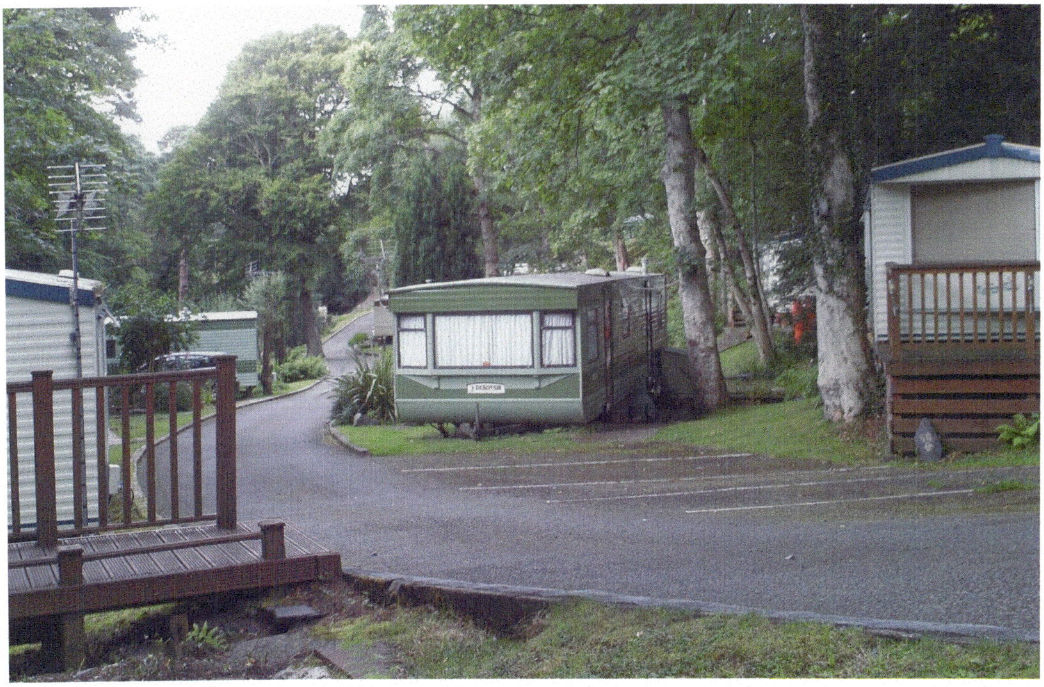

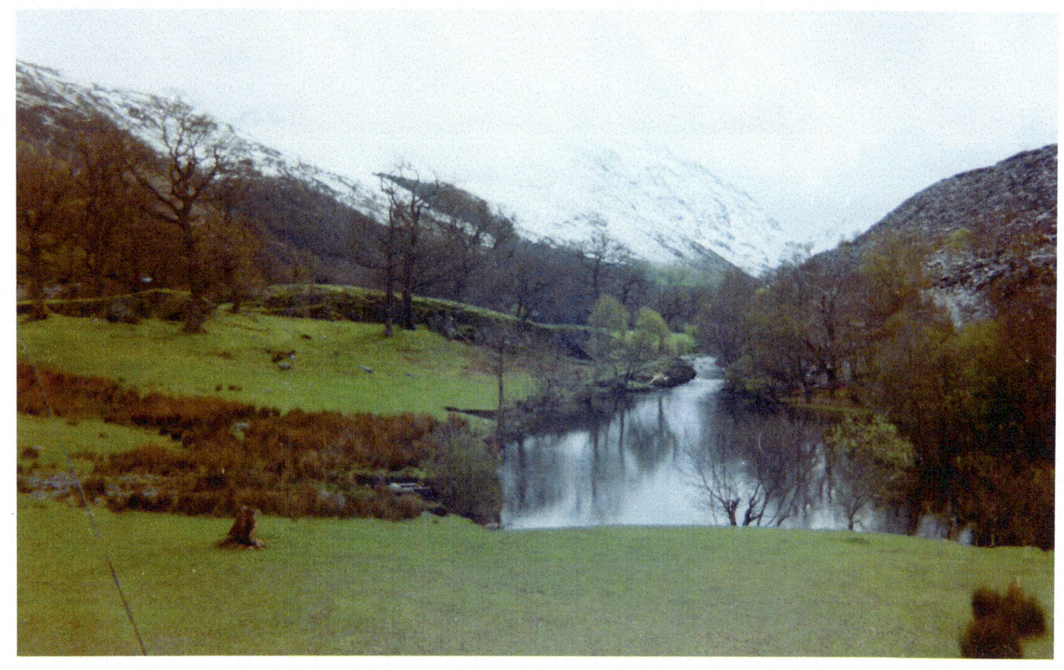

Ogwen Bank and Penrhyn Quarry, 1997

This view of the Carneddau Mountains, looking towards the Nant Ffrancon Pass, is taken from the junction of the A5 and the entrance to Ogwen Bank Caravan Park. To the right is the Penrhyn Slate Quarry and the spoil heaps that surround it. The photograph of 1997 was taken in April and shows us how severe the weather can be in the Ogwen Valley when conditions are unpredictable. When the weather is more favourable it is a great picnic location with tremendous views.

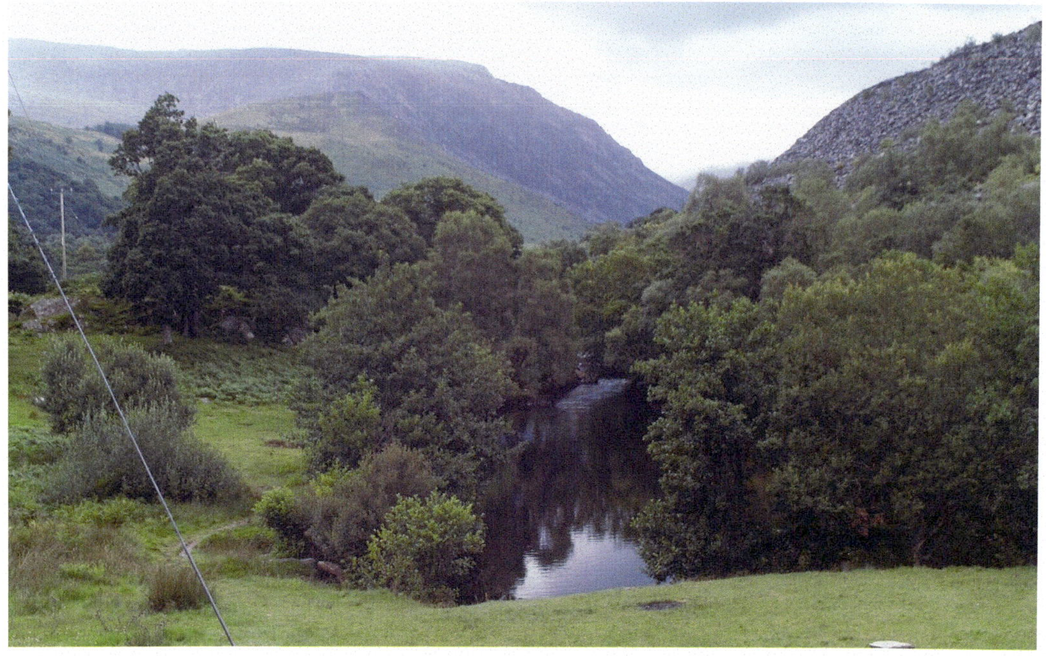

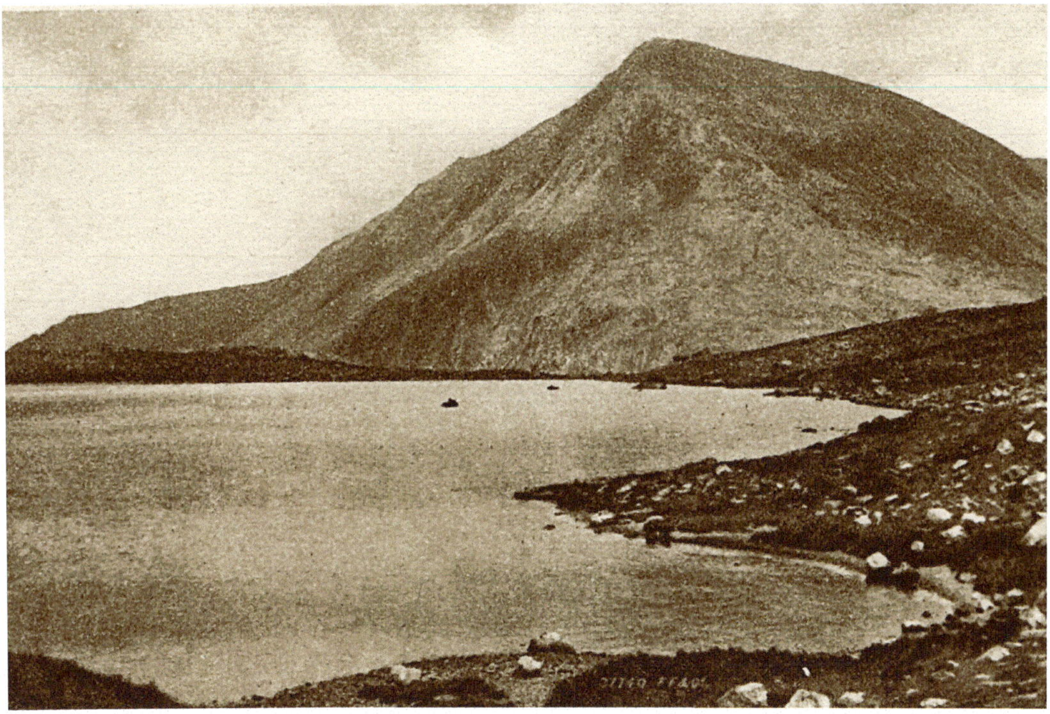

Llyn Idwal (Lake Idwal), near Bethesda, *c.* 1960

A small glacial lake, it is named after Prince Idwal Foel, who was possibly cremated by the lake, after his death in battle. The lake is reached on foot from the A5. It is 800 metres (2624 feet) wide by 300 metres (984 feet) in length and is only 10.9 metres (36 feet) deep at its deepest point, with over 60 per cent of the lake less than 3.04 metres (10 feet) deep. It is held back by a large terminal moraine, with more glacial debris along the western shore.

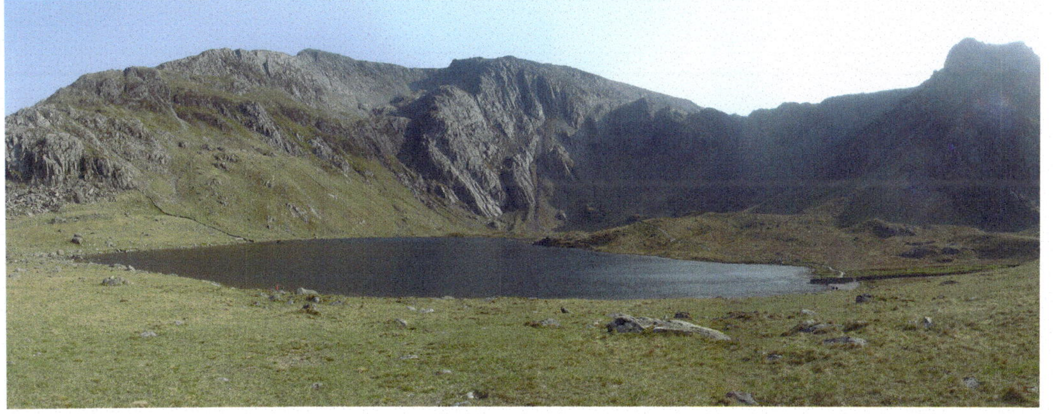

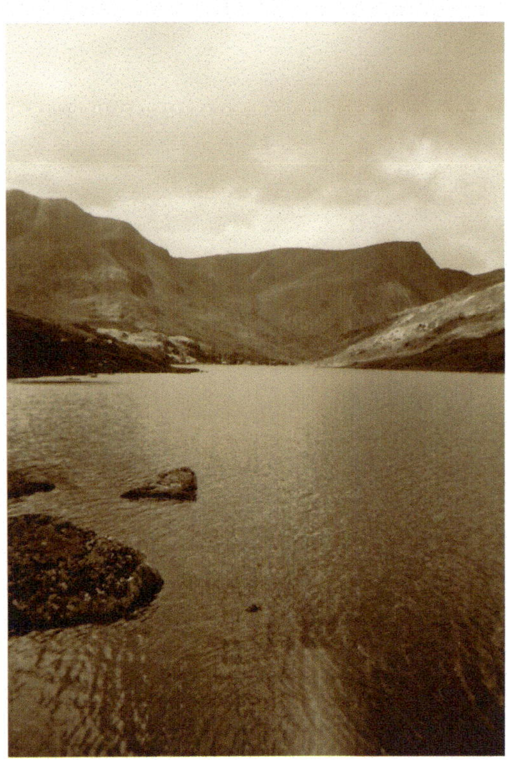

Llyn Ogwen (Lake Ogwen), Nant Ffrancon Head, 1961

The Nant Ffrancon Pass runs between Bethesda and Llyn Ogwen, which borders onto Gwynedd and Conwy. The summit is 312 metres (1,024 feet) at Pont Wern-gof, around a third of a mile beyond the eastern end of Llyn Ogwen. From here the road descends to Capel Curig and Betws-y-Coed. The A5, the Holyhead to London trunk road, was constructed by Thomas Telford in 1810–26. The original road through Nant Ffrancon was constructed by Lord Penrhyn in the late eighteenth century.

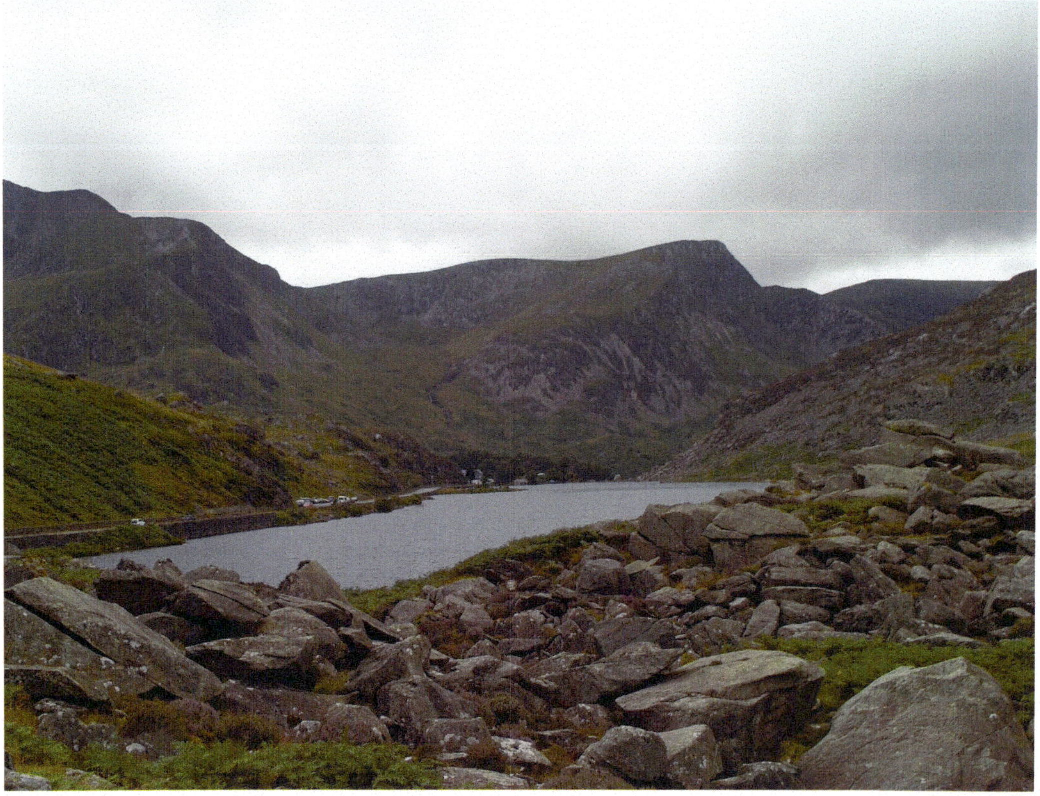

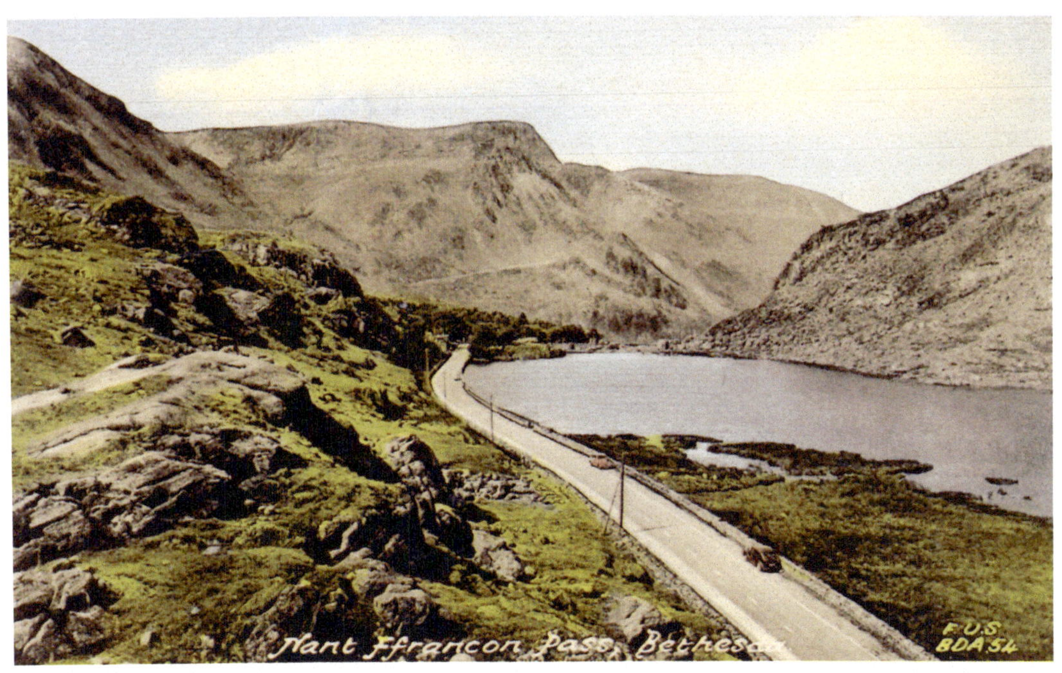

Nant Ffrancon Pass, Bethesda, *c.* 1930

The Nant Ffrancon Pass is a steep-sided glacial valley – typically 'u-shaped'. The pass drops into Bethesda between the Glyderau and the Carneddau mountains. The valley starts in Cwm Idwal, carrying water from Llyn y Cwn, through Twll Du and Llyn Idwal, to join the Ogwen Valley below the Rhaeadr Ogwen (Ogwen Falls), on Afon Ogwen. Nant Ffrancon is possibly the least agriculturally developed glacial valley in Gwynedd. Monuments from the Neolithic and Bronze Ages, as well as evidence of Iron Age hill forts and medieval settlements, have been found here.

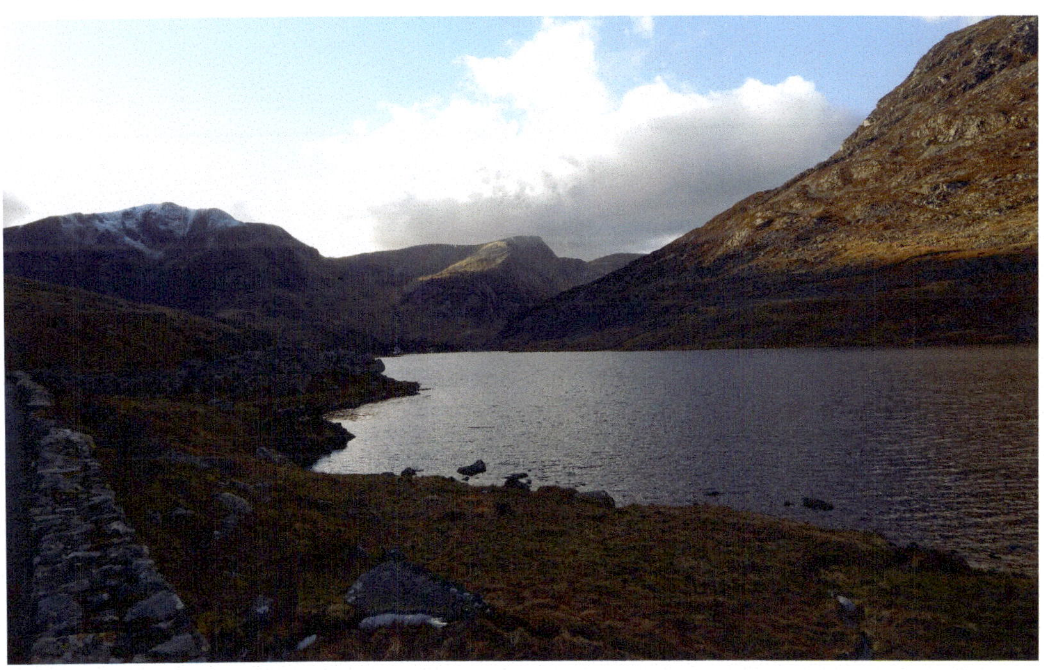

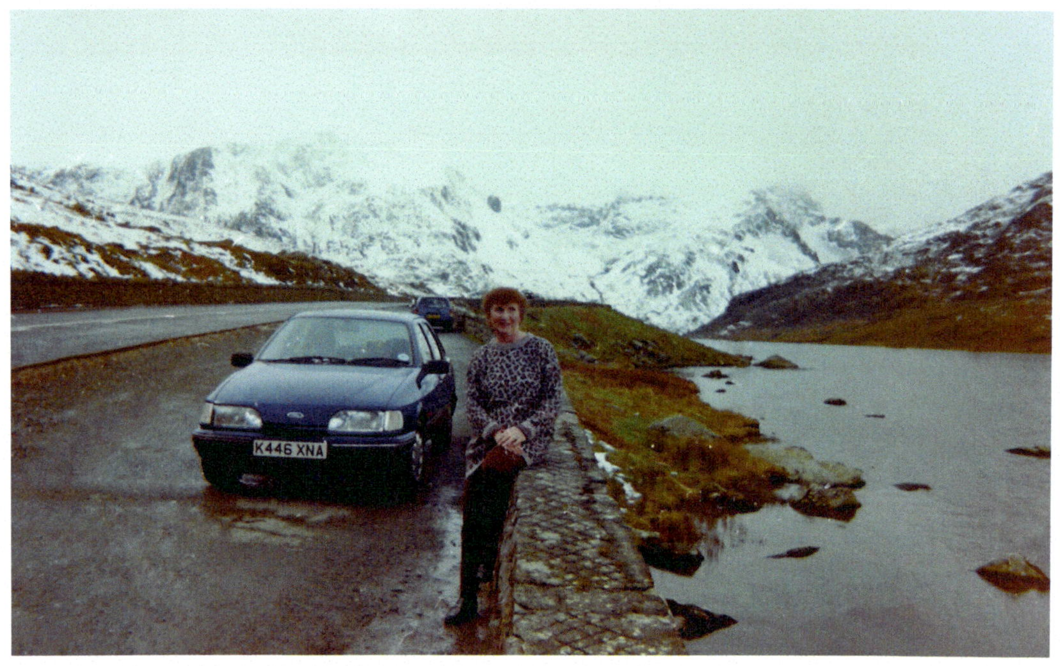

Llyn Ogwen (Lake Ogwen), Bethesda, April 1997

Llyn Ogwen has some dramatic views and is located to the south of Bangor. The Llyn is very shallow, with a maximum depth of around 3 metres (9 ½ feet). It is approximately 1.6 kilometres (1 mile) long and 310 metres (1017 feet) above sea level. Llyn Ogwen is the source of Afon Ogwen and legends link it to King Arthur. It is said to be the final resting place of his sword Excalibur. In the early twentieth century a dam was constructed to raise the water level, forming a reservoir.

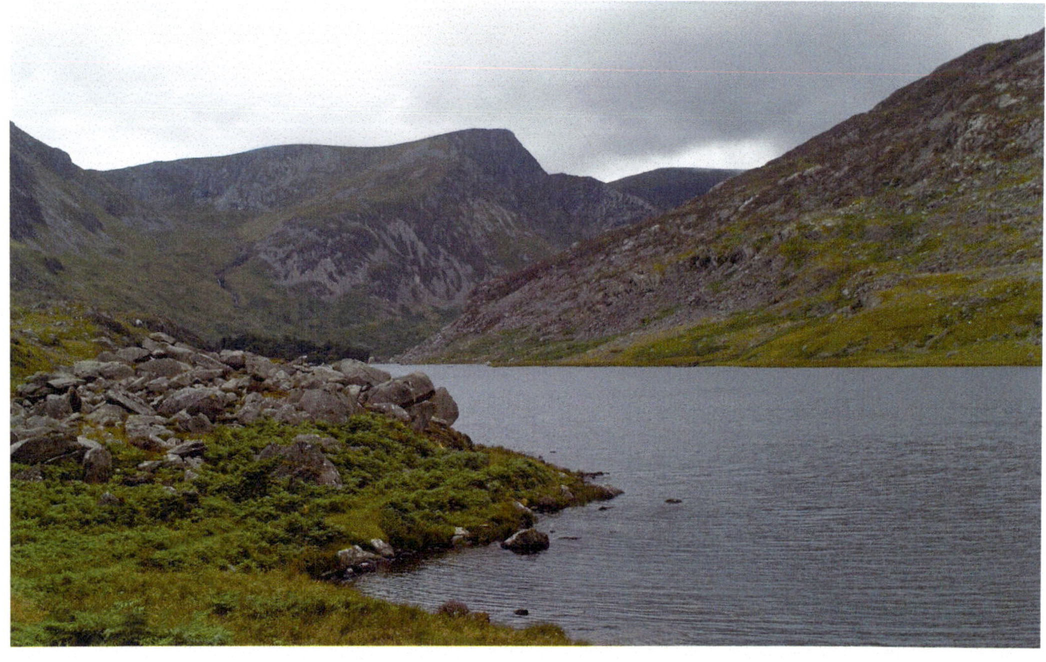

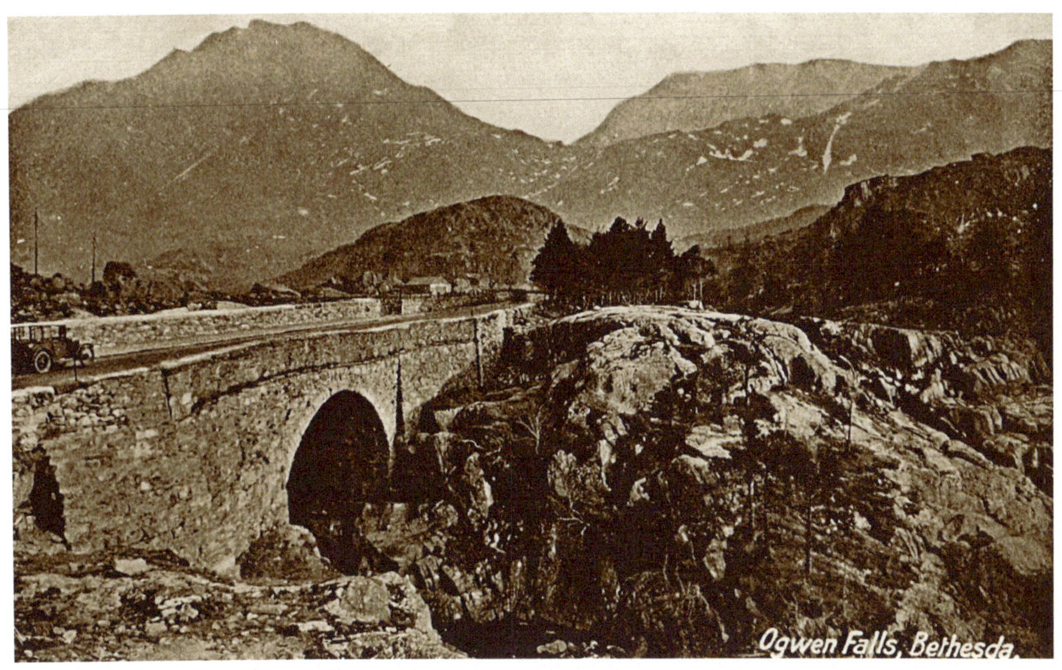

Rhaeadr Ogwen (Ogwen Falls) and Pont Pen y Benglog, Bethesda, 1934

The Rhaeadr Ogwen are situated at a point where the Afon Ogwen, emerging from Llyn Ogwen, begins to flow along the Nant Ffrancon Valley towards the sea. Nant Ffrancon is a steep-sided, u-shaped, glacial valley, said to be one of the finest examples in Wales, and drops into Bethesda between the Glyderau and the Carneddau mountains. The Afon Ogwen passes through the town of Bethesda and the villages of Tregarth, Tal–y–Bont and Llandygai, before reaching the Afon Menai.

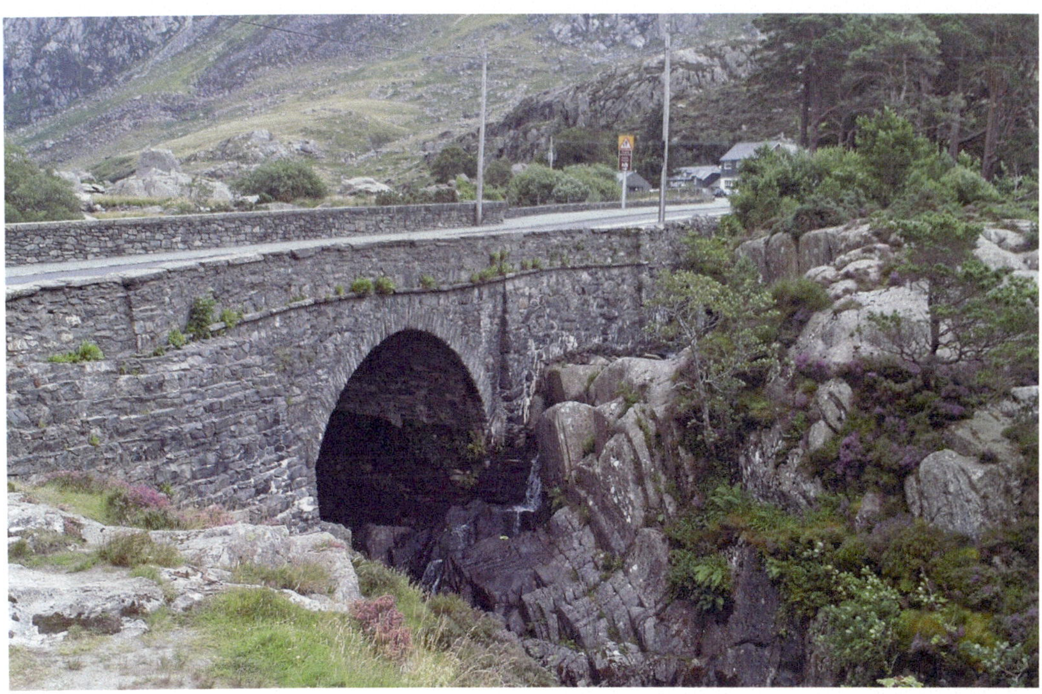

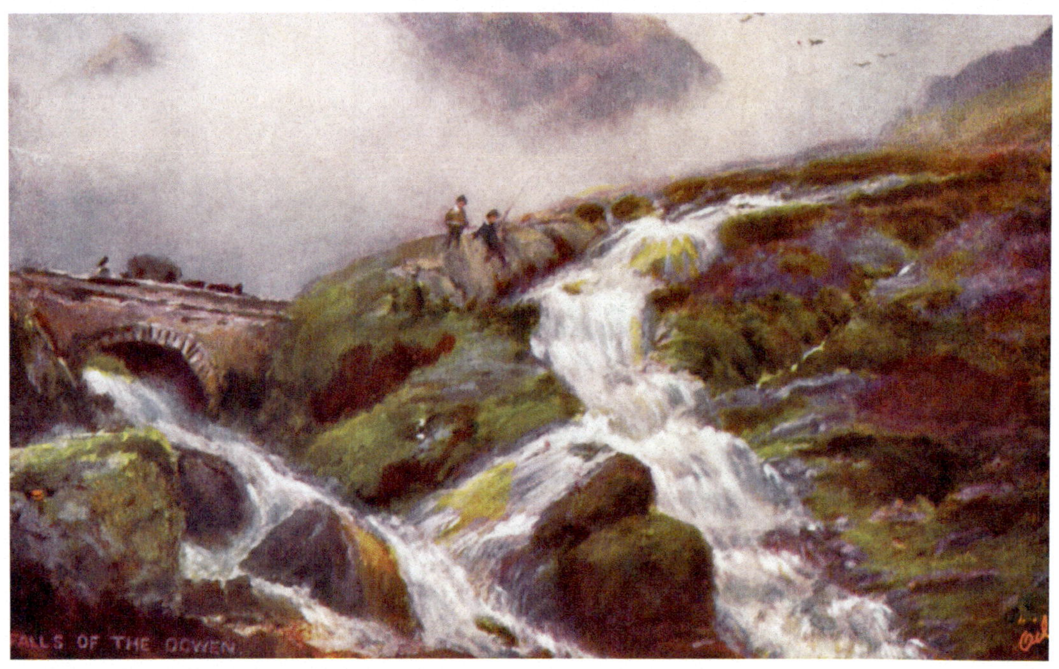

Rhaeadr Ogwen (Ogwen Falls), near Bethesda, *c.* 1900

The Afon Ogwen flows out of the western end of Llyn Ogwen and descends rapidly down a series of waterfalls known as the Rhaeadr Ogwen (Ogwen Falls). From the falls the river flows on in a north-westerly direction towards the steep-sided and glacial Nant Ffrancon valley. It eventually discharges into the Afon Menai, near Bangor. The Afon Ogwen contains Salmon, Brown Trout and Sea Trout. The Rhaeadr Ogwen remains popular with both climbers and walkers.

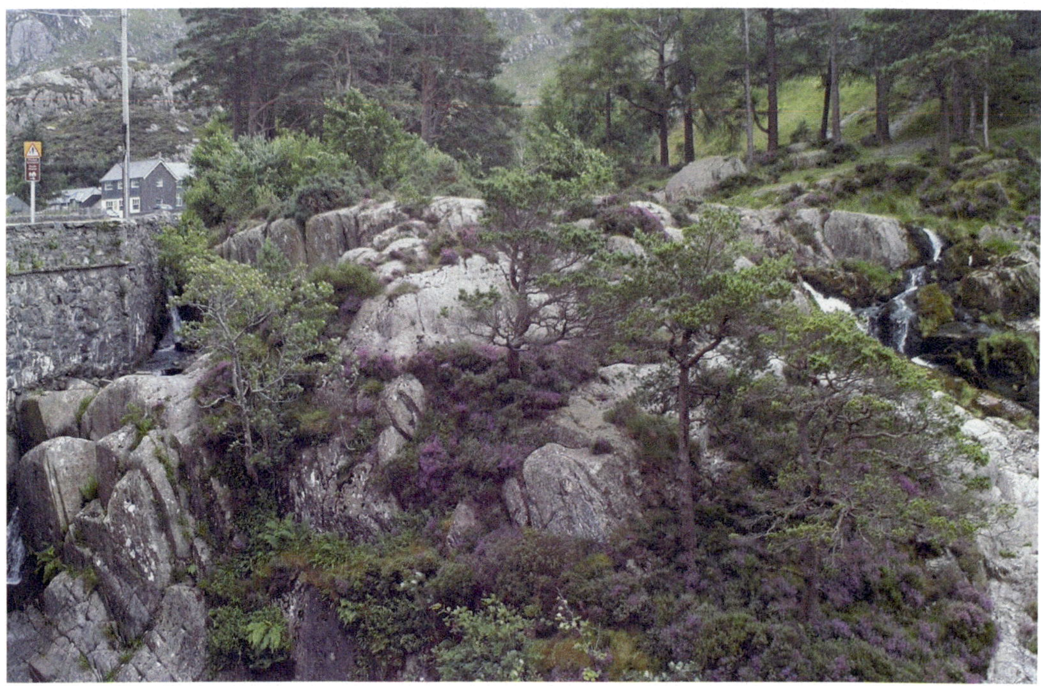

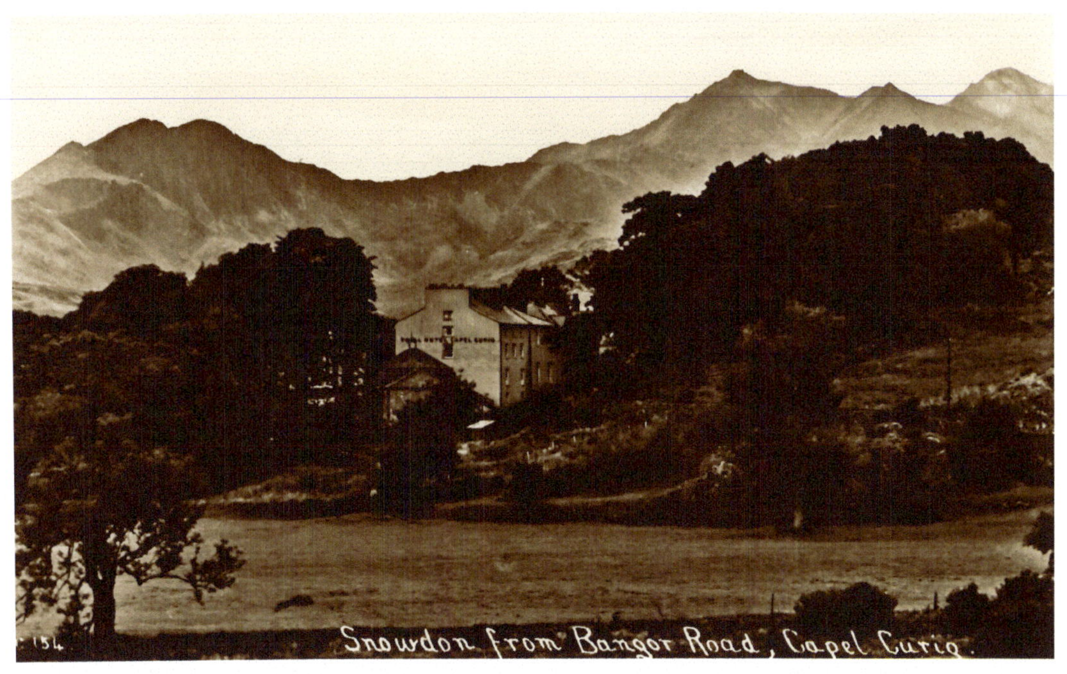

Yr Wyddfa (Snowdon) from Ffordd Bangor, Capel Curig, 1931

Snowdon (Yr Wyddfa) is the highest mountain in Wales, at 1,085 metres (3,560 feet) above sea level. It is located in the Snowdonia National Park (Parc Cenedlaethol Eryri), Gwynedd. It was formed of volcanic rock in the Ordovician period, with the massif extensively affected by glaciation, creating the pyramidal peak of Snowdon and the arêtes of Crib Goch and Y Lliwedd. It is popular with climbers and walkers and the summit can be reached by a number of well-known paths.

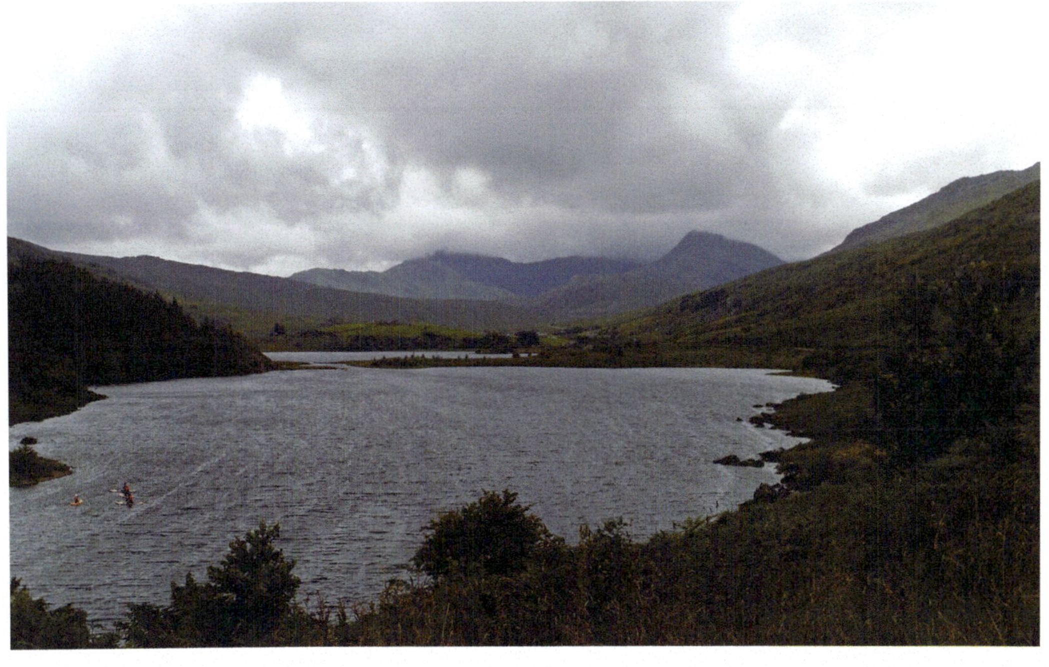

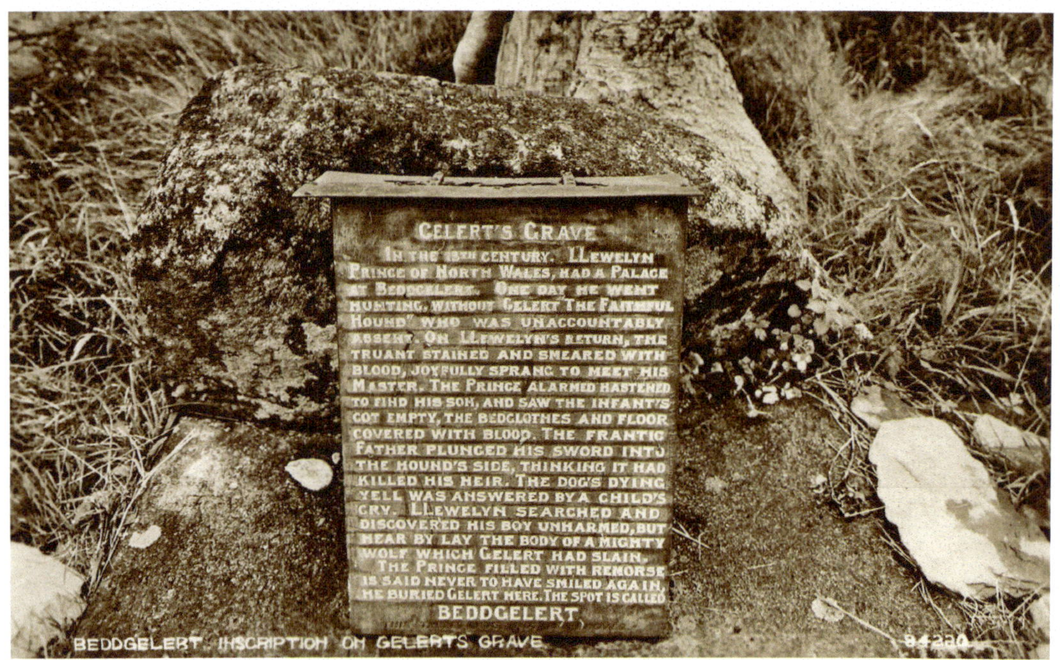

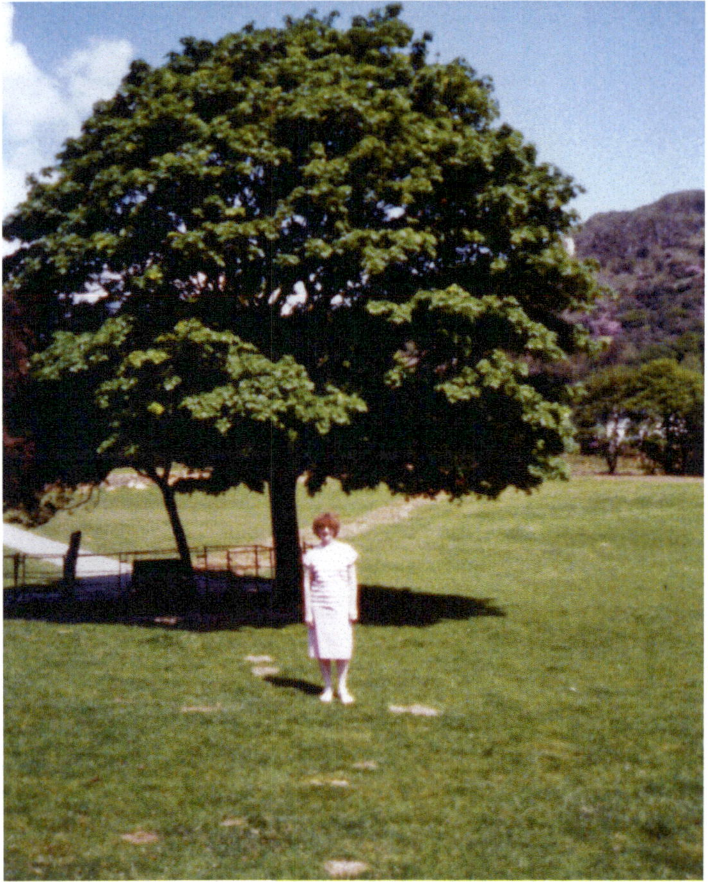

Beddgelert (Gelert's Grave), *c.* 1950

The village is one of the stop-off points on the Welsh Highland Railway. A short walk south of the village, following the footpath along the banks of the Afon Glaslyn, Beddgelert is also known for 'Gelert's Grave'. According to the thirteenth-century legend, the stone monument in the field marks the resting place of Gelert, the faithful hound of the medieval Welsh prince Llewelyn the Great. Gelert was slain after the prince mistakenly believed he had killed his infant son.

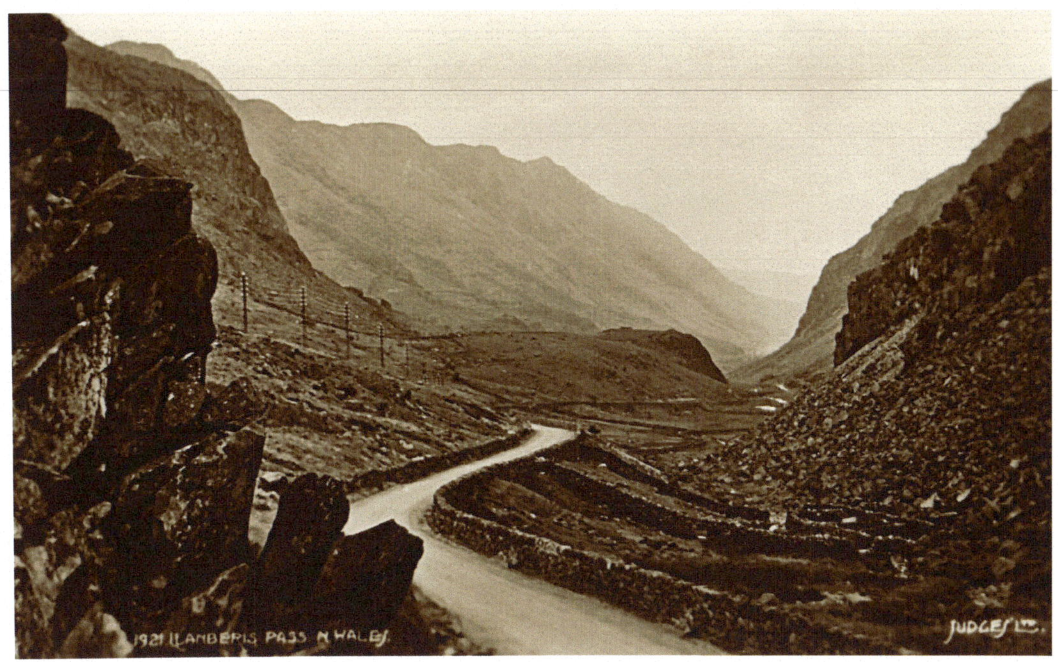

Llanberis Pass, *c.* 1920

The pass runs for just over 5 miles from Llanberis to Pen-y-Pass, providing some picturesque mountain views. The twin lakes of Llyn Padarn and Llyn Peris cut through the mountain ranges of Yr Wyddfa and Glyderau, which form the pass. At Pen-y-Pass, the highest point in the pass, stands a youth hostel converted from an old coaching inn, the Gorphwysfa Hotel. At the village of Nant Peris is the ancient, fourteenth-century church of St Peris, with the twelfth-century Dolbadarn Castle nearby.

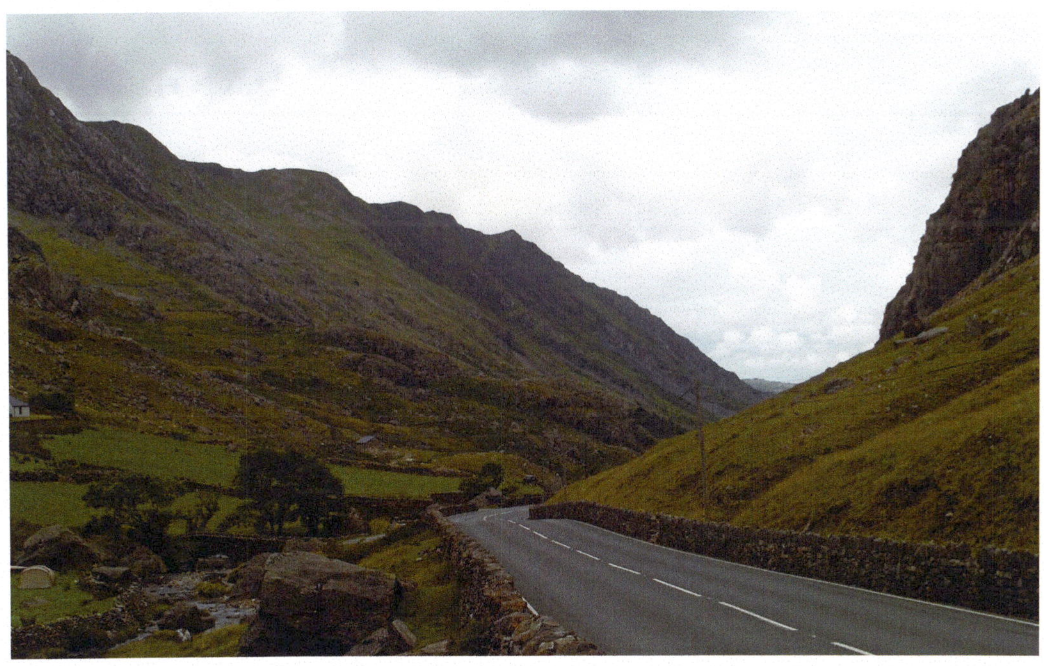

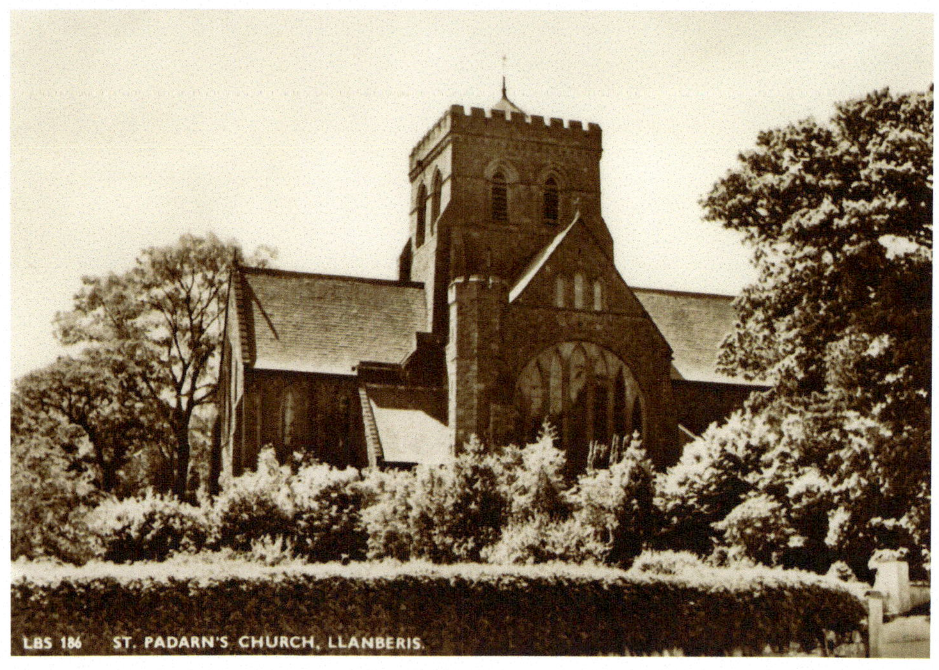

St Padarn's Church, Llanberis, *c.* 1950

The foundation stone was laid in 1884 and the Grade II-listed building was dedicated on 24 June 1885. St Peris was the original parish church. Llanberis' population grew as a result of slate quarrying, so a new parish church was required. The medieval font from St Peris was transferred to St Padarn. Funded by the Assheton-Smith family, the building was designed by Arthur Baker and supervised by his cousin, Herbert John Baker, later knighted. His son-in-law, Harold Hughes, enlarged the building in 1914.

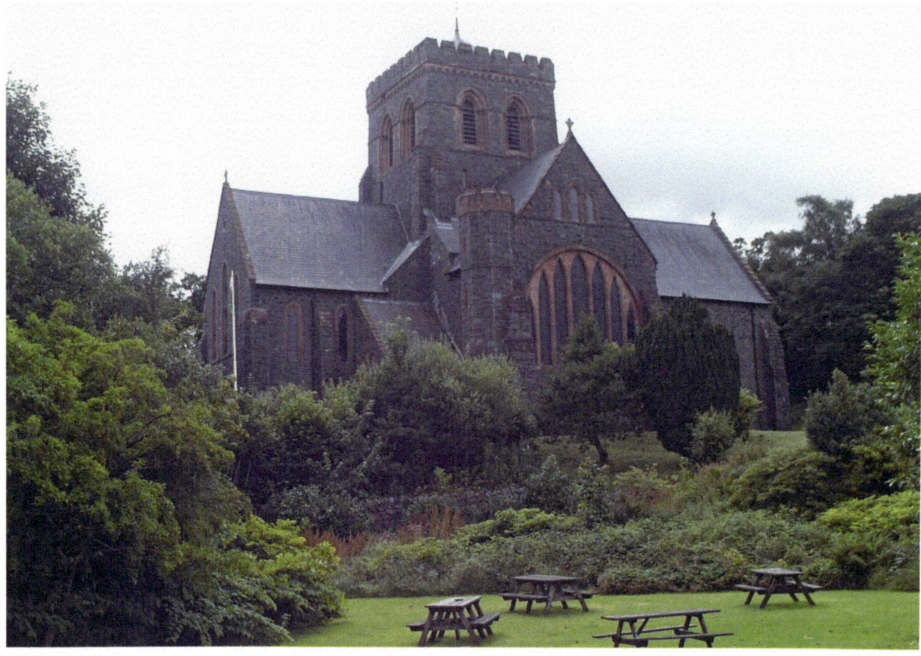

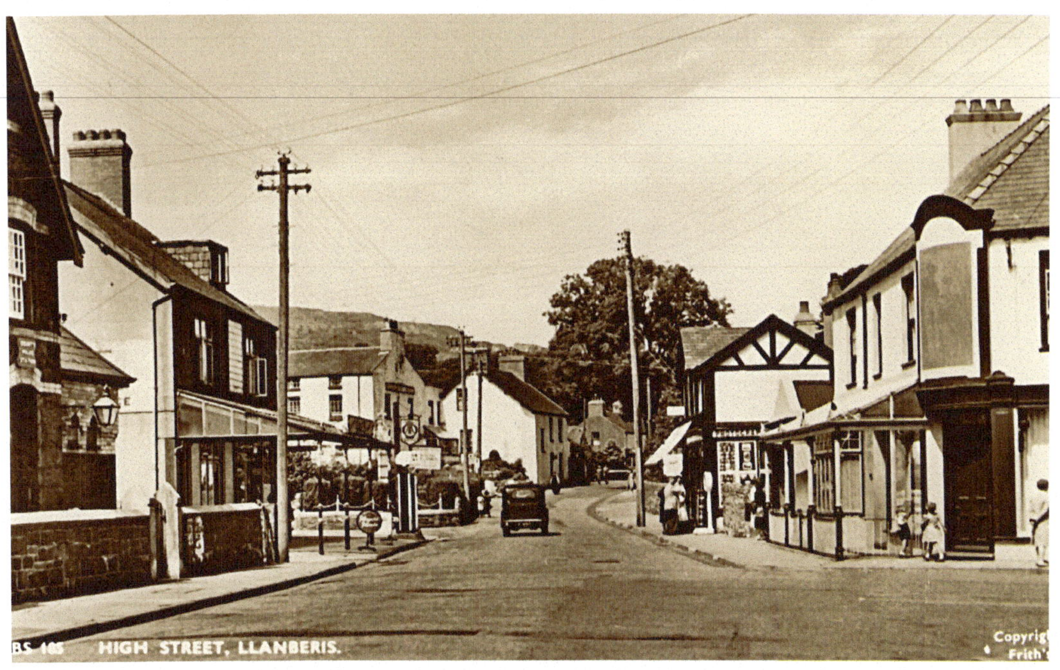

Stryd Fawr (High Street), Llanberis, *c.* 1950

Thousands of walkers and climbers use the village each year as a centre for exploring the nearby Snowdon massif. The Welsh Slate Museum is situated in the former workshops of the Dinorwig Quarry, showing much of the original machinery and equipment. Also nearby, Dolbadarn Castle was built by Llewelyn the Great in the thirteenth century, an important military symbol, with a fine example of a Welsh round tower. It was taken by Edward I in 1284 and raw materials from it were used for Caernarfon Castle.

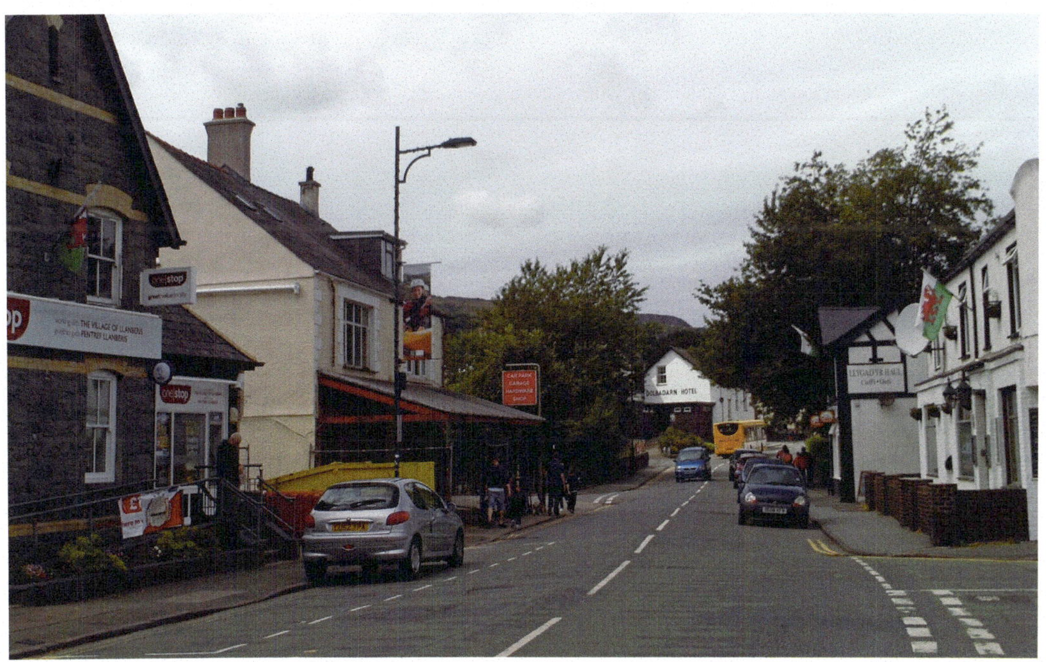

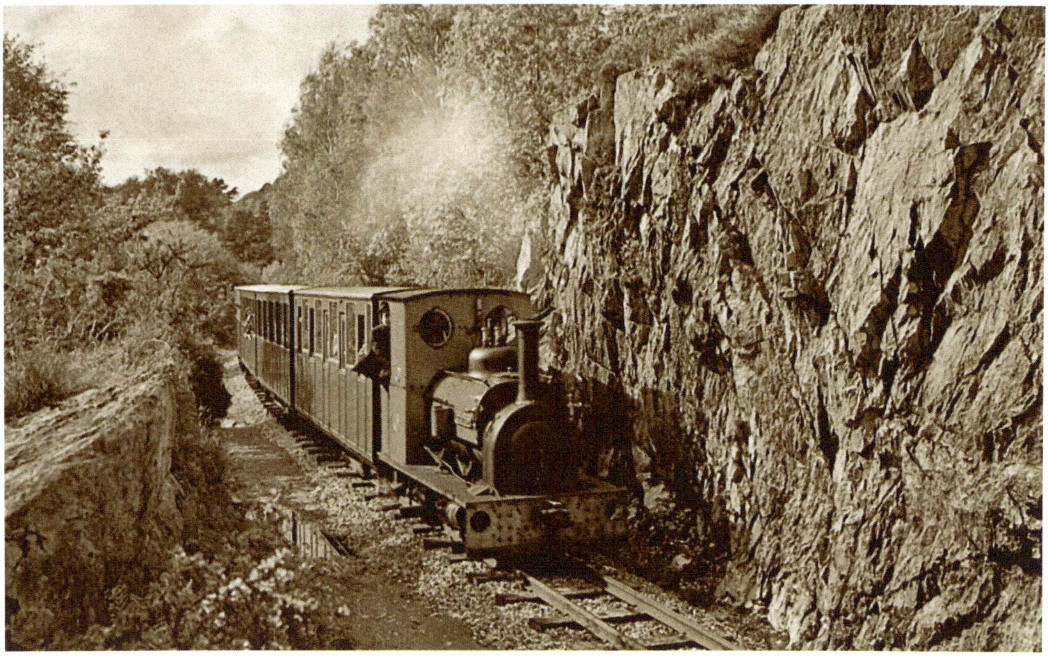

'Dolbadarn', Llanberis Lake Railway, *c.* 1971

The Llanberis Lake Railway is a sixty-minute, 8-kilometre (5-mile) journey, alongside Llyn Padarn and past the thirteenth-century Dolbadarn Castle. The railway runs through the Padarn Country Park, joining the 1845 slate railway route, following the shores of Lyn Padarn to Penllyn, where there are views of Yr Wyddfa across the Llyn. The train stops briefly at Cei Llydan and at Gilfach Ddu, where passengers can visit the National Slate Museum. Steam engines were rescued from the Dinorwig slate quarries.

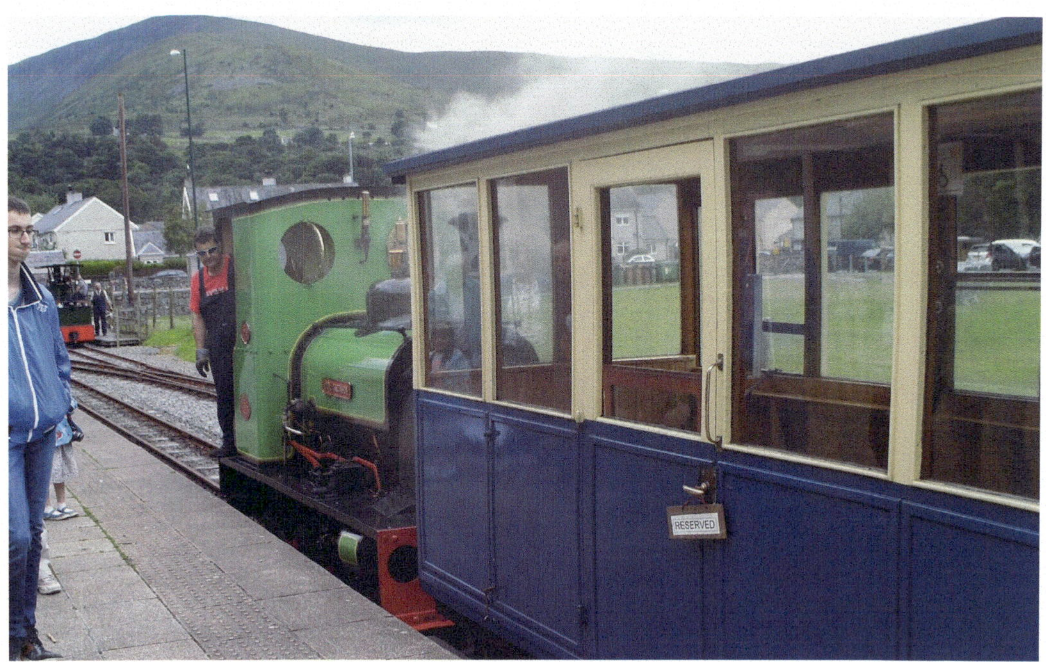

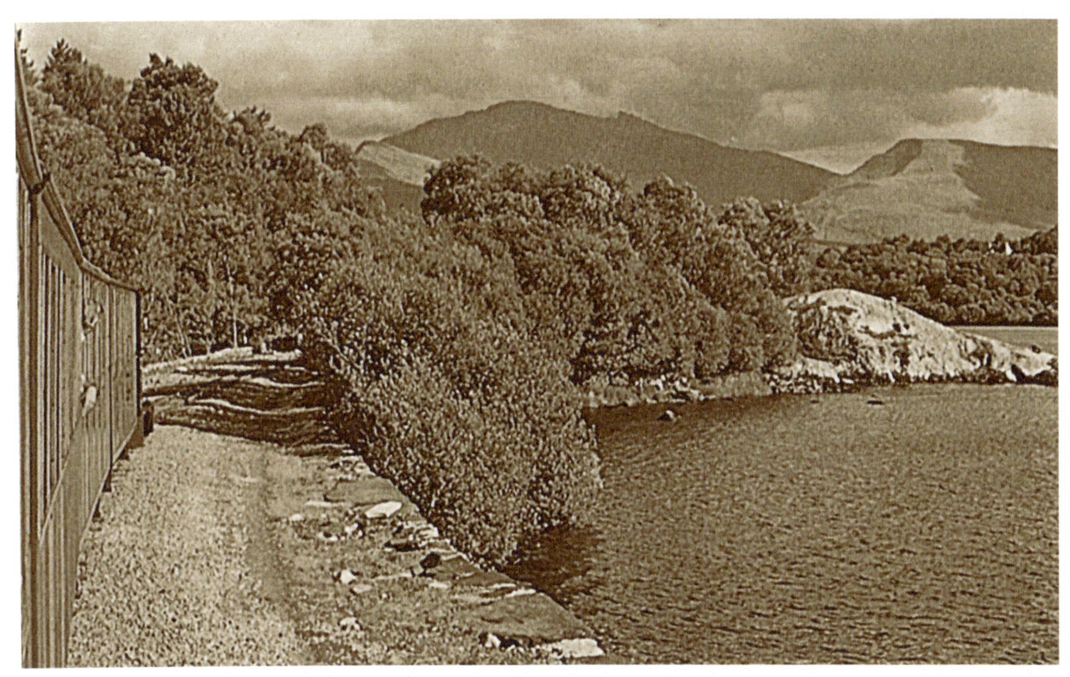

Llyn Padarn and Yr Wyddfa (Snowdon) from Llanberis Lake Railway, *c.* 1971

Llyn Padarn and Llyn Peris cut through the mountain ranges of Yr Wyddfa and Glyderau, which forms Llanberis Pass. Llyn Peris is a glacial lake, flanked on one side by the old slate quarry of Dinorwig, and is around 1.8 kilometres (1.1 miles) long. It forms part of the lower reservoir of Dinorwig Power Station. The Llyn takes its name from St Peris, an early Christian saint who settled here. The village of Llanberis sits between Padarn Peris, with the railway, opened in 1971, 4 kilometres (2.5 miles) long.

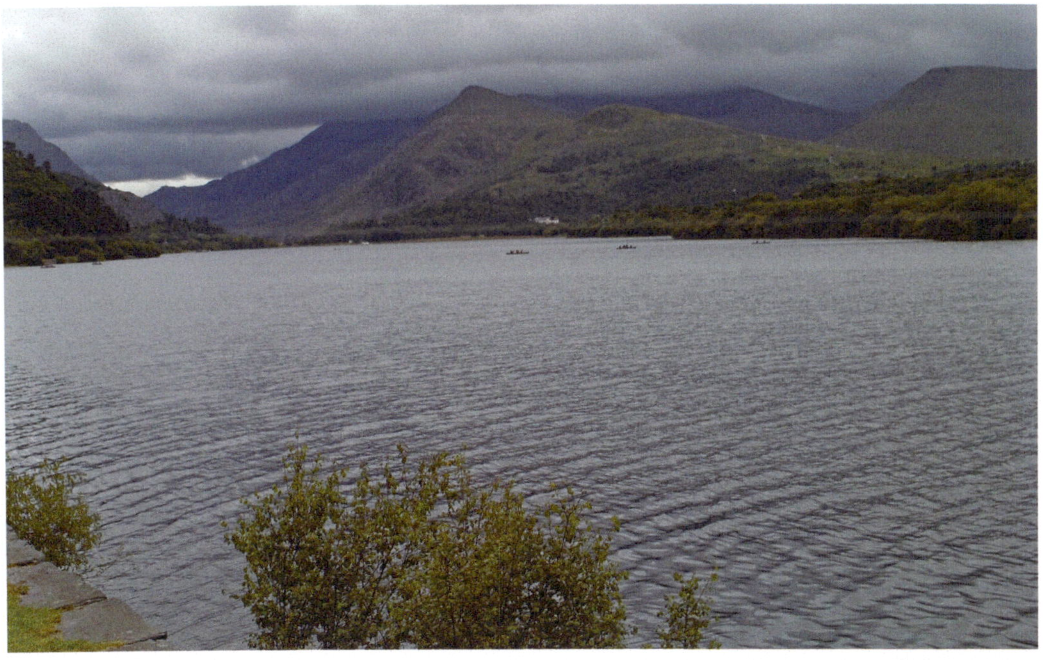

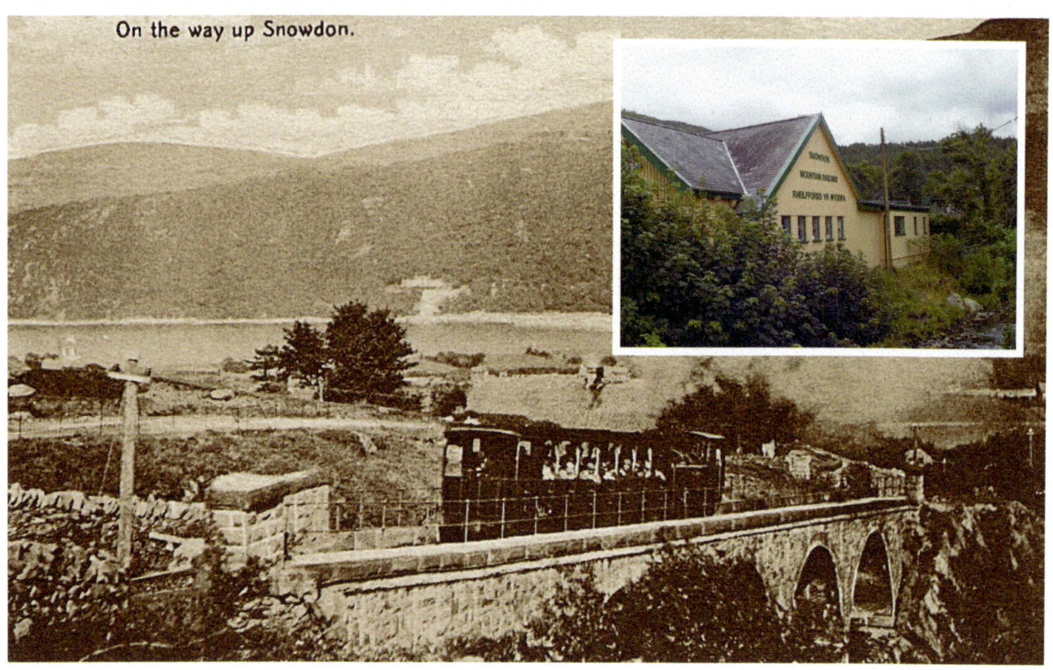

Ascent of Yr Wyddfa (Snowdon), *c.* 1910

The Rheilffordd yr Wyddfa (Snowdon Mountain Railway) is a narrow gauge rack and pinion mountain railway, opened in 1896, which carries passengers the 7.6 kilometres (4.7 miles) from Llanberis (*inset*) to the summit station. The summit also houses a café, built in 2006, to replace the one from around the 1930s. The railway usually operates to the summit station from Whitsun to October and is dependent on the weather and customer demand. It carries more than 130,000 passengers annually, by either steam or diesel locomotives.

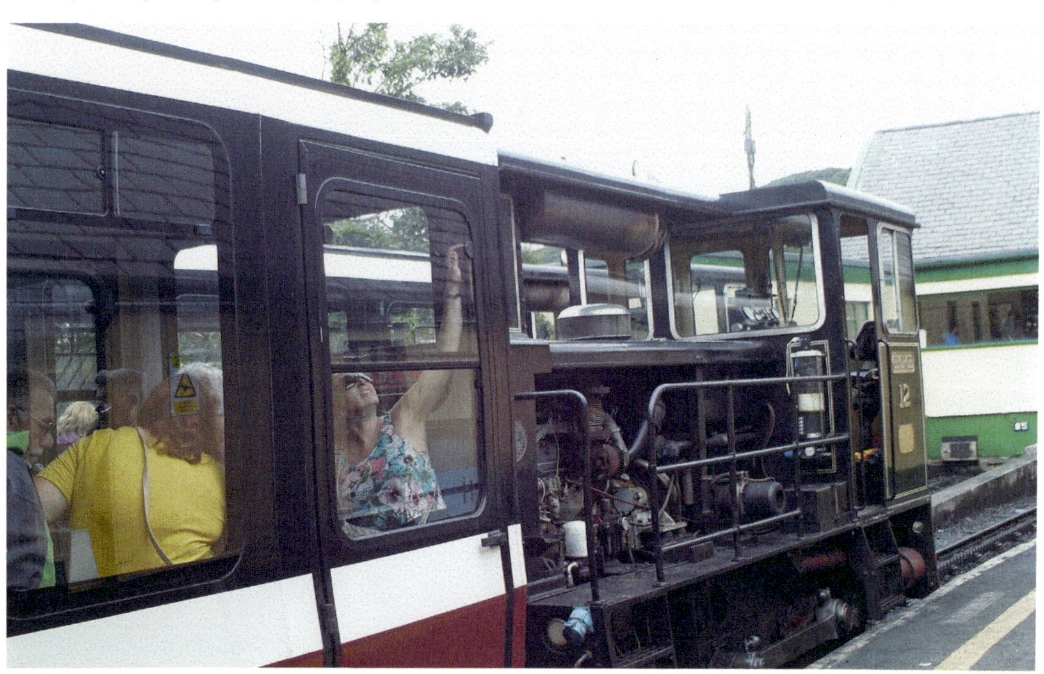

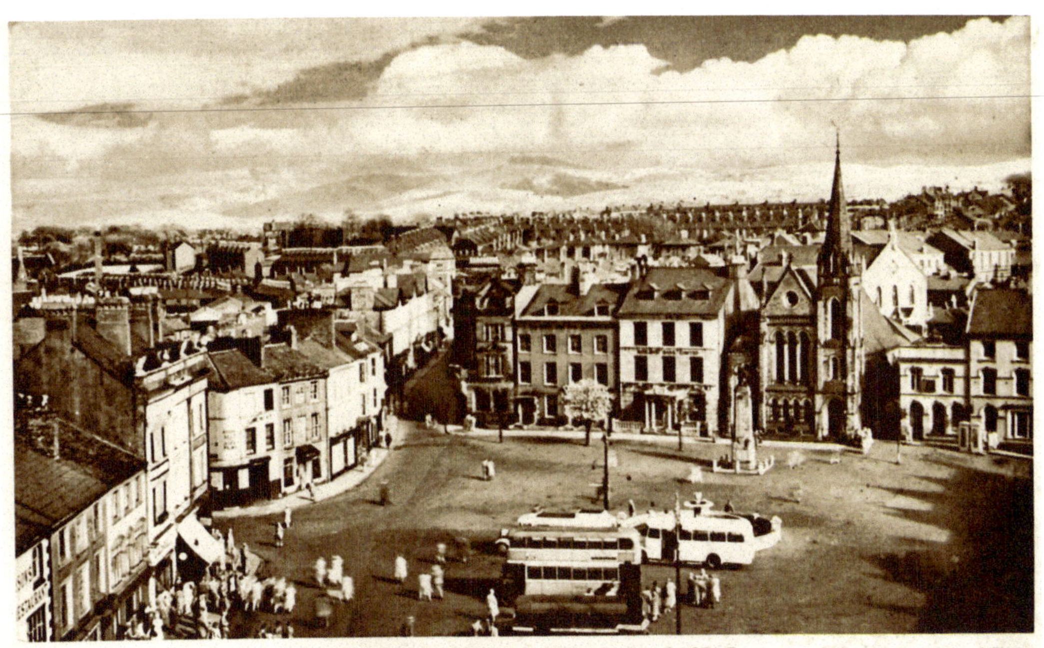

Castle Square, Caernarfon, *c.* 1940

Castle Square is commonly referred to as the '*Maes*' by local people. The square holds a market every Saturday and also on Mondays in the summer. It was modernised in 2009 at a cost of £2.4 million, but traffic and parking problems continue to afflict it, with issues relating to road safety the result of the removal of road barriers separating pedestrians and road traffic. The removal of an old oak tree from the Maes – a historic feature of the town – also caused some controversy.

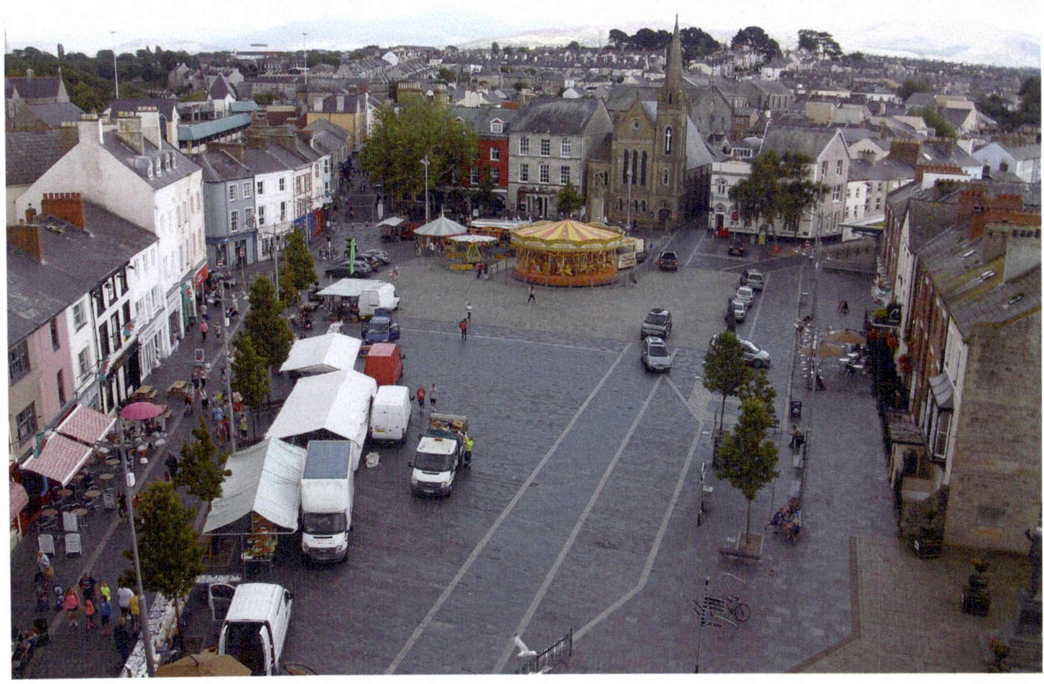

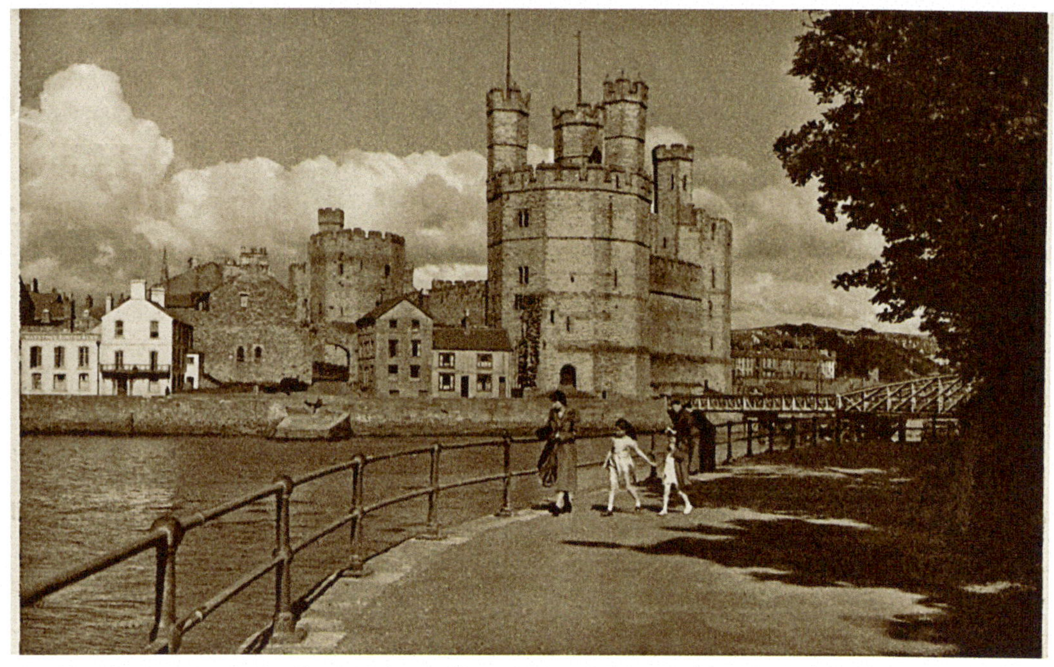

Caernarfon Castle, Bridge and the Anglesey, *c.* 1950

The castle has world heritage status. King Edward I deliberately made its appearance intimidating, as an expression of his power. Polygonal towers were built, with the Eagle Tower the most significant. It was previously the site of a Norman motte-and-bailey castle and before that a Roman fort stood nearby, ease of access to the sea explaining the reason for the locations popularity. The first English Prince of Wales was born in the castle in 1284. In 1969 Prince Charles' investiture took place here.

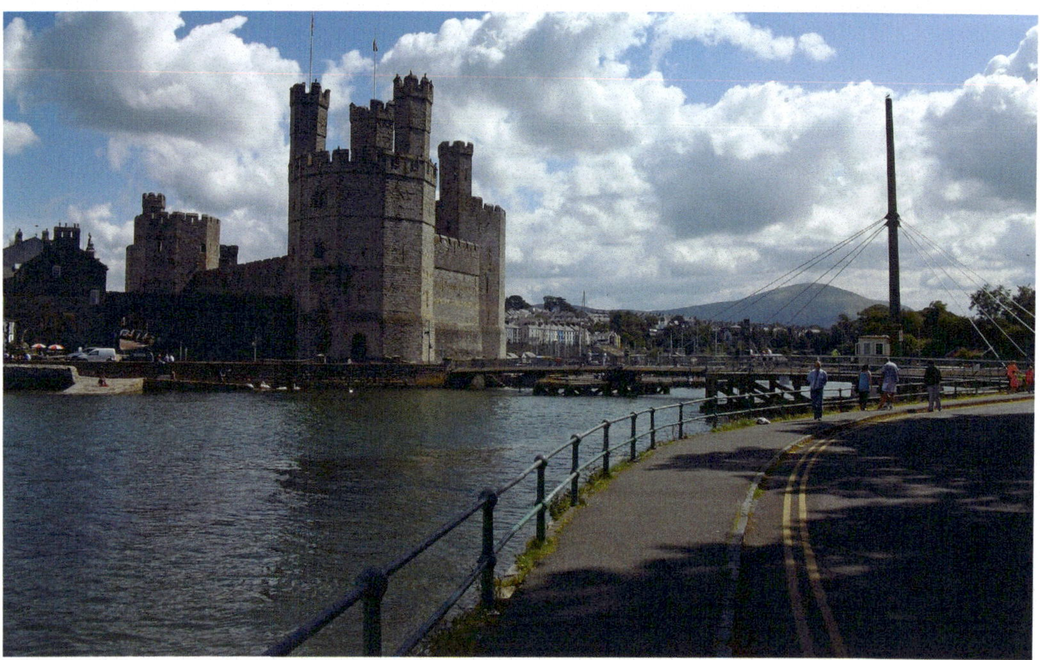

Rhaeadr Fawr (Big Falls), Aber Valley, Abergwyngregyn, 1904
At Abergwyngregyn, on the northern edge of the Carneddau mountain range, the Princes of Gwynedd once had a court. The Aber Valley (centre right on the panoramic view) is an area of special scientific interest. It is situated in a steep-sided valley on the Coedydd Aber Nature Reserve. The Afon Goch cascades over an escarpment 36.5 metres (120 feet) high (*inset*) into a marshy area where, joined by two tributaries, it becomes Afon Rhaeadr Fawr. In winter it can freeze enough to attract ice climbers.

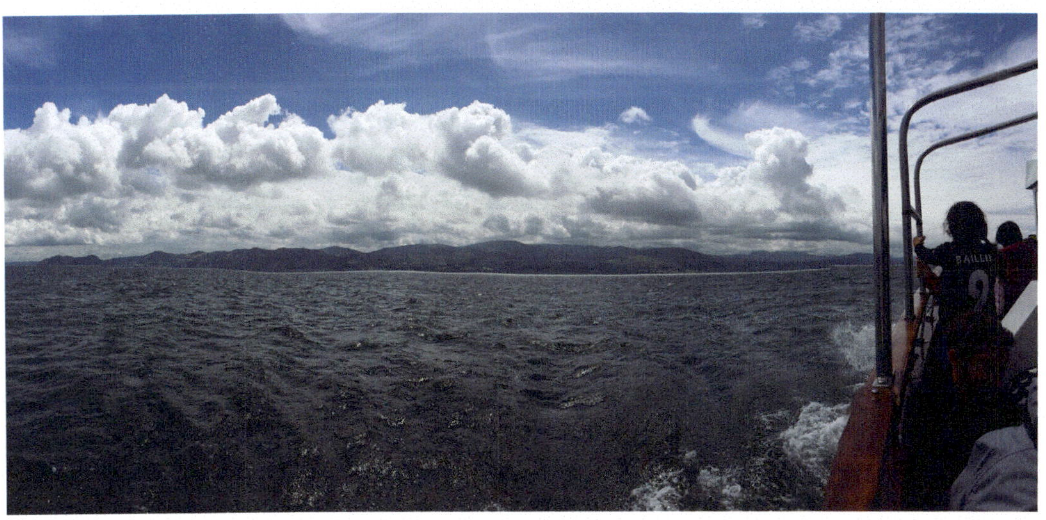

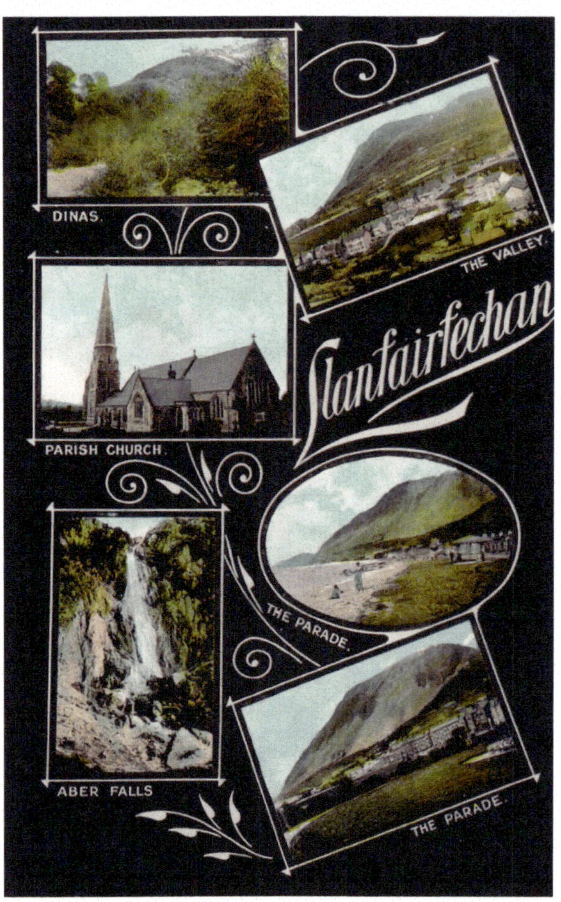

Views of Llanfairfechan, *c*. 1900
The biggest development of Llanfairfechan began in the mid-nineteenth century, coinciding with the building of the toll road to Ireland. In 1845 the building of the railway made the town even more accessible, although it did not stop at Llanfairfechan originally, but at Abergwyngregyn. Some prominent businessmen bought local estates once the railway had opened up the town, causing a station to be constructed. As a result, Llanfairfechan became a popular tourist resort and the promenade was developed.

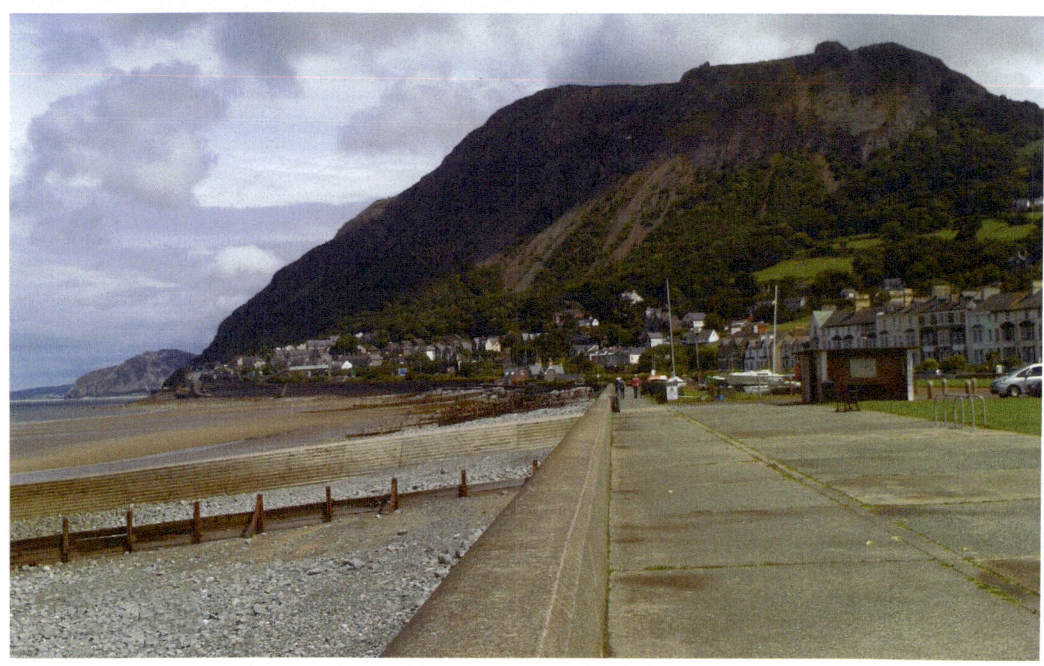

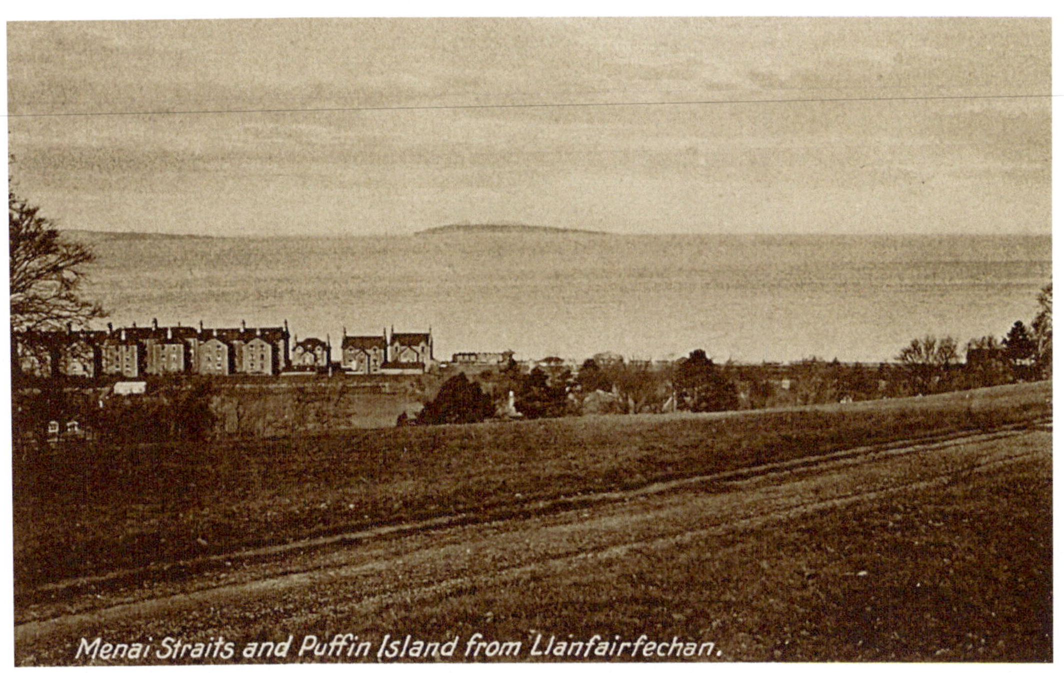

Afon Menai and Ynys Seiriol (Puffin Island) from Llanfairfechan, *c.* 1905

Off the coast of Anglesey, Puffin Island is uninhabited and is designated a Special Protection Area on account of its large Cormorant population. Other sea birds, such as Guillemot, Razorbill, Shag, Kittiwake and Eider Ducks are found. Puffins were decimated by the accidental introduction of rats in the late nineteenth century but a poisoning programme has helped the Puffins recover in recent years. Several were seen on a summer boat trip around the island. Seals, dolphins and porpoise can also be observed.

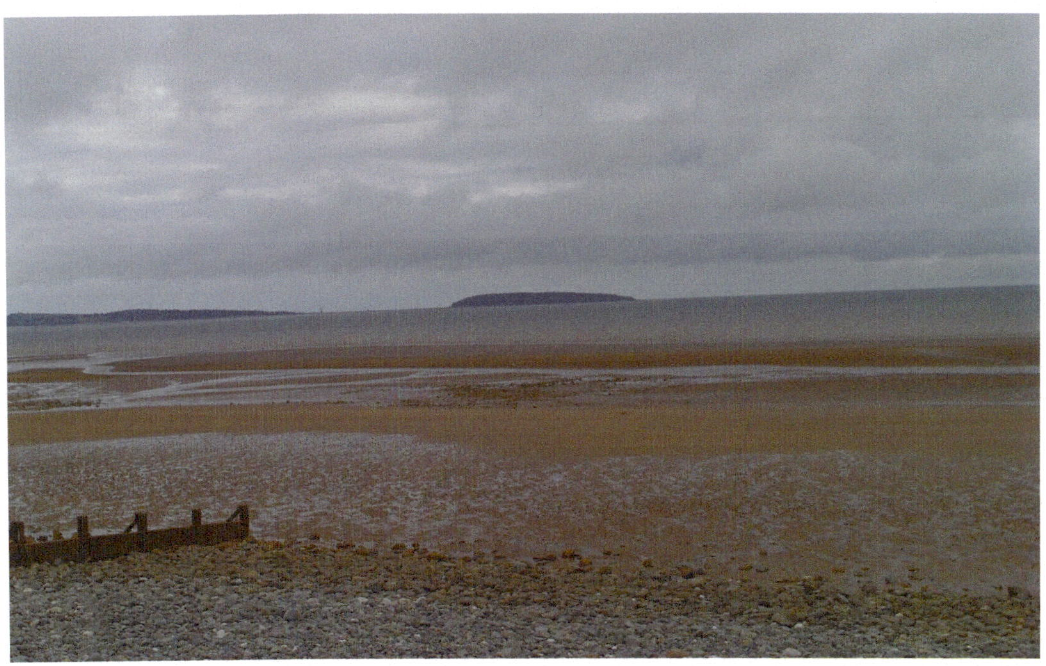

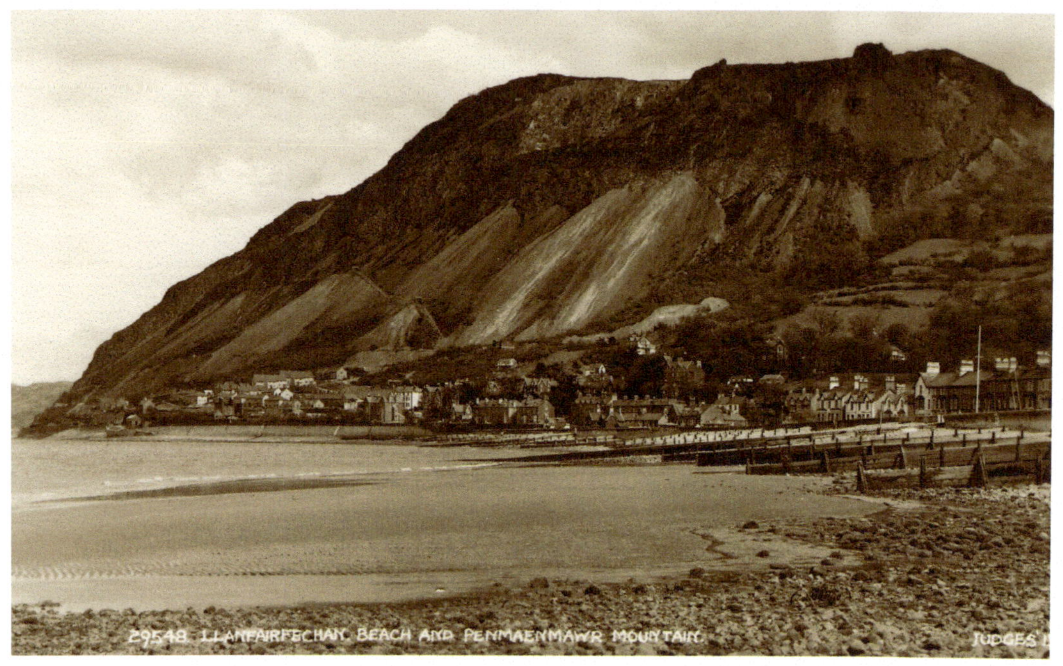

Llanfairfechan, Beach and Penmaenmawr Mountain, *c.* 1910.

Llanfairfechan is a Victorian seaside town, with a long, wide, sandy and sheltered beach beneath the 434-metre (1,423-foot)-high Penmaenmawr Mountain. At low tide the long stretch of sandy beach gives some spectacular views of Anglesey, the Menai Strait and the Great Orme. The beach is next to the North Wales Coastal Path and Traeth Lafan Nature Reserve, popular with ornithologists. Good launch facilities mean sailing and wind-surfing are popular pursuits. There is also a dinghy park.

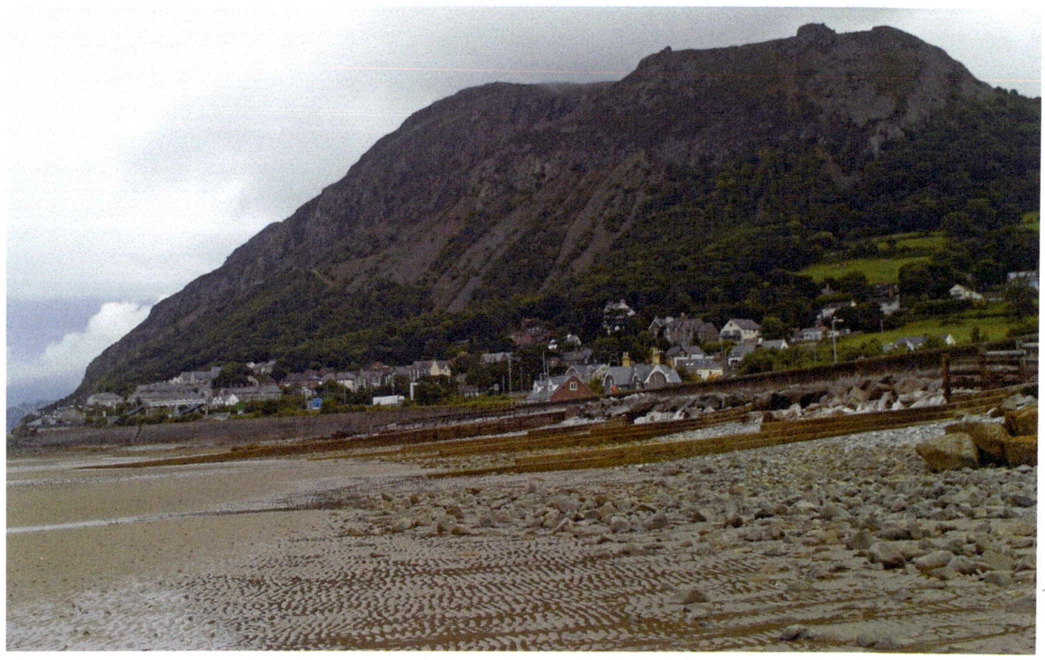

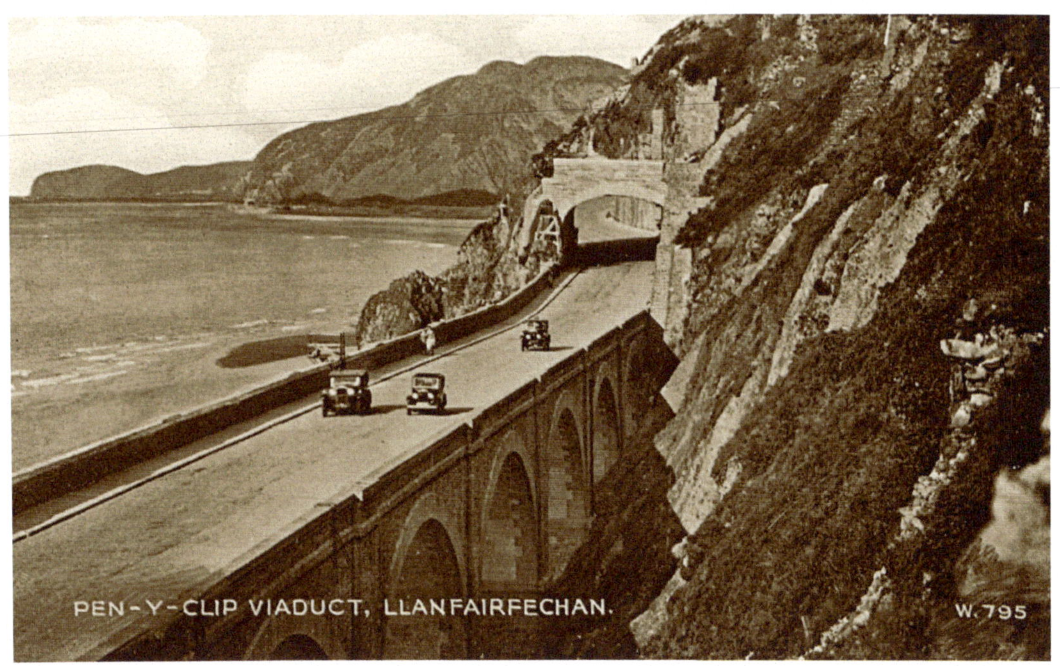

Pen-y-Clip Viaduct, *c.* 1936. *Inset*: from Llanfairfechan Beach

The viaduct opened on 5 October 1935. A very narrow carriageway, climbing at a gradient of 1:11 with a difficult bend, had made the early road treacherous. The new road was opened by Caernarvonshire County Council, comprising two tunnels and a 213-metre (700-foot) viaduct on six arches, 27.4 metres (90 feet) high. The piers are of solid concrete and the arches are in concrete sections. Facings are of local microdiorite and limestone, similar to the railway viaduct on its left. Small rockfalls continue to be a problem.

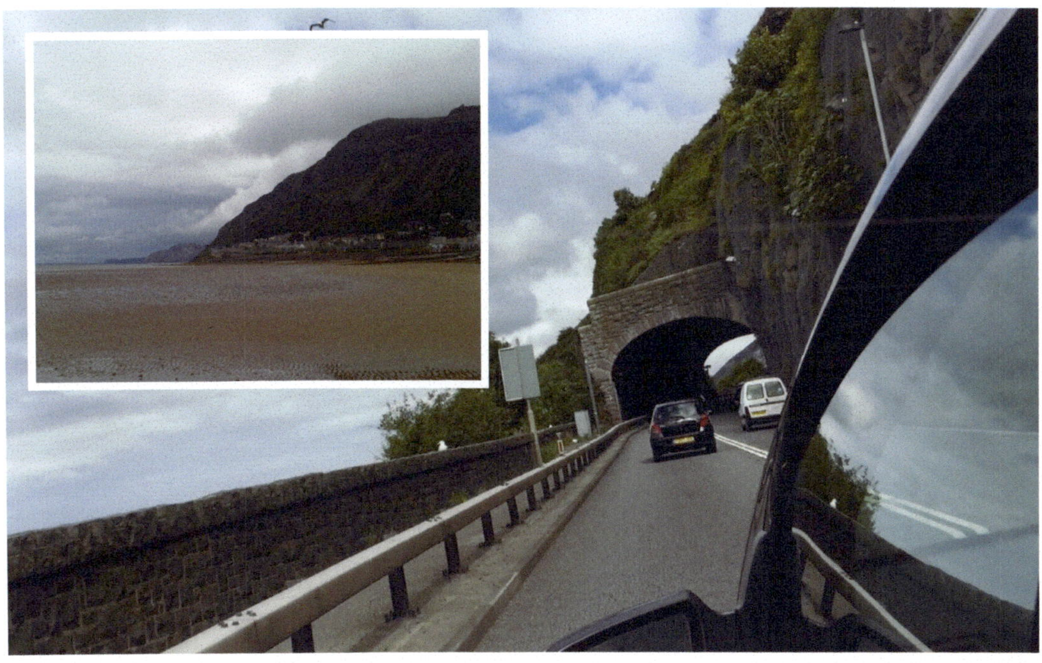

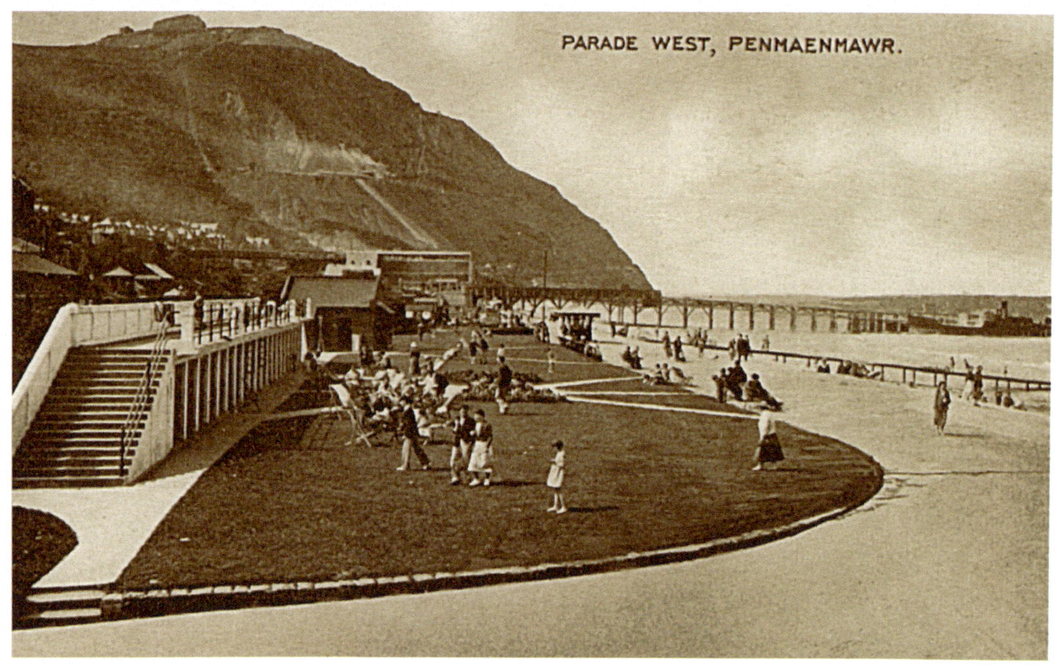

West Parade, Penmaenmawr, *c.* 1920

The first evidence of stone quarrying at Penmaenmawr Mountain dates to 1833. Two independent quarries were established, which concentrated on sett production and loose stone for ballast. By the early twentieth century the two quarries were amalgamated and linked by a railway. Later, by the 1930s, the eastern workings were abandoned. The western side produced aggregate for road construction and railway ballast. The mountain summit has been reduced by approximately 121.9 metres (400 feet) and the prehistoric hill fort of Braich-y-Dinas destroyed.

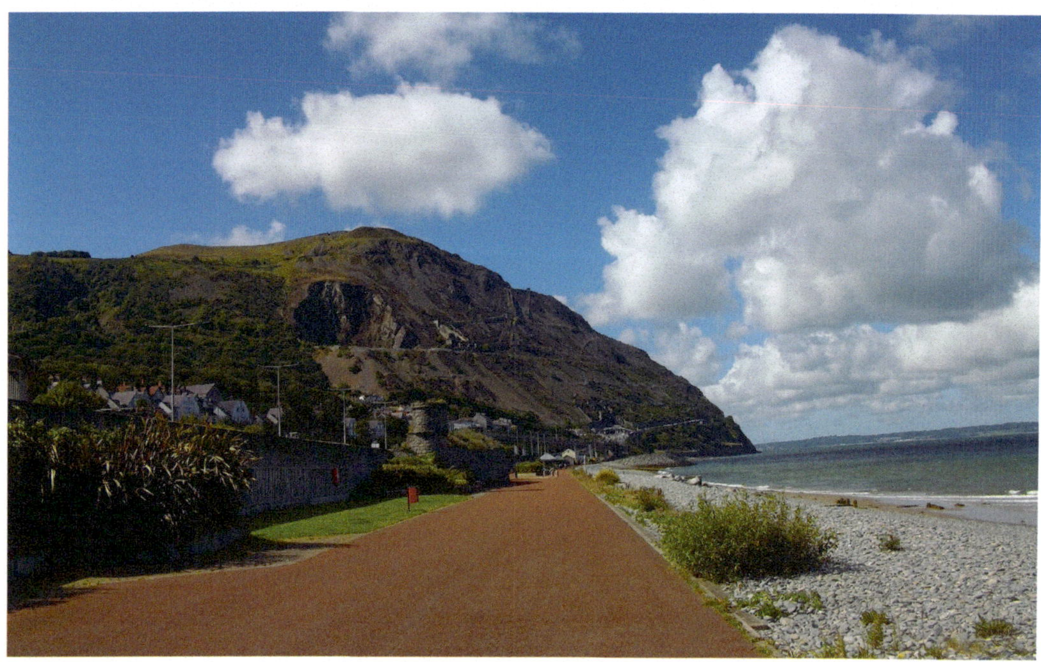

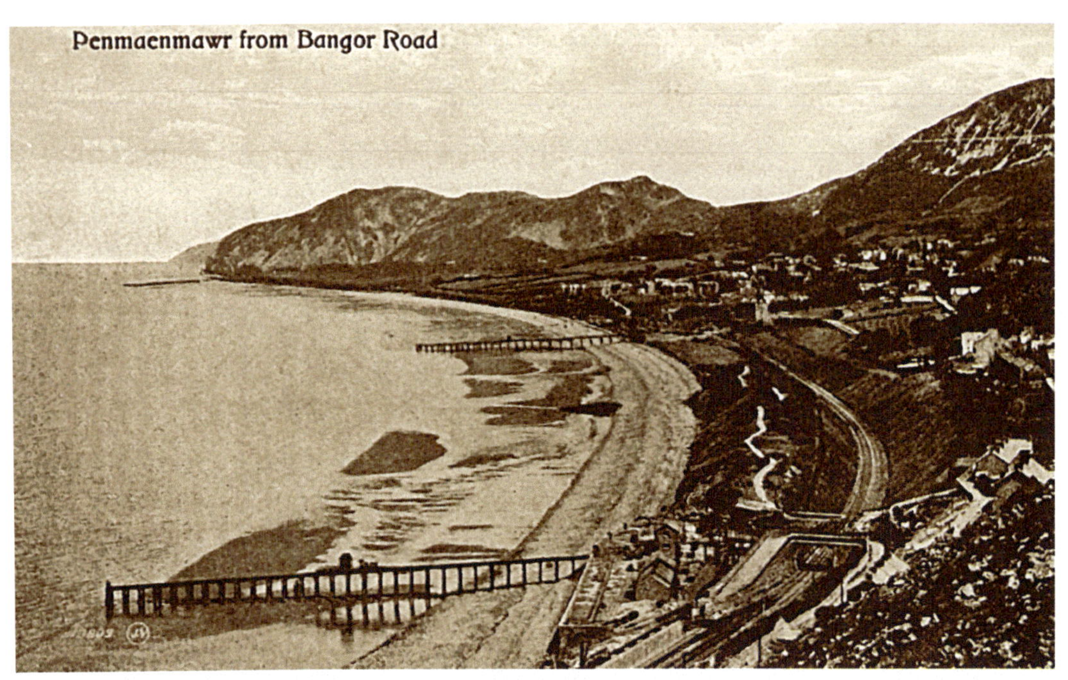

Penmaenmawr, from Ffordd Bangor, Penmaenmawr Mountain, *c.* 1910

The western half of Penmaenmawr is characterised by quarry workers' dwellings, with holiday villas, boarding houses and hotels in the eastern half. Penmaenmawr's quarry is no longer a major employer. The A55 Expressway and the railway dominate transport links, with the resort buildings mainly late nineteenth and early twentieth century. The main street's covered walkways, supported by cast-iron pillars, copied those of Llandudno, but construction of the Expressway in the 1980s meant Penmaenmawr lost its old Edwardian promenade, replaced by a modern one.

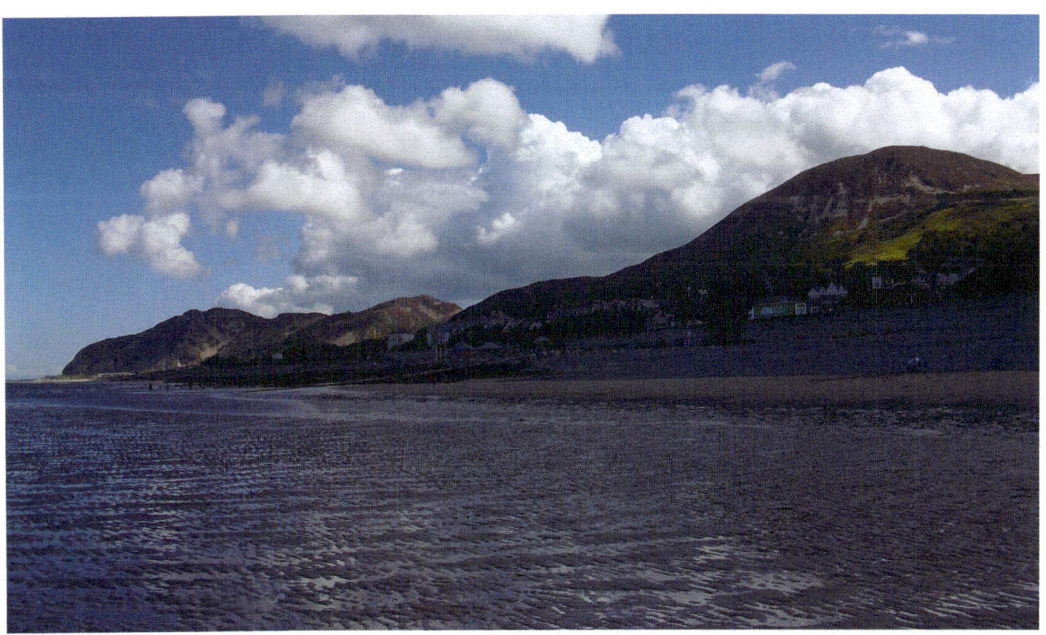

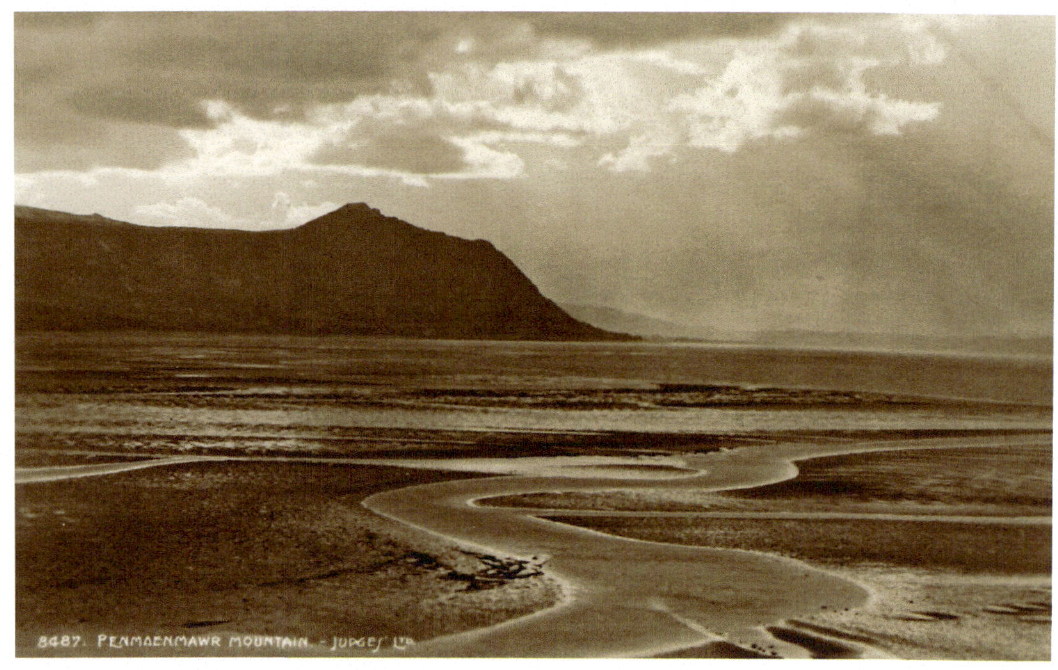

Penmaenmawr Mountain, looking west towards Bangor, *c.* 1930

It was Colonel Darbishire who developed the quarrying sites at Penmaenmawr, forming the Penmaenmawr and Welsh Granite Co. in 1911. By the early twentieth century around 1,000 men worked at the quarry. Ships continued to load at the jetty until 1976 but any infrastructure was removed by the building of the Expressway in the late 1980s. Prime Minister William Ewart Gladstone holidayed at the town eleven times from 1855–96, increasing its reputation as a resort for the well-to-do.

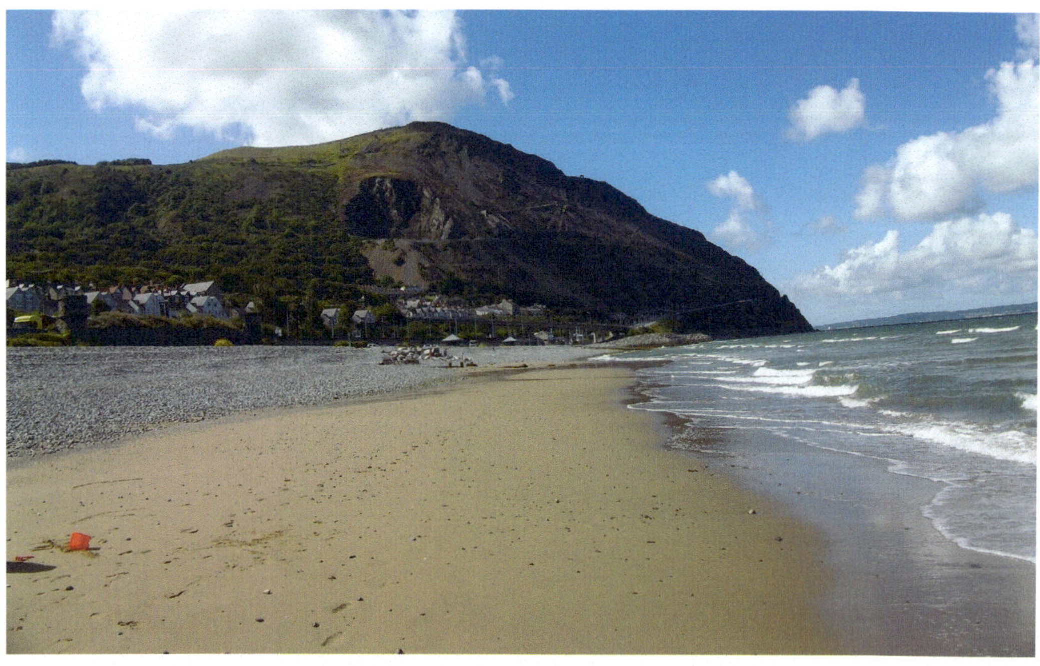

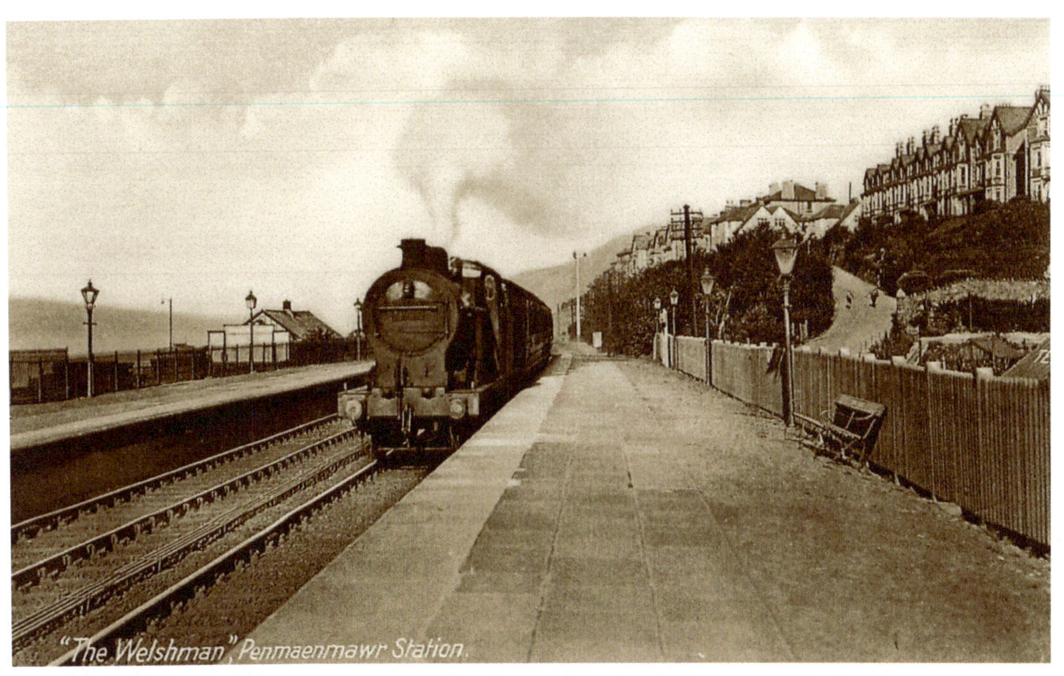

Penmaenmawr Railway Station, junction of Station Road and Paradise Road, *c.* 1910

The station was opened in 1849, a year after trains began running along the Chester to Holyhead Railway as far as Bangor. The train journey from Prime Minister Gladstone's home in Hawarden, Flintshire, took just over two hours, or five hours from London. The railway's ability to transport passengers quickly to the town was a major reason for Penmaenmawr's growth as a genteel resort, with picturesque walks and good bathing. The Edwardian promenade is now dominated by the Expressway, and new infrastructure.

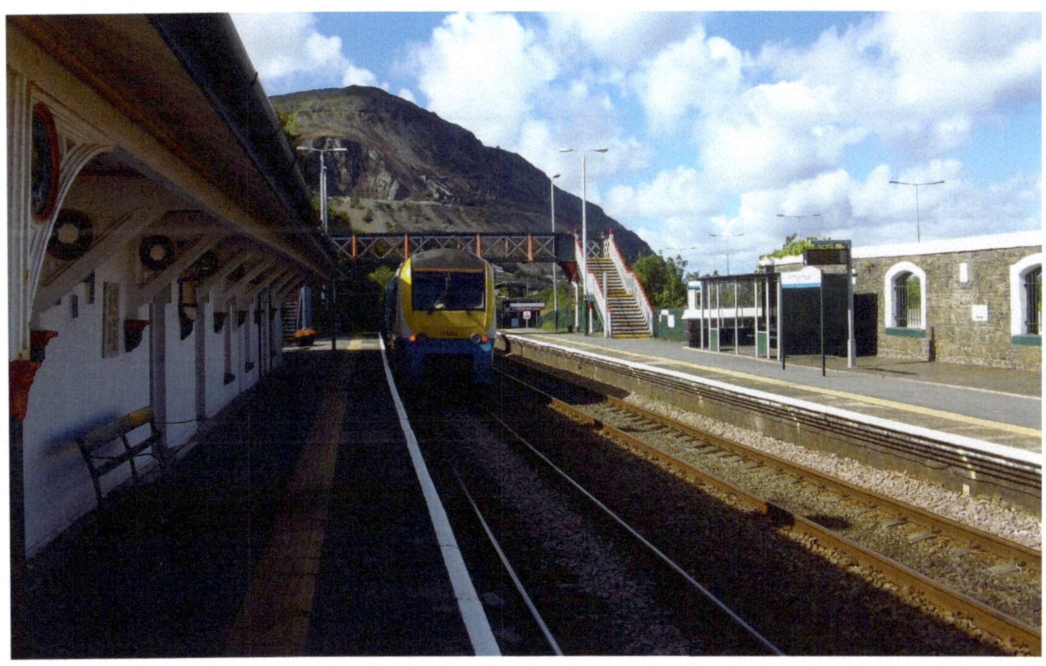

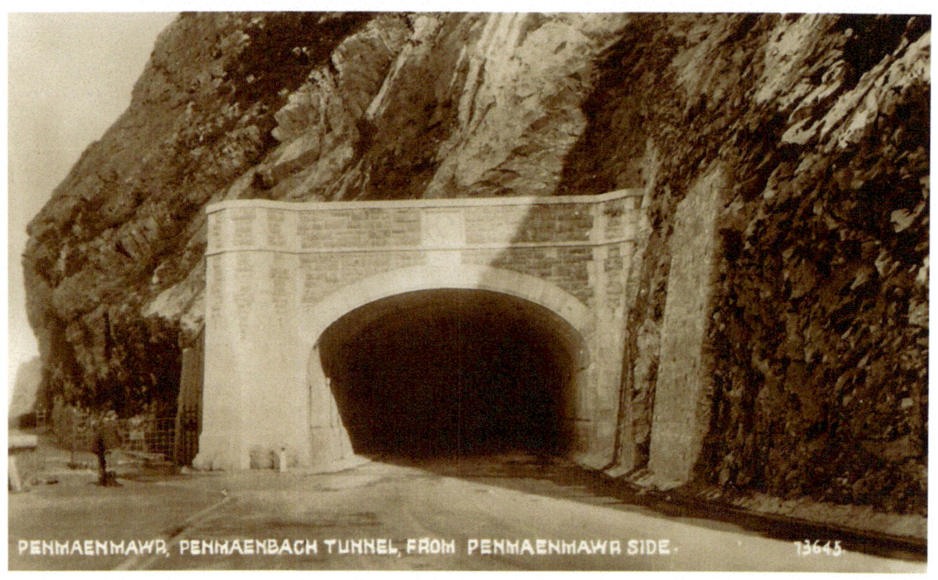

Penmaenbach Tunnel from the Penmaenmawr Side, *c.* 1936

Penmaenbach Tunnel is now part of the A55 North Wales Expressway (Gwibffordd Gogledd Cymru), which originally linked Chester to Bangor but now extends into Anglesey, reaching Holyhead in 2001. There have been major civil engineering works west of Conwy, at Penmaenbach Point and Penmaenan Point, in order to create this route. Penmaenbach Tunnel, built in 1932, carried motor traffic to Penmaenmawr. Two smaller tunnels through Penmaenan Point opened in 1935 and extended to Llanfairfechan, thus relieving pressure on Thomas Telford's early nineteenth-century Irish Mail coach road.

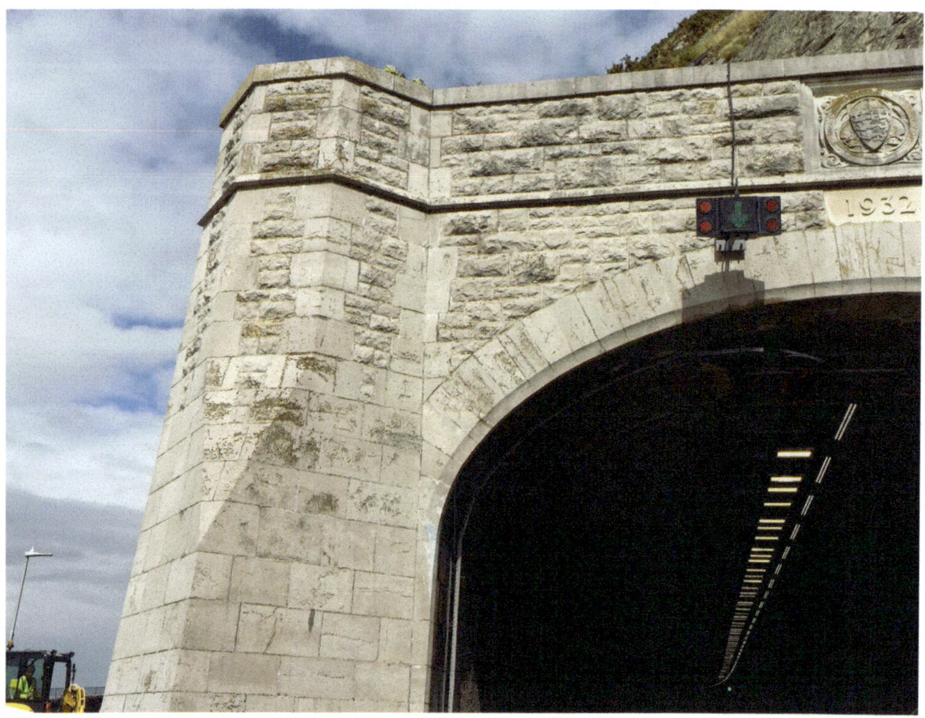

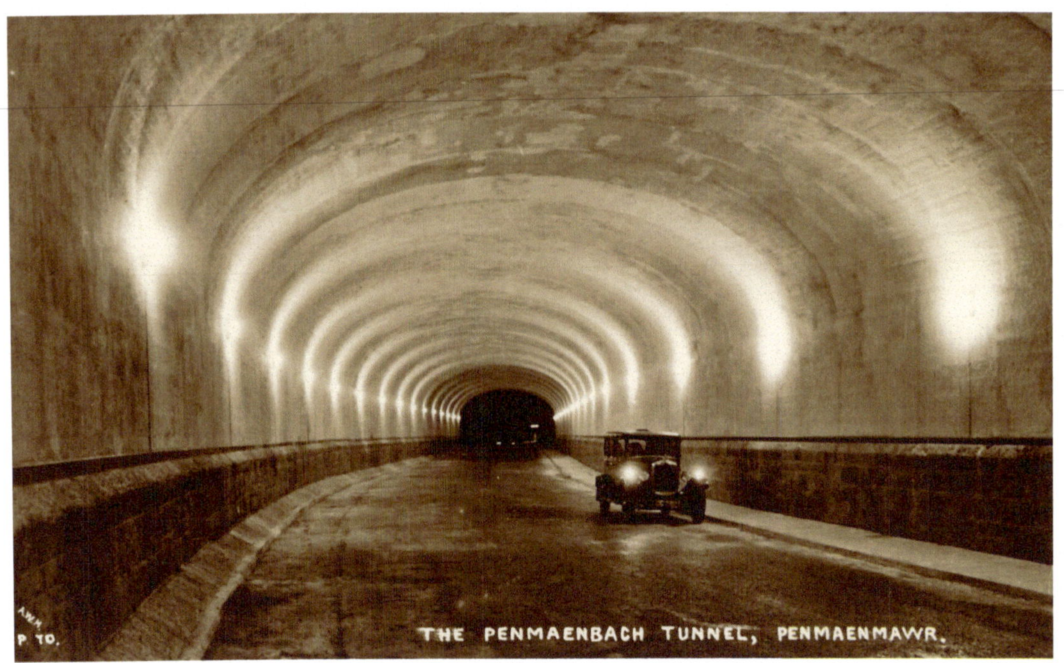

Penmaenbach Tunnel, *c.* 1936

Telford's route, cut into the cliffs by hand, is now part of a cycleway. The 1930s alignment was used until a new two-lane Penmaenbach Tunnel opened in 1989 for westbound traffic. Eastbound traffic continued to use the 1932 Penmaenbach Tunnel, utilising both lanes. Four years later the Pen-y-Clip Tunnel was completed, carrying westbound traffic, while the original road carried vehicles in the opposite direction, as at Penmaenbach. At present this sharply turning route is subject to speed restrictions.

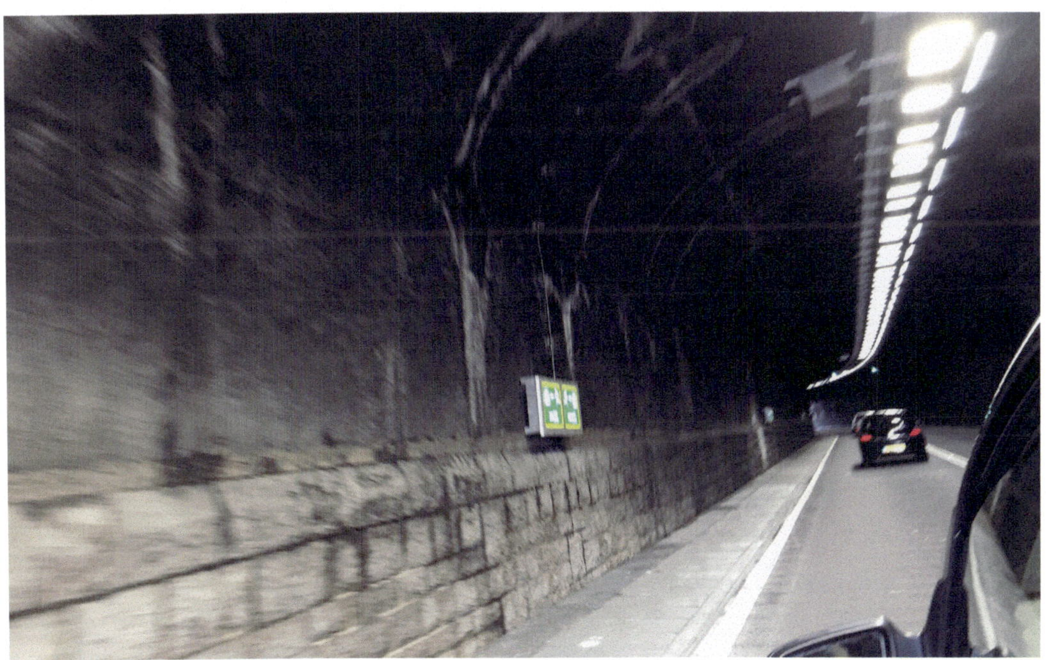

About the Author

Steven Dickens lives in the Flixton area of Manchester. However, his father's family hail from the town of Bethesda, in Gwynedd. Braichmelyn, Bryn Awel, Gerlan, the Penrhyn Slate Quarry and Rachub are all local names associated with the family, and Steven has been visiting this beautiful area of north Wales and his Welsh family members for many years. Author of several *Through Time* volumes, Steven is married to Sarah; they have three sons and three daughters.

Printed and bound by CPI Group (UK) Ltd, Croydon, CR0 4YY
16/07/2026
02169566-0007